SEASONAL
GUIDE
TO
THE
NATURAL
YEAR

One of the several coneflowers of the summer and fall prairie, this one attracts many butterflies, including the black swallowtail shown here.

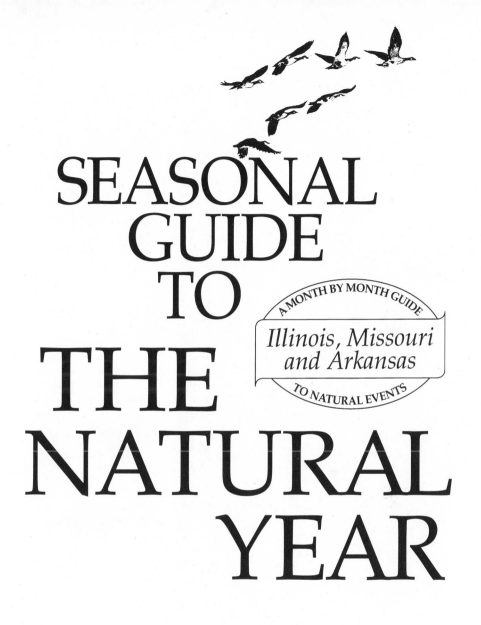

SEASONAL
GUIDE
TO

A MONTH BY MONTH GUIDE

Illinois, Missouri and Arkansas

TO NATURAL EVENTS

THE
NATURAL
YEAR

Barbara Perry Lawton

FULCRUM PUBLISHING
Golden, Colorado

Cover photo of Burden Falls in the Shawnee National Forest, Illinois
copyright © 1996, Richard Day/Daybreak Imagery
Photographs by Barbara Perry Lawton
Cover design by Deborah Rich

Library of Congress Cataloging-in-Publication Data

Lawton, Barbara Perry.
    Seasonal guide to the natural year : a month by month guide to natural events—Illinois, Missouri, Arkansas / Barbara Perry Lawton
       p.   cm.
    Includes bibliographical references (p.) and index.
    ISBN 1-55591-156-0
    1. Natural history—Illinois—Guidebooks. 2. Natural history—Missouri—Guidebooks. 3. Natural history—Arkansas—Guidebooks. 4. Seasons—Illinois—Guidebooks. 5. Seasons—Missouri—Guidebooks. 6. Seasons—Arkansas—Guidebooks. 7. Illinois—Guidebooks. 8. Missouri—Guidebooks. 9. Arkansas—Guidebooks.   I. Title.
QH104.5.M47L38   1994
508.77—dc20   94-4158
                                                  CIP

Printed in the United States of America

0 9 8 7 6 5 4 3 2

Fulcrum Publishing
350 Indiana Street, Suite 350
Golden, CO 80401-5093
800/992-2908

Dedicated to Cindy and Bill,
whose encouragement and enthusiasm I appreciate.

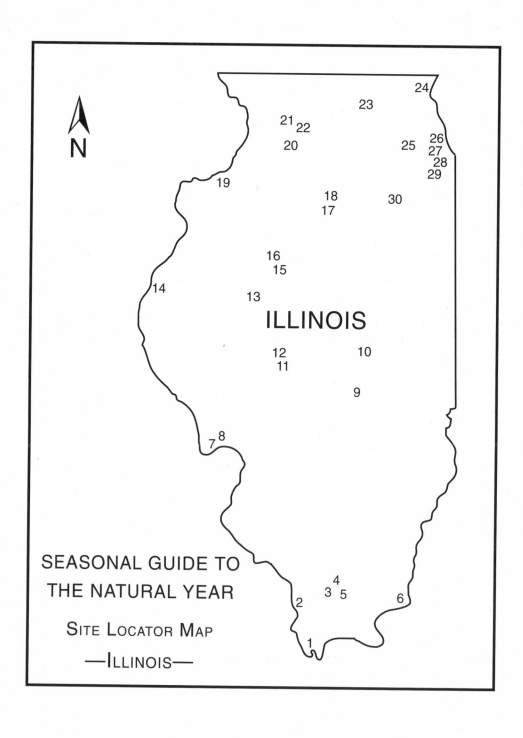

N

ILLINOIS

SEASONAL GUIDE TO
THE NATURAL YEAR

SITE LOCATOR MAP

—ILLINOIS—

LIST OF SITES
Illinois

Abbreviations: EDA—Environmental Demonstration Area; NWR—National Wildlife Refuge; SP—State Park; WR—Wildlife Refuge

1. Horseshoe Lake WR
2. Trail of Tears State Forest
3. Giant City SP
4. Crab Orchard NWR
5. Ferne Clyffe SP
6. Cave-in-Rock SP
7. Mark Twain NWR Complex
8. Pere Marquette SP
9. Eagle Creek SP
10. Robert Allerton Park
11. Washington Park Botanical Garden
12. Washington Park in Springfield
13. Chautauqua NWR
14. Cedar Glen Eagle Roost
15. Wildlife Prairie Park in Peoria
16. Forest Park Nature Center in Peoria
17. Matthiessen SP
18. Starved Rock SP
19. Upper Mississippi River National Wildlife and Fish Refuge
20. Nachusa Grasslands
21. White Pines Forest SP
22. Castle Rock SP
23. Moraine Hills SP
24. Illinois Beach SP
25. Morton Arboretum
26. Chicago Botanical Gardens
27. Jackson Park in Chicago
28. Lincoln Park in Chicago
29. Markham Prairie
30. Goose Lake Prairie State Natural Area

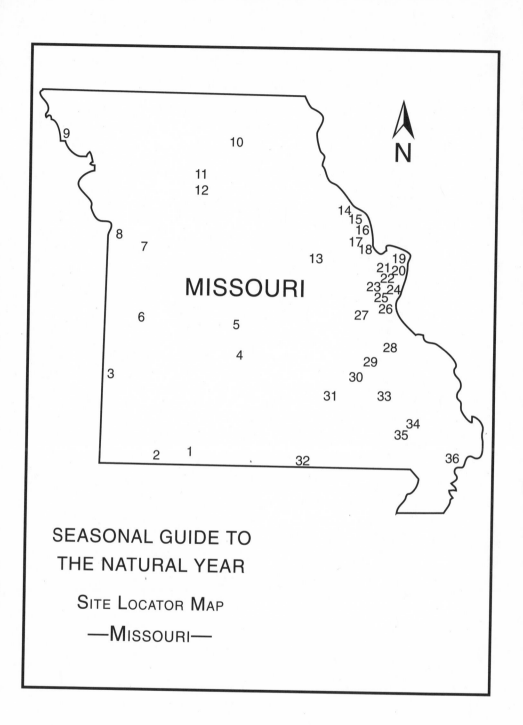

N

MISSOURI

SEASONAL GUIDE TO
THE NATURAL YEAR

SITE LOCATOR MAP

—MISSOURI—

LIST OF SITES
Missouri

Abbreviations: EDA—Environmental Demonstration Area; NWR—National Wildlife Refuge; SP—State Park; WR—Wildlife Refuge

1. Table Rock SP
2. Roaring River SP
3. Prairie SP
4. Bennett Spring SP
5. Lake of the Ozarks SP
6. Taberville Prairie Conservation Area
7. Powell Gardens
8. Swope Park in Kansas City
9. Squaw Creek NWR
10. Thousand Hills SP
11. Pershing SP
12. Swan Lake NWR
13. Graham Cave SP
14. Clarksville Locks and Dam 24
15. Clarence Cannon NWR
16. Mark Twain NWR Complex, Annada District
17. Cuivre River SP
18. Winfield Locks and Dam 25
19. Riverland EDA
20. Tower Grove Park in St. Louis
21. August A. Busch Memorial Wildlife Area
22. Dr. Edmund A. Babler Memorial SP
23. Rockwood Reservation
24. Missouri Botanical Garden's Shaw Arboretum
25. Missouri Botanical Garden
26. Mastodon SP
27. Meramec SP
28. Hawn SP
29. Elephant Rocks SP
30. Johnson's Shut-Ins SP
31. Ozark National Scenic Riverways
32. Grand Gulf SP
33. Sam A. Baker SP
34. Mingo NWR
35. Lake Wappapello SP
36. Big Oak Tree SP

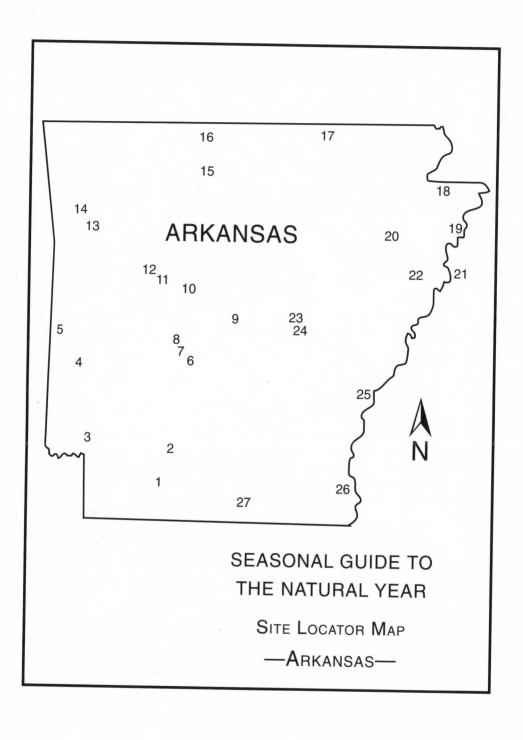

16
17
15
18
14
13
ARKANSAS
20
19
12
11
10
22
21
9
23
5
24
8
7
6
4
25
3
2
N
1
26
27

SEASONAL GUIDE TO
THE NATURAL YEAR

SITE LOCATOR MAP

—ARKANSAS—

LIST OF SITES
Arkansas

Abbreviations: EDA—Environmental Demonstration Area; NWR—National Wildlife Refuge; SP—State Park; WR—Wildlife Refuge

1. Logoly SP
2. White Oak Lake SP
3. Millwood SP
4. Cossatot River SP and Natural Area
5. Queen Wilhelmina SP
6. Lake Catherine SP
7. Hot Springs National Park
8. Lake Ouachita SP
9. Pinnacle Mountain SP
10. Petit Jean SP
11. Holla Bend NWR
12. Mt. Nebo SP
13. Lake Fort Smith SP
14. Devil's Den SP
15. Buffalo National River
16. Bull Shoals SP
17. Mammoth Spring SP
18. Big Lake NWR
19. Hampson Museum SP
20. Lake Poinsett SP
21. Memphis Botanic Garden
22. Wapanocca NWR
23. Railroad Prairie State Natural Area
24. Warren Prairie
25. White River NWR
26. Lake Chicot SP
27. Felsenthal NWR

The bald cypress at Wapanocca Wildlife Refuge, just four miles west of the Mississippi River in northern Arkansas, are large and sturdy, offering visitors insights to this type of southern ecosystem.

CONTENTS

CONTENTS

List of Maps

ACKNOWLEDGMENTS

This book owes a great deal to the enthusiasm and generosity of members of many natural history organizations and associations, not the least of which is the Webster Groves Nature Study Society, often called "Wigness" after its initials. This organization is a multifaceted group of hundreds of nature lovers of all sorts—birders, botanizers, insect enthusiasts and others. Although WGNSS appears to be a loosely constructed group, it is tightly bound by the dedication of its members to their impressive field trip schedule. The monthly newsletter has schedules of meetings and field trips, and also includes regular reports from several of its subgroups—the botany group and the birders are the two most active.

Although WGNSS originated in the St. Louis suburb of Webster Groves, its membership includes people from through-out the region and, indeed, from other parts of the country as well. Each week throughout the year, bands of WGNSS members go to favorite hotspots to find wildflowers, birds and other wildlife. Through WGNSS, many of us have been able to develop a natural history network that has been a great source of enjoyment and knowledge.

In addition, the people of the state and local Audubon Societies have a multitude of contacts and tips that they gladly share. Members of the American Birding Association also are generous with their information and expertise. In the plant arena, the native plant societies are a big help in identifying places to find wild plants. It's difficult to separate the members of the various wildlife organizations because so many natural history buffs enjoy cross memberships in several organizations.

The Missouri Department of Conservation people also have been helpful, as have their peers in Arkansas and Illinois. The expertise of their specialists is well documented in an ever-growing supply of reprints, booklets and books on subjects ranging from mosses to owls. Staff members have been helpful in pointing me toward other natural history experts in far-flung corners of the heartland states. Staff members of the state parks in all three states have provided a wealth of information and good leads. The same is true for the people who work with the National Wildlife Refuges.

Many thanks to Richard W. Coles, Ph.D., director of Tyson Research Center and adjunct professor of biology at Washington University, for checking the science of this book. Dick made some valuable suggestions which improved several parts of the book.

Special thanks go to the many people who have helped me in many ways, and to those who have been kind enough to review this material and correct my sins of both omission and commission— I accept full responsibility for the remaining mistakes.

INTRODUCTION

Each fall, along the great rivers and lakes of Illinois, Missouri and Arkansas the cries of migrating Canadian geese mark seasonal changes as they fly south in ragged chevrons. The haunting calls hint of faraway places, of distant fields and broad waters.

If your ears are in tune to the wild things, you can hear the geese even though you may be on a busy city street. You look up and there they are, thousands of feet above the noisy traffic—dozens of geese in their traditional formations, muscling their way south along those great sky paths known as the Central and Mississippi Flyways.

Millions of birds make these semiannual trips south and north through the central part of the United States. We notice the geese more because of their loud chatter as they fly. When you hear them you realize that the rush of migration is near and countless other migratory birds are also on the great paths, silently winging their way to warmer climates for the winter. In the spring they will return north to nesting grounds scattered all the way to the far reaches of Canada and Alaska.

The mysteries of migration have not all been solved. Bird banding and studies show that many of our smaller migratory birds travel far into South America—how they travel such great distances puzzles both scientists and birders alike. Observe these great waves of birds as they make their fall and spring treks; this is one of the most awesome of natural events.

ABOUT THIS GUIDE

We hope that our Seasonal Guide will raise your curiosity about the natural world in these heartland states and help you to really *see* what you are looking at. We hope it will inspire many naturalist expeditions in search of the events we describe. We will tempt and tantalize you into learning more about the land, its climate and its plants and animals. Lists of wildlife refuges, parks, forests, nature centers and recreation areas will point you toward places to go. Lists of private preserves and organizations will suggest contacts in a number of specialized areas. Birding hotlines and participating in some of the annual regional bird counts are among the ways you can meet people who are experienced birders.

Birding, botanizing and otherwise studying the things of the natural world provide a good excuse to get outdoors and a purpose for walking. This Seasonal Guide will help those who live in Illinois, Missouri and Arkansas learn more about where they live. It should help visitors enjoy the great range of habitat, plants and animals that we residents enjoy. Most importantly, this book will help you teach your children, grandchildren, and other young people more about the natural world and how we fit into it.

America's heartland states of Illinois, Missouri and Arkansas are located at an environmental crossroads, a natural meeting place of northern, southern, eastern and western plant and animal species. Here you may find plants such as the pawpaw or animals such as the water moccasin at the northernmost reaches of their territories. Both eastern and western box turtle species coexist and often interbreed. You will find black-capped chickadees north of the Missouri River and Carolina chickadees south of the river, with a predictable area in the middle where there is quite a mix of the two chickadees. It is possible for birders in this crossroads area to see as many as six hundred different bird species if the accidentals that stray in from other areas are included.

This region also represents the meeting of western prairies and eastern woodlands, the junction of glaciated and unglaciated land and the place where the ancient Gulf Coastal lowlands and Mississippi Embayment meet the Ozark Mountains.

Each month of the year welcomes new and exciting events of the annual cycle. *Seasonal Guide to the Natural Year—Illinois, Missouri and Arkansas* will lead you to many of these events. Joining an organization or group of people interested in field trips will give you the opportunity to learn from those who are more experienced. You will meet people of many sorts in your pursuit of natural events—those who specialize in certain groups of plants or animals almost exclusively and others who are interested in everything the natural world has to offer, from fossils to birds to mosses. Increasingly, I've noticed that there is a lot of cross-pollination between the specialized groups. Birders are going botanizing, rock hounds are searching for mushrooms and many naturalists are becoming interested in more and more plant and animal groups.

EQUIPMENT

Field guides and a certain amount of equipment will help you enjoy learning more about the natural world. Some good field guides and references are listed in the bibliography at the back of this book. For most of us, one or two guides is not enough—the libraries of most birders, botanizers and rock hounds continue to grow as new books are published. In recent years there has been a trend toward regionalized natural history guides. Unlike the more generalized books that focus on the entire country or a whole quadrant of the country, the region-specific guides are great for helping you decide precisely where to go to find the habitats, plants and animals you are looking for.

Joining the Audubon Society, American Birding Association or other organizations dedicated to birding, botanizing or other forms of natural history will give you a bridge to the local and regional experts. Knowing these experts and going on field trips with them is the best way to learn about local "hot spots" as well as the local flora and fauna. There is a list of these organizations in the Appendix.

Audiotapes of bird and amphibian calls are a boon, since the songs and calls of wild birds, frogs and toads will help you know where to look for them. Videotapes of plants and animals in the wild are becoming more common and will help beginners recognize common species. Perhaps you will want to make your own recordings in the wild—as reminders and to help you learn.

Binoculars are a must for observing wildlife—in some circumstances, such as wet and swampy areas, they are useful for identifying plants that are unreachable. Binoculars and telescopes are often useful for studying mammals and can also be helpful in identifying butterflies and moths. Before choosing binoculars, find an opportunity to try out different magnifications, fields of view and light-gathering power. Ask other natural history buffs if you can try out their binoculars when you're in the field.

The older porro-prism binoculars have prisms set at 90-degree angles to one another. The newer roof-prism binoculars, with small prisms in line in the optical tube, are sealed and so comparatively dust and moisture proof—an advantage if you plan field trips in all sorts of weather. Roof-prism binoculars tend to be more compact and lightweight than the older type. Porro-prism binoculars offer a slight edge in brightness, particularly noticeable at dawn and dusk. Since more powerful binoculars tend to be heavier, the choice in binoculars is a compromise of price, magnification, brightness and weight.

The numbers on binoculars, such as 7x50 or 10x40, refer first to the maximum magnification possible and, second, the size of the field of view (diameter in millimeters) and thus the light-gathering power of the front lens. Most people find that a magnification somewhere between seven and ten is sufficient. Be sure that your binoculars have rubber guards on the oculars for comfort and safety, especially if you wear glasses. A soft, comfortable yet sturdy neck or chest strap will pay off if you are on extended field trips.

A spotting scope or telescope on a tripod is helpful when you are in fields, meadows, prairies and along shores of rivers and lakes where plants and animals can be seen at considerable distance. Although spotting scopes are almost useless in the tight quarters of woods and forests, it's fun to set up a scope on a deck or porch at home for special situations—as when a pair of kestrels nested in a dead oak about 150 yards from my deck.

You will find that the magnifications of telescopes used in birding will range from 20x to 40x or even more. Most people find 20x to 25x adequate. The object lens (or objective) of good birding scopes is usually somewhere between 50 and 70 mm in diameter. The larger they are, the heavier the scope, so there is yet another compromise for those of us who carry all our own gear. There are zoom scopes that will bring objects much closer than the average telescope, but remember that the higher the magnification, the smaller the field of view—this can make even a large bird or animal difficult to find.

A small tape recorder can help birds find you. If you play a bird's calls and territorial songs it often will fly in to investigate, thinking there is an intruder present. Although some ornithologists believe that you should never try to attract birds by playing their songs and calls, most believe it does no harm to do this occasionally, especially with our more common birds. Of course, this should not be done too frequently since it can disturb birds' breeding habits, and it would be unwise to use this method for rare birds.

A 10x hand lens, the kind you can wear around your neck, is handy for all sorts of natural observing. It will help in appreciating and identifying plants, insects and fossils. A sharp pocketknife is handy for dissecting twigs and buds, prying a clinging fungus from dead wood and unearthing small insects and grubs. It's also immensely handy for cutting up apples to share—once it's cleaned, of course. A small ruler will help determine different species of trees and other plants. If you go mushrooming a trowel is handy, as well as a basket and waxed paper for rolling up individual mushrooms or small fungi.

If you are going to be roaming quite a distance from your car, a small day-type backpack is handy for carrying everything from lunch and thermos to field guides. "Dress for the weather and the environment" is good advice no matter where you are birding or botanizing. In Illinois, Missouri and Arkansas, however, dressing for the weather can be a challenge, since it can be a balmy 70 degrees Fahrenheit in the morning when you leave home and a bone-chilling 30 degrees with wind by afternoon. Watch the weather maps and anticipate the possibilities. Layered clothing is a necessity in such extremes.

Many amateur naturalists like to list all the birds and plants they have discovered on field trips. Field guides are handy for this since you can simply mark the species in the index for later reference. A small notebook is useful for recording a few pertinent details about each field trip—it's fun to look back, see what the weather was like and remind yourself of what you saw. Notations would include the date, the weather, where you went, who was on the trip and how many of what you saw. Some people use tape recorders for this information.

Some amateur and professional naturalists are dedicated to getting their finds on film—stills, videotape or movie film. This is another whole breed of cat for whom many books have been written. There are camera clubs that have subgroups dedicated to wildlife and plant photography and natural history organizations with subgroups devoted to photography. If you are interested, a few inquiries will head you in the right direction.

GENERAL TIPS AND CAUTIONS

If you want to study plants and animals on private land, you must get permission. Respect landowners' wishes and property. Fortunately, Illinois, Missouri and Arkansas all have marvelous local, state and national parks, refuges and preserves that offer a great range of habitats, so you probably won't even be tempted to stray onto private property. When on these public lands, respect both the wildlife and the posted rules. Stay on the trails and do not thoughtlessly intrude upon nesting birds or other wildlife. The best naturalists are those who leave no mark of their presence.

It helps to know the hunting seasons in the states where you plan to seek out the month by month natural events. If you must go birding during a major hunting season, be sure to wear a hunter-orange vest and hat. I prefer not to go birding or venture into any hunting area during deer or turkey season, but I'm not as concerned during rabbit, squirrel or quail seasons.

If you plan to explore by canoe or some other type of boat, follow the rules of water safety, using a personal flotation device even if you are a strong swimmer. Some of the streams in the Ozarks have treacherous rapids that are particularly hard to negotiate when trees are down. Even if you are an expert boater, do not go out on streams or rivers during floods.

You probably will want maps that are more detailed than those provided for general travel. The United States Geologic Survey topographic maps give the most detail. They show buildings, contours and every passable road as well as some that are probably not passable. The USGS maps are most commonly available in 7.5-minute quadrangles that cover an area of about 6.5 by 7.5 miles.

Since USGS maps are both large and expensive, you might wish to look for the state atlases published by the DeLorme Mapping Co. Their scale is more manageable (1:150,000) than USGS quads (1:24,000). The DeLorme Company is working west in its aim to complete maps of all of the states. The atlas and gazetteer for Illinois have been published, but those for Missouri and Arkansas are not yet in the works. The Illinois atlas has ninety-six pages of detailed maps of the entire state. The details include natural features, public lands, recreational sites and fishing hotspots.

The most important thing when birding, botanizing, or looking for other natural events is to use common sense. In cold weather, carry extra clothing and dress in layers. In all weather, carry drinking water and food if you plan to be gone for many hours. Know where you are going and let others know where you are going if exploring a remote area. It is wise to canoe or travel into more primitive areas with at least one other person. Finally, enjoy yourself and share your pleasure with others.

A REQUEST FOR HELP

Scott Weidensaul, author of the first book of this series, *Seasonal Guide to the Natural Year—Mid-Atlantic*, which covers six states, set the pattern for seasonal guides to other states. He noted in his introduction that while we make every effort to see that our research and fieldwork results in accurate information, things change.

Landmarks may disappear, bridges wash out, and other conditions may alter some of the places we have described.

Please help us keep future editions of these seasonal guides as accurate and up-to-date as possible by sending corrections to the author, c/o Fulcrum Publishing, 350 Indiana Street, Suite 350, Golden, CO 80401.

If you know of other natural events that we should include, please let us know so that we can include them in future editions. Include detailed directions and as much background information as possible. We have only scratched the surface of the natural world to whet your appetite—there are bound to be many other events that are at least as notable. Remember that these events should be consistent from year to year, be of unusual interest and occur on public land or private land that is open to the public.

LAND, WATER, ROCKS AND WEATHER—
AN OVERVIEW OF THE HEARTLAND ENVIRONMENT

The heartland states of Illinois, Missouri and Arkansas are crossroads for both plant and animal life from biological, environmental, geological and climatological points of view. The three-state region represents the meeting place of five different *biomes*—areas that represent common sets of plants, animals and environmental conditions. The biomes are the forests and swamps of the Gulf coast lowlands; southwestern deserts; western prairies and grasslands; northern evergreen forest; and deciduous forest of the eastern temperate region.

Because of its varying geology and climate, the region includes many habitats and environments. Prairie, woodland, riparian, wetland and mountain ecosystems all fall within the three-state area. Where these biomes and ecosystems meet, a particularly rich population of plants, birds, and other wildlife exists. The regions where they meet are called *ecotones* and include natives of both regions plus, often, hybrids of the two.

Although political boundaries such as state lines are important economically, they seldom delineate the important physical features of the region. Exceptions to this are those places where major rivers or lakes have become state lines.

WATERWAYS AND WETLANDS

Arkansas has the mighty Mississippi as its eastern border and a bit of the Red River on its southwestern corner. Illinois and Missouri share the Mississippi River as their western and eastern boundaries respectively, and Illinois has a bit of Lake Michigan on its northeastern border. Missouri's northwest boundary is the Missouri River.

Internally, Arkansas has the Arkansas River that comes in from Oklahoma at Fort Smith and joins the Mississippi southeast of Little Rock. Within Illinois the Illinois River runs from north of Peoria south to Alton just above Mississippi River Locks and Dam 26. And Missouri has the Missouri River that bisects the state between Kansas City and St. Louis. These rivers, their tributaries and associated wetlands provide many likely spots for birding and botanizing.

The Mississippi-Missouri river system is the semiannual migratory path of many birds as they escape harsh winter weather by flying south in the fall, then returning to breeding grounds throughout North America in the spring. The Mississippi Flyway begins in northern North America, then runs along the Great Lakes and down the Mississippi Valley to the Gulf of Mexico. Some of the birds seen on this flyway spend their summers in the far northern reaches of Canada and Alaska, then travel south as far as Mexico, Central America and South America. Ducks, geese, shorebirds and many songbirds follow the watery path. Birders living near this flyway, one of the world's great migration routes, are richly rewarded each spring and fall.

The wetlands and bottomlands associated with rivers, lakes, streams and ponds are marvelous gathering places for shorebirds. Dowitchers, plovers, greater and lesser yellowlegs and an assortment of sandpipers are among the migratory visitors to wetland areas. Cranes, egrets and herons fish in shallow waters of the heartland states throughout the warm seasons and many of these birds also breed here, often in large rookeries.

THE LAND AND ITS GEOLOGY

Aside from the Mississippi River system and its many tributaries, the most striking feature of the three-state area is, to many people, the Ozark Mountains, also called the Ozark Plateau. Rugged hills, swift streams and deep valleys typify these ancient mountains. The Ozarks, which have many clear, spring-fed streams, occupy much of the northwestern quadrant of Arkansas, a small bit of southern Illinois and most of the southern half of Missouri. The forests that used to cover the eastern United States still inhabit much of this area.

The Missouri, Mississippi and Arkansas rivers delineate the south, east and north of the Ozarks. The prairies of Kansas and Oklahoma are to the west. Scorpions—more commonly found in southwestern deserts—are not uncommon on shallow-soiled Ozark glades. There are over a dozen native fish species that thrive in isolated glory in crystalline Ozark streams, but wouldn't survive in the muddier waters of the major rivers. Buttonbush and water tupelo, plants of the south, grow in Ozark bogs. The ice ages pushed plants growing farther north down into the Ozarks. Many factors have combined to provide an unusual environment where plants and animals from other regions thrive in mutual harmony in these rugged hills.

Beginning at the southern edge of our heartland states, Arkansas comprises two main areas from a geological point of view. There are the lowlands of the southern and eastern areas and the Ozark highlands of the northern and western part of the state. The eastern Ozarks of Arkansas and Missouri slope down to the Mississippi Alluvial Plain, a hot, rich land. The Missouri Bootheel and Arkansas land to its south have long been noted for lush cotton and rice crops that have made fortunes for planters for well over a century. The moist bottomland of eastern Arkansas boasts a gigantic population of migratory waterfowl. In the southwestern Ozarks are the Boston Mountains, a tilted plateau of steep and forested slopes. The Ouachita Mountains rise just south of the Arkansas River. The Arkansas Valley that divides the Ouachita from the Ozark highlands is broad and rolling.

Except for its Ozarkian southern tip, Illinois consists mostly of gently rolling Central Plains that were smoothed and enriched by the irresistible forces of the deep ice age glaciers. The glaciers scooped out the Great Lakes as they advanced and receded. This land with its incredibly fertile black soil is part of the Corn Belt that extends east to Ohio and west to Kansas and Nebraska. Slow-moving streams drain the area.

Only a few areas of Illinois were not flattened by glaciers—a small hilly section in the northwest corner of the state and another hilly area between the Illinois and Mississippi rivers just north of their junction. There is in the southern part of Illinois a bit of alluvial plain that is shared with Arkansas and Missouri—it represents the northernmost reach of the Gulf Coastal Plain. This area is often called Little Egypt because of the similarity of that land around Cairo (pronounced Kay´row), Illinois, to the Nile River Delta.

Glacially formed plains extend from Illinois across much of the northern half of Missouri with the Missouri River as their southern border. Before the ice ages the mighty Missouri flowed much farther north. Unglaciated rolling prairies, south of the Missouri River and west of the Ozarks, are known as the Osage Plains.

Missouri includes the greatest portion of the Ozark Mountains with their many beautiful streams, giant springs and caverns. Lake of the Ozarks, one of America's largest artificial lakes with its 1,672-mile shoreline, and other man-made lakes plus their associated parks offer excellent opportunities for seeking area plants and animals.

Thousands of freshwater springs bubble up through the rocky Ozarks, adding to the flashing clear water of the streams and often creating microenvironments where you can find unusual plants and creatures. Hundreds of caves lace the limestone formations of the Ozarks, carved from the stone by water. Some caves are host to such strange animals as the blind cricket and blind catfish.

The Ozark Mountains are, from a geological point of view, one of the oldest mountain ranges on earth. They are thought to have been many thousands of feet higher eons ago. Originally formed by volcanic activity, these ancient hills have been so eroded that some of the oldest rock on earth, rock from the Precambrian Period over five hundred million years ago, can be found in southern Missouri. Although there are no signs of fossils in Precambrian rock, the Ozarks and, indeed, other parts of our heartland states are rich in fossils. Highway cuts throughout the region are particularly rewarding for those seeking the mineralized remnants of ancient plants and animals.

The Ozark Mountains are also called the Ozark Plateau because of the way the contours have formed. Water and wind erosion cut deeply into the ancient plateau, forming the cliff-edged streams that now run far below the original land surface. At the same time the high plateau itself was eroding, so that the Precambrian granite now lies exposed in the central Ozarks. Thus the region was formed more by erosion than uplift.

THE ICE AGE

The influences and effects of the Wisconsin Ice Age in Illinois, Missouri and, secondarily, Arkansas are profound. This last great ice age, which occurred some seventy-five thousand years ago and lasted until about ten thousand years ago, shaped the land, smoothed its sharpness, lowered its hills, scooped out lakes and generally softened the contours of the land as it advanced and receded.

At the height of the ice age, the massive glaciers crept southward under the pressure of their own weight, picking up all manner of rocks, pebbles and plant life. These were the "teeth" of the glacier that striated the land so thoroughly in some areas. These teeth plus ice, water and the weight of the thick glacier proved powerful enough to sculpt the land in ways that remain visible today.

When the glaciers melted and receded, they dropped boulders and stones far from their origin. These erratics, as they are called, can be found in northern parts of Missouri and Illinois—their origins are often traceable to specific rock formations in northern United States and Canada. At the southern ends of the great ice sheets the glaciers dropped moraines—accumulations of gravel and stones pushed ahead of the icy snouts—in many shapes and sizes.

The grinding power of the slowly moving glaciers ground rocks into a fine powder called loess. Thick deposits of wind-blown loess are found in northwestern Missouri, its next door neighbor, Kansas, and many other parts of the world. In some places, such as the northern prairies of Missouri, the glaciers scoured the earth, then melted and formed depressions called kettles. These shallow, round and oval depressions became ponds and bogs. In addition to making great watering holes for all wildlife and good locations for moisture-loving plants, these kettles are valuable stopovers for migrating birds and offer breeding places for amphibians as well.

The great ice sheets changed the climate and habitats of the land they covered and also the adjacent surrounding lands. Animals and plants from northern regions moved south ahead of the glaciers and, in many cases, remained there when the ice melted and warmer weather ruled once again. Some of these plant and animal relicts, as they are called, are found to this day in the Ozarks where they retreated as the Wisconsin Ice Age advanced.

When ice age glaciers pushed the Missouri River south to its present location, their oppressive scouring weights did not reach the Ozarks. Remnants of plant and animal life that fled before the great stretches of that Wisconsin Ice Age can still be found in the Ozarks. Beech trees, normally found farther north and east thrive in some of the cool valleys of Ozark streams. River birches that also are usually found in more northerly climes grow in some of the Ozarks' cool hollows. Arctic lichens exist on some north-facing rocky cliffs.

THE CLIMATE

Although the latitude and altitude of the land have a great deal to due with day lengths and the extremes of temperatures through the seasons, the continental climate of these three states is another determining factor for what kinds of plants and animals we can find. The region is noted for its warring weather systems. Warm moist air from the Gulf of Mexico slides north and clashes with cold polar air that may thunder across the plains. Greater weather battles often result in monumental thunderstorms or even tornadoes. At other times, a warm southern wind may bring hints of spring in January as temperatures rise to 60 or even 70 degrees Fahrenheit.

One of the reasons for our having such intemperate weather is that our mountains run in a north-to-south direction, unlike Europe where the mountains are in a generally east-to-west configuration. The European mountains buffer the weather that comes in from the north, making southern European weather far milder than the corresponding weather at the same latitude in our country. The geography of North America, on the other hand, allows winds and weather systems to sweep out of the Arctic and slide south in the funnel of the Great Plains.

There are days when you may leave home in a light sweater with the smell of spring in the air and come home only hours later shivering in temperatures that have plunged into the 20s or 30s with winds that create subzero chill factors. Weathermen call these fast-moving cold fronts Arctic Clippers for good reason. The jet stream, that swift highway of cold air that sweeps from west to east, often performs a sinuous hula over the heartland. From a weather point of view, this is surely a robust region.

Rainfall, in many years, seems as capricious as the temperatures. One season may be drought and the next, flood. Snowfall is heavier in northern Illinois near Lake Michigan. In Missouri there may be several winters in a row when there is hardly enough snow to hide a mouse, while other winters may be destructively icy and snowy. One odd thing that often happens in the winter is that the clash between Gulf air and the Arctic cold fronts can result in snows that are greater and longer-lasting in southern Missouri and Arkansas than they are in areas farther north.

Plant cover throughout the world is greatly dependent upon the annual rainfall as well as the timing of rains during each year. It helps to know that if rainfall is below an average of 12 inches annually, the plants that are most likely to grow are desert plants. If the annual rainfall averages 12 to 36 inches, dominant plants tend to be grasses. When rainfall averages over 36 inches each year, the plant cover is most likely to be trees. When you look at a rainfall map of Illinois, Missouri and Arkansas, you will see that most of the area has rainfall over 36 inches annually—so it is not surprising that much of the area is or was in the past forested. Periods of drought plus other factors of soil also affect plant growth and, because many woody plants (trees and shrubs) are not genetically tuned to tolerate extremes, they will not grow on some lands even though they get enough rain in some seasons.

As wags are likely to say, the weather in this region is too hot, too cold, too wet and too dry. That is why the month by month natural year is often so hard to predict—certain natural events are triggered by temperature and moisture as well as hours of sunlight. However, knowing something about the geology, climate and environmental attributes of the land is a giant step toward learning what to look for and where to find it in the natural world. We and all living things are extremely dependent upon our geology and climate.

JANUARY

January Observations

1

Bald Eagles

One cold winter morning I stood on a bluff southwest of the Mississippi River Lock and Dam No. 24 at Clarksville, Missouri. A sharp wind from the northeast blew straight from the dam toward the bluff creating a strong updraft as it hit the steep hillside. A half dozen adult eagles were flying around the dam, probably looking for fish in what little water remained unfrozen. As I watched, the eagles circled and then, flapping vigorously, headed straight for the bluff where I stood. After gathering speed, they set their wings and glided toward the bluff. As the strong updraft caught them, they swooped up the hill and over my head. Then they circled for a few minutes as if they were saying to each other, "Hey, did you see me fly up that hill?"

Any thought that this was a coincidence was soon dispelled as the eagles flew back to the dam and repeated their play again and again. I was reminded of otters that play on snowy river banks, sliding time after time into the water. The eagles were having a wonderful time with the wind and updrafts—there is no doubt about it.

Many migrant bald eagles spend the winter in parks and wildlife preserves along the major rivers and lakes of Illinois, Missouri and Arkansas, especially when the weather is very cold and waters are frozen. Then, hunger drives eagles farther south. In recent years we have been regaining resident eagles, thanks to the efforts of many professional naturalists and biologists. Since fish are a major component of their diet—which also includes carrion—bald eagles are most often found near open water in harsh winter weather. The colder the weather, the more eagles you will see near open water.

The locks and dams of the Mississippi River above St. Louis are excellent places to find eagles since the water below the dams remains open throughout the winter. I have seen them as thick as tree-top chickens along river slues.

From a distance, all you can see at first is dark lumps on the tree branches. Then the lumps move, slide away from the branches and their dark-brown wings spread to an awesome span. When the chalk-white head, large yellow bill and white tail appear, you know that you are seeing the unmistakable field marks of the adult bald eagle. These impressive birds are large and have tremendous soaring ability. The females have a wingspan of nearly 8 feet, are up to about 3 feet tall and weigh approximately 15 pounds. The male eagle is typically smaller with a wingspan of about 6 feet, stands under 3 feet tall and weighs roughly 10 pounds.

Take time to observe eagles. One of the first things you will see is that, associated with the white-headed adults, there are a number of younger birds that lack the striking white head and tail. Bald eagles take four to five years to mature and fully realize their adult coloring. Yearlings are dark in color and may be confused with the golden eagle. If in doubt, look for some blotchy or mottled white on the underneath side of the wings—this white marking is more distinct, like a flash of white at the base of the primaries in the juvenile golden eagle. The undersides of the bald and golden eagles are uniformly dark in the adults.

Until the turn of the century, bald eagles were found in all of the lower forty-eight states. A decline in their population followed and, by 1966, there were only about six hundred breeding pairs, according to U.S. Fish and Wildlife statistics. The U.S. Fish and Wildlife Service, Dickerson Park Zoo in Springfield, Missouri and the Missouri Department of Conservation were among the sponsors of programs that began in the early 1980s to restore eagles to the heartland area. Between 1981 and 1990, seventy-four eagles were released.

Thanks to programs like these, the bald eagle is once again resident in parts of the heartland states adjoining rivers and lakes. Reports of eagle nests are becoming more common along waterways where they often live in tall waterside trees such as cottonwoods. Eagles' nests can be huge affairs 20 feet high, weighing more than a ton and a half and measuring up to 9 feet in diameter. An eagle brood usually consists of two eggs but may range from one to three.

HOTSPOTS

Winter is the best time to look for bald eagles—the migratory eagles join the residents, boosting the population to its annual highs. On particularly severe winter days it's not unusual to see dozens of bald eagles or more at some of the listed hotspots.

Big Lake NWR, part of the Northeast Arkansas Refuge Complex of the U.S. Fish and Wildlife Service, is in the northeast corner of the state. Interestingly, Big Lake was formed by the infamous New Madrid earthquake of 1811–1812 that also formed Reelfoot Lake, Tennessee, not far away. You can reach Big Lake by driving north from Memphis or south from St. Louis on I-55. Take Arkansas Route 18 from near the Arkansas-Missouri border to 18 miles west of Blytheville, Arkansas. That will bring you to the refuge office where you can get current updates on good spots to search for eagles and other attractions. For the past three years or so, a pair of eagles has been nesting at a spot that is easy to observe from one of the roads in the refuge. The 11,038-acre refuge, which extends 10.5 miles north to the Missouri border, has some spectacular stands of virgin bald cypress, and includes about 3,000 acres of timbered swampland and some 3,000 acres of open water. Spring floods may result in much of the refuge being under water.

Wapanocca NWR, south of Big Lake, comprises 5,485 acres around a shallow oxbow lake of the same name. Willow and cypress swamp surround Lake Wapanocca and the remaining acres of the refuge include bottomland hardwoods and croplands of the refuge's farm unit. In winter, the bald eagles roost in cypress trees. To get there, take I-55 and watch for the Turrell-Twist exit about 16 miles north of West Memphis at Highway 42. Go east for 2 miles, crossing Highway 77. The Northeast Arkansas Refuge Complex will be on your right past the railroad overpass. Stop at the visitors' center and ask about current eagle activity around the lake.

In Illinois, the Nature Conservancy's **Cedar Glen Eagle Roost** on the Mississippi River just south of Keokuk, Iowa, and across from the mouth of the Des Moines River, is a top spot of riverside roosting sites for bald eagles. The 790-acre preserve includes restored prairie and Mississippi islands as well as the eagle roosting sites. Managed by Western Illinois University, Cedar Glen is reached by Highway 136 west from Macomb, continuing 41 miles to Hamilton. From there, take the Great River Road about 4 miles to the field office where you can get current information.

Chautauqua NWR, a 4,400-acre preserve, is another good Illinois bald eagle hotspot. Bordered on the west by the Illinois River and featuring the 3,500-acre Lake Chautauqua, this area includes both floodplains and uplands. Large springs keep some of the lake's eastern shoreline free of ice even in the worst winter weather, which makes this a good spot for wintering eagles. To reach this refuge in west central Illinois, take Manitou Road from Havana north about 10 miles to the refuge entrance, then you turn left and follow signs to the office.

In southern Illinois, **Crab Orchard NWR** is a hotspot for bald eagles. Fall and winter find thousands of waterfowl as well as eagles feeding and resting in the 43,000-acre refuge. A mixed bag of croplands, wilderness, pasture, natural areas and lakes, Crab Orchard is easily reached by taking the Route 13 Exit west from I-57 in Marion for just under 2 miles. Turn left on Route 148 and go 1 mile to the refuge office.

Bald eagles are commonly seen at the **Mississippi River locks and dams** where the water remains open even in the coldest winter weather. In Missouri, the Missouri Department of Conservation sponsors Eagle Days each year at several locations throughout the state. Local Audubon Societies and similar organizations also are active in this event. In addition, the U.S. Army Corps of Engineers participates in Eagle Days by having experts present to answer questions at the locks and dams at Clarksville and Winfield in Missouri, where the overlook access for visitors offers an excellent vantage point.

The **Winfield Locks and Dam 25** and **Clarksville Locks and Dam 24** are easy to reach from the St. Louis area by taking I-70 north to Missouri Route 79 that goes north along the river toward Hannibal. Watch for signs near the town of Winfield, some 25 miles north of St. Louis, that direct you to the visitors' area of the dam. About 30 miles farther north is the town of Clarksville where the locks and dam are located at the foot of the town's main street. The raised overlook allows you to get a good view of the dam and thus the eagles.

The best spot for viewing bald eagles and many other birds in the St. Louis area is the **Riverland Environmental Demonstration Area (EDA)**, established in 1988 by the Corps of Engineers just upstream from the new **Melvin Price Locks and Dam** that replaced the old Locks and Dam 26 a couple of miles upstream at Alton, Illinois. Riverlands is 1,200 acres of floodplain that the Corps is restoring and re-creating to a mosaic of bottomland, marsh, native prairie and forest. Riverlands is located just south of Missouri Route 367 which goes between I-270, a circumferential highway around St. Louis and

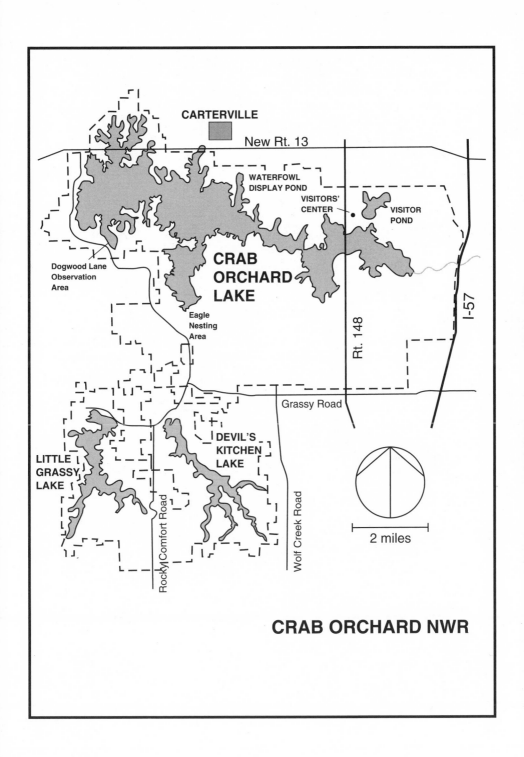

CRAB ORCHARD NWR

Alton. When visiting Riverlands, look for the visitors' center where you can learn more about what you can expect to see. In January and other cold months, eagles are most likely to be roosting in the trees of the Riverlands area known as Ellis Island.

Mingo NWR, a good eagling site in southeastern Missouri, is in an ancient abandoned channel of the Mississippi River separated from the current channel by an area called Crowley's Ridge. From Puxico, go north on Highway 51 for 1.5 miles to the office and visitors' center. The habitats include 21,676 acres of bottomland, swamp and steep hills. The remaining croplands are gradually reverting to their natural state.

Bald eagles can also be seen in numbers at **Squaw Creek NWR**, located in northwestern Missouri, where nearly 7,000 acres of marsh attract large numbers of migratory birds, especially waterfowl. This area has one of the largest U.S. populations of bald eagles—as many as three hundred during winter months. To get there, take I-29 from Mound City south 4.5 miles to Highway 159 (Exit 79), then go west on Highway 159 to the refuge headquarters.

2

Woodpeckers

We have six resident woodpeckers in Illinois, Missouri and Arkansas, seven if you count the rare and endangered red-cockaded woodpecker that can be seen in some parts of Arkansas. In addition we have a migrant woodpecker, the yellow-bellied sapsucker, that breeds farther north and winters farther south. The sapsucker might be seen in northern Illinois in the summer and in the southern extremes of Illinois, Missouri and Arkansas during winter months.

Woodpeckers are usually easier to see in the winter when leaves are off the trees. Their calls and the sound of their rapping on wood in search of insects and other small creatures will catch your attention. Then you can follow their hop-and-creep progress up and down the trees as well as their distinctive flight. These are flashy birds, featuring touches of bright red plus patterns of black and white. Although woodpeckers are solitary birds, downy woodpeckers travel as couples or, when their offspring are fledged but still young, as families.

Follow the chattering calls or drumming with your eyes to see woodpeckers on the sides of trees, going up and down, hopping and circling in a remarkably dexterous style. Their stiff tail feathers are used as props, making tree-side acrobatics easier. Their sharp-clawed toes are arranged two in front and two behind, which gives them a great advantage in clinging to tree bark.

In flight, woodpeckers have a distinctive undulating pattern of "flap-flap-flap-closed wings." This odd flying style plus the flashes of red, black and white make recognition easy. Their habit of landing upright on the sides of trees or bird feeders is equally distinctive.

Woodpeckers have strong chisel-like bills with sharp points, well suited for drilling, picking and chipping into tree trunks and branches. The bill and remarkably long barbed-tip tongue make it possible for these birds to find and eat wood-boring insects and other creatures that live in the superficial layers of trees. Their diet may include berries, acorns and sap as well as insects.

Woodpeckers nest in the hollows of trees, often in cavities that are chiseled well down into the trunk or branch. In the spring, they lay their eggs directly on the wood chips at the bottom of their excavations.

The red-headed woodpecker, about 9 inches long, handsome and flashy with its brilliant red head, white belly and wings of black and white, is found in orchards, open woods and in fields of scattered trees. The sexes are alike in coloration. Throughout the year the red-head's diet consists of about one-third animal and two-thirds vegetable matter, including acorns, fruit and corn. This bird may store some of its food under loose bark, in knotholes and tree cavities.

The pileated woodpecker, largest of North American woodpeckers at over 16 inches long, has a bill at least as long as its head and a bright red crest on top of its white-striped black head. The male's red "mustache" differentiates it from the female. The flashy white of the underwings bordered by black flight feathers are in contrast to the dark upper wings, body and tail. Their diet consists primarily of ants, beetles and their wood-boring larvae. The pileated and the flicker are the only woodpeckers regularly seen feeding on the ground—both like to tear open anthills to savor the ants and their larvae. The pileated woodpecker is a forest dweller, living almost wholly within the treetop canopy. It is alert, furtive and rather silent in the summer and easily eludes observation. The "Woody Woodpecker" call and loud drumming are usually clues to its presence.

The red-bellied woodpecker, a bit over 9 inches long, has red, black and white as part of its main color scheme. Its belly is buff, not red, and it is one of the so-called ladder-backed woodpeckers. The male has a red cap and nape while the female has a gray head and only a bit of red on the nape. The loud "clucks" of the red-bellied woodpecker announce its presence in woodlands, including swampy areas and bottomland woods. Its diet consists of insects and larvae as well as vegetable matter.

The Northern flicker's deeply undulating flight and loud repetitive call quickly draw attention to this handsome 12-inch-long bird. In flight, the white rump is obvious as are the yellow underwings. The gray cap has a red crescent below it on the back of the head. A black bib tops the black-speckled breast and the brown and black colors of the back and wing tops give a tweedy look to the flicker. The male's black "mustache" distinguishes it from the female. Flickers are found in lightly wooded areas and also the wooded edges of open country. In winter flickers seek the shelter of woodlands. Ants, ground beetles, bugs, grasshoppers and crickets comprise nearly two-thirds of their warm-season diet, the rest consisting of seeds and wild fruits. In the winter the fruits of poison ivy are a favorite food.

The smallish yellow-bellied sapsucker, slightly smaller than the hairy woodpecker at about 8 inches long, gives the impression of being primarily black and white with a large white wing bar. The belly is yellowish and the forehead is marked by a striking red patch. The male has a red throat while the female's throat is white. This migratory bird breeds in the North, including northern Illinois, and winters in the South, including the extreme southern parts of our heartland states. Its habit of drilling rings of holes in ornamental and fruit trees to eat the sap causes this bird to be more than a little unpopular with some farmers and landowners.

The downy woodpecker, a black and white bird only 6 1/2 to 7 inches long, is the most common and most sociable of our native woodpeckers—look for it in all wooded areas. The male has a red patch on the back of its head while the female and juvenile do not. The bird's back is white and the cheeks have two white stripes, one along the jaw line, the other above the eye. The wings appear to be banded with white and black. The downy woodpecker, a sprightly little bird, is most often found in shade trees, orchards and at the edge of woods. Most of the downy's diet is wood-boring larvae, weevils, ants, caterpillars and other small, mostly destructive creatures.

The description of the downy is about the same for the larger (9 or more inches long) hairy woodpecker. The hairy woodpecker is different in that its beak is comparatively larger and longer, about the same length as the head, and it has a generally coarser, rangier look. Agile and strong, this bird is more active and noisier than the downy—its swift darting manner helps it dodge behind tree trunks as you try to get a glimpse of it. Watch the way it throws itself backwards as it leaps from tree trunk into flight. The voice of the hairy woodpecker is comparable to the kingfisher, a long rattle that runs together. This is a rather shy bird that can be found in deciduous woods, old orchards and open forests. Most of the hairy's food consists of injurious insects—the rest of fruit, grain, seeds and miscellaneous vegetable matter.

The pileated and sapsucker can be readily identified by the rhythm of their drumming alone. The drumming of other species—territorial displays that are usually heard in the breeding season—are not such a sure thing. The drum roll of the pileated consists of a dozen or so strokes that begin slowly and loudly, then increases in speed as it diminishes in volume. The sapsucker's drumming intersperses spaced pecks with rapid drumming, giving it an odd stuttering effect.

HOTSPOTS

Look for the greatest number of woodpecker varieties in bottomland woods and forests. Here you will find the best combinations of the needed habitat of these marvelous birds. Warm winter days when there is little wind are ideal for searching for woodpeckers.

If you want to see the red-cockaded woodpecker, visit the forests of **Felsenthal NWR** in Crossett, Arkansas, where it is a year-round resident. This rare bird was once widespread from Virginia to Texas. Now colonies of these small wood-boring birds are found on forestlands in Arkansas, the Carolinas, Louisiana and Mississippi. Logging and urban development reduced this woodpecker's habitat and, in 1973, it was among the first animals listed for protection under the Endangered Species Act. In early 1993, The U.S. Department of Interior approved a plan by Georgia Pacific Corporation, the nation's largest timber company, to maintain at least 10 acres of trees and brush around the known colonies of red-cockaded woodpeckers on its forest lands. Most of the estimated ten thousand red-cockaded woodpeckers live in national forests and timberlands on military bases in the South, but a substantial colony of these birds lives in Felsenthal NWR. You can reach Felsenthal from U.S. Highway 82 which bisects the refuge on an east-west plane between Crossett and Strong. Stop at the refuge headquarters, about 5 miles west of Crossett, for information and a map.

In Illinois, you can see pileated woodpeckers as well as other woodpeckers and bald eagles at **The Nature Conservancy's Cedar Glen Eagle Roost**, Warsaw. (See Chapter 1 for directions.) The preserve and **Kibbe Life Sciences Station** are both managed by Western Illinois University. For information and a map, ask the resident manager or contact The Nature Conservancy Field Office.

Mingo NWR in southern Missouri is a great place for seeing a wide variety of woodpeckers. (For directions, see Chapter 1.) Stop at the visitors' center north of Puxico on Highway 51 for directions to the trails on the forested oak-hickory hillsides and bottomlands where you are most likely to see woodpeckers. Downy, red-headed and red-bellied woodpeckers are common, and both hairy and pileated woodpeckers are seen occasionally.

The Missouri Botanical Garden's Shaw Arboretum at Gray Summit, Missouri, offers a wonderful bottomland woods area along the Meramec River. To get there, take I-44 southwest of St. Louis to the Gray Summit Exit. That is about 25 miles southwest of I-270. Turn left and go over I-44, then bear right. The gate and visitors' center are a few feet away and well marked. The arboretum's trail map will lead you to the woods along the river where you are likely to see a number of woodpeckers.

3

Animal Tracks

Early one winter morning after a snowfall, I walked through an open area near some woods just after the sun broke through the clouds. Miniature rabbitlike tracks in the snow began near a clump of tall grass. Like rabbit and squirrel tracks, the hind feet overreached the front, making the characteristic pattern of hopping mammals. Between hops, the mark of a long tail appeared identifying the animal as some kind of mouse. The tracks wandered about, moved in a circle, then totally disappeared. Around the final set of tracks were two soft, shallow, brush-like marks. My guess is that during the night an owl, hunting on silent wings, swooped down and captured the small rodent.

Snow, even just a sprinkling, offers rare opportunities to learn more about wildlife. The snowy times of winter are no time for the curious to sit inside. The tracks of birds and animals tell where they've been, where they are going and, often, what they have been doing. The private lives of both animals and birds become more public when there is snow on the ground. Look for tracks, but also look for urine signs and scat, good clues for identifying different creatures.

Tracks cross or intertwine as animals appear to meet or follow one another. Signs of interactions or predations between species may appear as animal tracks wander across fields and through woods. Under trees, confusing marks that look like tracks may be the marks left by snow sliding from leaves and branches. It takes some careful sleuthing to read the snow signs.

Birds and animals take cover during bad storms or cold windy

The tracks of cottontail rabbits are common throughout our three-state region. You will find rabbit tracks close to brush, deep thick grass, or other places that offer quick shelter and protection from hawks, owls, coyotes and other predators.

weather. Birds will huddle on the lee side of trees and small mammals may take refuge in tree hollows, burrows in the earth or under the snow in tunnels through grasses, leaves and brush. Larger mammals seek thickets, fence rows or brush piles under which they can find refuge from the wind and cold.

White-tailed deer may gather in deer "yards" when the snow is deep and use common paths so that the snow becomes packed, allowing them to get around more easily. When hiking during snowy times, look for signs of deer lying down and also for their scat and signs of browsing.

Deer tracks are easy to identify since deer are the only wild animal in the region that are two-toed. The deer, when walking, often place each hind foot in the print of the front foot. When running, the hind feet overreach the front—bounding deer often leave 8 to 12 feet bet-ween each leap—and they can pop over 5-foot fences with an ease that Superman might envy. Tracks are of different sizes, with those of older bucks being quite a bit larger than those of does and youngsters. Large, heavy deer and those running fast usually leave tracks that include their dew claws—the two hind toes above the rear of each hoof. Deer droppings are dark black oblong pellets.

Deer look for places that are warm, often a south-facing slope—protected, yet near young trees, grass or other browse. When snows are deep and available grass is scarce, deer will browse on the buds and twigs of deciduous trees and also the foliage of evergreens. You can tell the difference between twigs chewed by deer and twigs chewed by rabbits and other rodents: rodents make clean bites with their sharp central incisors while foliage and twigs chewed by deer are more ragged because deer use their molars to gnaw the woody material.

The tracks of deer, canids, felines and other trotting animals appear to be single footprints in a somewhat straight line with fairly equal distances between tracks. The gallop of most animals will show up as sets of four footprints set apart from each other by varying distances that depend upon the speed.

Canid tracks—fox and coyote as well as dog tracks—all are oval and have four toes and claws that show in the tracks. They are difficult to tell apart. Wild canids tend to have tracks in a straight line whereas dogs tend to have varying spans or straddles between their right and left legs. Use other clues to tell you if the tracks are from foxes or coyotes—dog tracks are likely to be out in the open or near people tracks and show indications of playing or bounding. The wild canids are more likely to show evidence of stealth and wariness. Coyotes might go along the edge of woods where, in a moment, the animal could disappear in the brush. Foxes trot most of the time and tend to follow edges of the landscape—walls, banks, swamp edges or ridges.

Feline tracks show four toes but no claws in their round prints. The bobcat is the only wild cat that can be found in wilder wooded areas of Illinois, Missouri and Arkansas—mainly in the southern swampy areas. The tracks are easy to tell from domestic or feral cats by size alone. Domestic cats usually have paw prints that are about 1 inch in diameter, while bobcat tracks are about 2 inches in diameter.

Raccoons and opossums are common mammals found pretty much all over the three states in wooded areas, often near water. Raccoon tracks will show five toes on both front and hind feet. Opossum tracks have five toes on the front feet and four toes plus a thumb on the hind feet. Raccoons usually place their smaller front paws beside the larger hind paws, and opossums also often travel with that same odd gait. There one sure way you can tell these two apart—the opossum's nearly hairless tail sometimes drags, whereas the raccoon's furry tail never does.

Muskrats and beavers will be near water, as a rule. Muskrats' tails often drag and their hind feet usually step in the prints of the front feet. Beavers' large webbed hind feet with narrow heels are quite triangular in shape, and usually slightly overreach the front paws.

HOTSPOTS

Country roads, farmlands and even the smallest parks in suburban areas can be keen spots for tracking animals after a snow. If you are planning to visit private land, be *sure* to get permission.

The wildlife refuge areas along the rivers in all three states are ideal sites for studying the signs and tracks of mammals and birds. **Mark Twain NWR Complex** includes nine different sections for a total acreage of about 23,500 along some 250 miles of the Illinois and Mississippi rivers. Parts of this gigantic complex, whose main office is in Quincy, Illinois, are within easy reach of much of our three-state area.

These riverside habitats are primarily bottomland and often flooded. The lakes, backwaters and sloughs, surrounded by deciduous forests and croplands, are ideal for tracking mammals and birds after snowfalls. The mammal and bird populations of all nine sections are generous. The various offices will provide brochures and information for their respective areas.

Three district offices, located in Brussels, Illinois, Annada, Missouri and Wapello, Iowa, manage the divisions. The **Brussels District Office** is located in Calhoun County, the picturesque peninsula area between the Mississippi River and the lower Illinois River, about 4 miles southeast of Brussels, very near County Road 754 and about 30 miles northwest of St. Louis. Batchtown, Calhoun and Gilbert Lake are the three divisions under this office.

Largest of the three is **Calhoun Division**—4,500 acres in Calhoun County on the Illinois River. A delightful way to reach this refuge is the Brussels Free Ferry. Take the Great River Road (Illinois Highway 3) north from St. Louis past Alton and Grafton to the ferry landing. The ferry, a relic of past days on the rivers, takes a limited number of cars and trucks across the Illinois River to Calhoun County. The 656-acre **Gilbert Lake Division** is on the east side of the river in Jersey County, Illinois. **Batchtown Division's** 2,249 acres lie on the west side of Calhoun County on the Mississippi River.

The **Annada District** of the Mark Twain Refuge Complex, headquartered north of St. Louis in Annada, Missouri, manages Gardner and Delair divisions and also **Clarence Cannon NWR**. The Gardner Division consisting of thirty-two islands is accessible only by boat. The Delair Division is closed to the public. Clarence Cannon

NWR, on the other hand, should be on your list. Located on the Mississippi River at Annada (watch for signs as you travel north from St. Louis on Missouri Highway 61). Nearly 4,000 acres of woods, grasslands, farmland, floodplains and wetlands support a wide variety of mammals and birds.

The **Morton Arboretum** in Lisle, Illinois, just 25 miles west of downtown Chicago, is an ideal place to look for winter signs of birds and mammals in the snow. Morton is a mile north of Lisle, three miles south of Glen Ellyn, and almost bisected by Illinois Route 53. The lakes, meadows and wooded hills, formerly farmlands, cover some 1,500 acres. Stands of evergreens—mostly pine and spruce— make it ideal for winter animal watching and tracking as the evergreens offer shelter from winter winds and snows. Morton offers marvelous opportunities for naturalists in many specialties.

In Arkansas, **Wapanocca NWR**, described in Chapter 1 is a top spot for tracking animals after a snow. The trails in **Lake Ouachita SP** in central Arkansas offer another opportunity for studying native animals in the winter. Lake Ouachita is Arkansas' largest man-made lake. The **Caddo Bend Trail** winds through four miles of forests and lakeshore that promise to give you plenty of animal tracks if there has been even a little bit of snow. To get there, take U.S. 270 3 miles west from Hot Springs, then go 12 miles north on Highway 227. The visitors' center offers trail guides and information.

In all parts of our three-state territory, city and county parks as well as many landscaped cemeteries also offer great opportunities for tracking animals in winter months after a snowfall.

4

Trees in Winter

It's comparatively easy to identify deciduous trees during the growing season, when they're clad in their full uniform of leaves and often adorned by flowers, fruits and seeds. In the winter, when your favorite shade tree is a stark mass of trunk and branches, and when the bark looks like the bark on every other tree, identification is another story indeed.

Identifying evergreens is easier, since most of them keep their leaves throughout the winter. The only native evergreen with needlelike leaves in our three-state area is the shortleaf pine. Junipers, the group that includes the eastern red cedar, have a different but needlelike look. The American holly is the only broad-leafed native in this region, a singularly easy small tree to identify in any season.

Bark patterns often become easier to understand and differentiate if you take the time to look closely at them. Some trees have distinctive bark that is hard to miss. The smooth gray bark of magnolias and beeches is handsome and easy to identify once you've studied them. The bark of hackberries, with its many little corky projections, is also easy. The handsome exfoliating bark of the sycamore makes this riverbottom tree a beautiful large and almost white landmark. Trying to identify oaks is a challenge but fortunately oaks tend to keep their leaves much longer than other trees, so you can use leaf shapes to help you even in the winter.

The sure way to identify deciduous trees in the winter is by their buds and twigs. Here you will discover that the leaf buds grow

— 19 —

on the ends (terminally) and the sides (laterally) of the twigs. The lateral buds that developed in the axils—the upper angle between leaves and stems—are usually smaller than the terminal buds. The buds may grow opposite each other or alternately—this is an important characteristic and may dictate the pattern of the twig. Lateral buds may give the twig a zig-zag appearance. A 10x hand lens, small pocket knife and ruler will help in making these identifications.

Flower buds are usually larger and rounder than leaf buds. Look for the scales that may grow over the buds to protect them. Some leaf buds lack scales. If so, the first leaves may curve inward to protect inner leaves. Sometimes you can't find any leaf buds at all—in those cases, the leaf buds grow within the twig and don't appear until growth starts in the spring.

Look for the leaf scars from last year's foliage—the corky places on the twigs where last year's leaves were attached. Look closely at the leaf scars to see if there are bundle scars, the remnant of the vascular bundles that carried water and nutrients to and from the leaves.

Let's look closely at a few of the easier trees. If you can identify a few simple ones, that foundation of knowledge will be easy to expand upon when you want to learn a few more.

The only native pine of southern Missouri and Arkansas is the shortleaf pine, which has needlelike leaves in bundles of two or three. The needles are between 3 inches and 5 inches long. They are not twisted in their growth pattern. All pines with needles in bunches of two or three are called yellow pines. Another name for the shortleaf pine is bull pine, because when these trees are grown in the open, they grow rapidly and have large bushy crowns.

The shortleaf pine was the dominant species of tree through-out the Ozarks until heavy logging in the late nineteenth and early twentieth centuries decimated the forests. Oaks replaced the short-leaf and are the dominant species today.

The eastern white pine, native to northern Illinois (and all of northeastern United States as far west as Iowa), has soft-looking foliage with five needles in each bunch. Highly adaptable to environmental conditions, this handsome tree is used in parks, forestlands, and home landscapes throughout our three-state region—far beyond its original territory.

We have grown so used to seeing other pines in our landscapes that many people assume they are native. Among the more common non-natives planted in Illinois, Missouri and Arkansas are the Scotch pine and Austrian pine. The number of needles in the

Common red cedars, which are juniper relatives, commonly grow in old fields such as this one.

needle bundle is an easy way to identify pines. Both the Austrian and Scotch pines, originally from Europe, have two needles in each bunch, and both are generally more stiff and bristly in appearance than the white pine.

The eastern red cedar and the Ashe juniper are also evergreen natives in our heartland area. Eastern red cedar is native to most of North America east of the Rockies. The Ashe juniper is found in western Arkansas and southwestern Missouri. Both have two types of leaves: the first scalelike about 1/8-inch long and the second needlelike and about 1/3-inch long. The eastern red cedar—actually a juniper as you can tell by its botanical name—*Juniperus virginiana*—is noted for the reddish or copper color in the center of its stems and trunk. Cut across a section of twig to see this. The center of stems and trunks in Ashe junipers is brown.

American holly, the only broad-leafed native of our region, is found in Arkansas and southern Missouri. It is dioecious, which means that the berries develop from flowers on the female tree while pollen comes from the male's flowers. The leaves are green and leathery with veins that end in sharp spines. Birds love holly berries and are very good at sowing holly seeds through their droppings.

The bald cypress is a deciduous tree of southern swamps, including those in southern Missouri and Arkansas. This is the tall tree that develops "knees" when it grows in water. It is a highly adaptable tree that once established can tolerate a wide variety of conditions, and so is often used in landscaping. The knees are thought to have something to do with providing oxygen to the tree, though exactly how they do that is not known. The pyramidal shape, scattering of dropped needles and swollen base of the trunk should be enough to identify this tree.

Some maples are native to Illinois, Missouri and Arkansas— red maple, silver maple and sugar maple are three that bear closer inspection. Their leaves are opposite simple and lobed—the leaf shape is called palmate, easy to remember because it looks much like the palm of your hand.

On the winter twigs, look for terminal buds, and leaf scars and buds that are opposite. Study the leaf scars and count the bundle scars. These maples have three to seven bundle scars in each leaf scar. The leaf scars are narrow and less than 1/2-inch across. The buds have several exposed outer scales and the twigs are brown or reddish.

The final two critical sets of characteristics will give the specific identity of these three maples. If the buds are rounded and there are often several in a cluster, the tree is a soft maple. If the twigs have an unpleasant odor and the mature bark is smooth rather than scaly, the tree is the silver maple. If the buds are elongated and pointed, the tree is one of the other maples. If the twigs do not have an unpleasant odor and the tree bark is smooth rather than scaly, you have identified a red maple. Elongated, pointed buds with shiny, slender, pale reddish brown twigs typify the sugar maple.

Another maple similar to the sugar maple is the black maple, which has twigs that are thicker, dull and grayish-brown. The black maple is very similar to the sugar maple, and therefore I think it's enough just to key a tree to a level that includes both.

The oaks comprise the largest group of trees in our area, with at least twenty different species native to the region. In addition, there are many hybrids, since oak species cross quite freely with one another. Oaks are the most important hardwoods in North America from an economic point of view, and they are certainly highly regarded from both environmental and ornamental points of view as well. Acorns, called oak mast, are of major importance as a food staple of wildlife, including deer and turkeys as well as squirrels and many other mammals and birds, to say nothing of the insect life that depends on such woody things as acorns.

Oaks are easier to understand if you first realize that they are in the same family as beech and chestnut trees, which have similar characteristics. The fruits have important similarities and the leaves grow alternately on the twigs. If you cut across a twig with a sharp knife, you will see the singular star shape of the pith—look closely to see wood rays radiating from the pith. The true oaks all have the characteristic nuts called acorns that form within a bumpy, scaly or fringed partial husk called a cup, or cupule, to use the botanical term.

Since so many oaks hold their leaves through much of the winter and the forest floor retains decay-resistant oak leaves as clues to identity, it's fair to include leaf characteristics as part of winter identification. The white oak group and the red or black oak group constitute the two main groups of oaks. Bur, swamp, white, post and chinquapin all are members of the white oak tribe. You can tell the white oak species because their leaves have lobed or wavy edges, and the ends and lobes are rounded. The true black oak and also the pin, northern red, southern red, willow, and blackjack oaks all are species in the red or black oak tribe. The red or black oak species have leaves that may be lobed or entire and all have little spines or bristles at the ends of lobes or leaves.

Let's take a look at just a few of the many oaks. The white oak, the mighty oak of legend, may grow to well over 100 feet high in the wild. Common in our forests, its twigs and smooth buds are dark red-brown and the bark on young branches does not peel off in large scales. The 4- to 8 1/2-inch leaves have five to nine rounded lobes and are about half as wide as they are long. Leaf buds are pointed and less than 1/4 inch long. The acorns grow singly or in pairs, have short stalks, and are 1/2 to 3/4 inch long with a cup that encloses about 1/4 of the slightly oblong nut. Another member of the white oak tribe is the post oak, a smaller tree (40 to 50 feet tall) than the white oak, which has dusty looking brown to gray-brown twigs. The 4- to 8-inch long leaves have two to three broad pairs of lobes—the middle pair is so much longer that the leaf has sort of a cross shape. The buds are reddish and not hairy. Most of the terminal buds are close to 1/4 inch long.

The true black oak, a member of the red or black oak tribe, is widespread and grows 50 to 60 feet tall. Its terminal buds are hairy, mostly about 3/8 inch long, and clearly pentagon-shaped in cross section. Four- to ten-inch leaves are deeply lobed with seven to eleven lobes and obviously spiny tips. The twigs are shiny and the buds brown to gray. This oak's oval acorns are half covered by their deep cups. Another member of this tribe is the pin oak, with leaves that are even more deeply lobed than the black oak. The indents between the lobes are U-shaped. The chestnut-colored buds grow from shiny red-brown twigs. The pin oak is a tree of bottomlands that grows 70 feet or more in height, and is another common introduction to parks and home landscaping.

Although there are many other native trees, these keys to the evergreen natives and two major deciduous tree groups, maples and oaks, will give you an opportunity to develop the kind of observation of details that will help you learn to identify trees during winter. I recommend two things that will help with tree identification at any time of year. First of all, look for places that have labeled trees— botanical gardens, horticultural study areas and some private gardens. Secondly, look for field guides and keys on native trees, increasingly common in most bookstores. (See also list of books in the Appendix.)

HOTSPOTS

As I just mentioned, it's easier to start out studying native trees in places where the trees are labeled. You will know exactly what the tree is and can study its shape and bark as well as the telltale clues I've described. Booklets and handouts on native trees may exist—ask for them at visitors' centers or gift shops.

In Arkansas, to my knowledge, there are as yet no botanical gardens, arboreta, or other public gardens with labeled trees. At the risk of cheating a bit on our three-state territorial limits, I recommend crossing over the Mississippi River and visiting **Memphis Botanic Garden**, located at 750 Cherry Road, Memphis, Tennessee. From Arkansas, go east across the river on I-40, then take the circumferential I-240 around Memphis. The botanical garden is located in Audubon Park near Memphis State University on the east side of the city—watch for signs. Here you will find both native and introduced trees, shrubs and herbaceous plants well labeled—a great help to those learning plant identification.

Morton Arboretum in northern Illinois has the state's best collection of native trees and shrubs. (See Chapter 3 for directions.) **Chicago Botanical Gardens** is another good place in this area to study trees in the winter. To get there, take Edens Expressway (I-94) about 22 miles north of the Loop and exit on Lake Cook Road—the botanical garden is just 1/4 mile from the highway. **Washington Park Botanical Garden** in Springfield is a likely place for studying trees in winter or anytime. Take I-55 to South Grand Exit at Springfield and turn west to Washington Park. Follow signs through park. **White Pines Forest SP** southwest of **Mount Morris** in northwestern Illinois features a significant stand of native white pines. From Illinois Route

2, between Rockford and Dixon, take Pines Road west for about eight miles. The park is between Oregon and Polo on Pines Road.

The **Missouri Botanical Garden** in St. Louis is another good place to study trees; tree labels and booklets are available. Get there by taking I-44 through St. Louis, then the Kings Highway Exit. From either direction, follow MBG signs to the garden located nearby on Tower Grove and Shaw avenues. **Powell Gardens**, an 835-acre botanical garden near Kansas City, has labeled trees and other plants, including natives, in the 14-acre garden area around the visitors' center and the perennial gardens. You can reach this comparatively new botanical garden by taking Highway 50 from Kansas City or Warrensburg—it's located on the north side of the highway between Highway 131 and County Highway Z.

Hawn SP, part of the Missouri park system, has a virgin shortleaf pine forest that is one of many distinctive highlights of this park's great diversity and beauty. In recognition of the pines, most of the park is designated the Whispering Pine Wild Area. Hawn State Park is located about halfway between Highway 67 and I-55, slightly southwest of the little hamlet of Weingarten on Highway 32.

5

January Shorttakes

Signs of Animals Eating Tender Growth

Look for signs of deer, rabbits and other animals eating the tender buds and twigs of saplings—rabbits make sharp cuts and deer make ragged cuts. If snow is on the ground, you can follow their tracks as they looked for food, then see what they chose. **Mount Nebo SP** on Highway 155 southwest of Russellville, Arkansas; **Robert Allerton Park** just four miles southwest of Monticello, Illinois; and **Thousand Hills SP** west of Kirksville, Missouri are good spots to look for signs of animals in winter. These and other places with mixed habitats are likely spots—the edges of woods are ideal for many animals.

Winter Birds Feed on Insect Larvae

Watch chickadees, woodpeckers and nuthatches feeding on the insect larvae they find in the crevices of tree bark. Study how they work their way around the tree, the way they cling to the bark and the directions they move. Visit some of the riverbottom parklands for good opportunities to see these birds at work. Warm winter days when there is little or no wind will be most comfortable for the birds and for you. **Cossatot River SP and Natural Area** near Wickes, Arkansas, with its many trails, is a good site for winter birding. In Illinois, the **Cedar Glen Eagle Roost** mentioned in Chapter 2 is a likely winter birding spot. **Bennett Spring SP**, which is also one of

Missouri's marvelous trout parks, reached via Highway 64 west of Lebanon, Missouri, is another good place to look for winter birds.

See also:

Chapter 14, Mourning Cloak and Spring Azure Butterflies. On warm days, you may see butterflies in or near woods and along brushy roadsides. Mourning cloak and comma butterflies hibernate in rock crevices, open buildings and tree hollows. The undersides of their wings are dull colors, helping to camouflage them from predators.

6

Breakout: Birds at Feeders

The sudden appearance of a snow bunting one snowy afternoon is the highlight of my bird feeding career. I saw it just that once and then only for a few minutes, but there was no mistaking it—no other bird looks like a snow bunting. The bunting appeared during a lull in a strong winter storm that dropped several inches of snow and closed down most of St. Louis. Chances are that it had become lost or confused and was blown this way by the winds out of the north. Although most winters won't bring such impressive accidentals to your feeder, you will have lively, entertaining company during those short and often gloomy winter days.

When winter weather defeats all attempts at outdoor activity, do your birding at home. When icy winds, snow and winter-slick roads are intimidating and hazardous, there will be more birds at your feeders than at any other time. The reason is simple. When the weather is good, birds can find insects and seeds more easily. When storms freeze and cover the food supply, many species of wild birds are only too eager to take a handout at the bird feeders.

Bird feeding used to be a very casual practice. We would toss toast crusts, a leftover pancake or doughnut or other extra bits of foods out on the ground—or on the porch railing if there were lots of cats in the area. The birds were equally casual, sometimes coming to take a bit of this or that and sometimes ignoring the offerings altogether.

Bird feeding today has become quite scientific and certainly far more elegant. In some circles it has become a competitive sport with friends vying with one another to see who has the most or the best birds at their feeders. Even those who are not inclined to be birders under other circumstances have become quite knowledge-able as to what birds to expect and what foods will attract certain species. Feeders will attract both resident birds like the cardinal, chickadee, goldfinch, Carolina wren and titmouse, and winter migrants like the slate-colored junco that summers in northern pine forests.

Bird feeders themselves are no longer simple platforms on which to spread seed and fruit. There are triple-barrelled tubular feeders that offer three different kinds of seed at once. There are enclosed feeders that protect the feeding birds from winter weather. There are special gadgets that will hold fruit and include a perch. Watering equipment is also available, including water heaters and special containers. Bird feeders come in all shapes, sizes and prices and range from the simple to the complex. Most are for winter feeding, but there also are summer feeders, the best known being the hummingbird feeders.

You can easily make your own feeders by cutting holes in gallon milk jugs and using them to dispense bird seed. Peanut butter can be slathered on a medium-sized branch 1 or 2 feet in length and hung as a feeder. A clay drainage saucer from a summer planter makes a fine feeder to place on a picnic table. There are many simple solutions if you'd rather make your own feeders.

When setting up bird feeders, make them convenient not only for the birds, but also for you. Put them where you can easily see them, in places convenient for checking out their behavior and the fine points of their plumage. Be sure not to place the feeders where you will be looking at them against a background of sky—that makes birds difficult to see. Place them also where they are easy to fill and conveniently near the supplies of seed. Place them near enough to bushes and trees so the birds have easy escape routes if hawks frequent the area. Put feeders high enough to prevent access by cats.

If possible, put feeders where squirrels can't get at them, or buy squirrel baffles or squirrel-proof feeders (though I doubt that there is an absolutely squirrel-proof feeder). The alternatives are easier. Offer the squirrels enough corn and other squirrel-type food to keep them from being interested in birdseed. The other alternative is to learn to love the squirrels. If you want to discourage starlings and blue jays from the feeders, use tube feeders with small perches. Chickadees, titmice and other small birds can easily feed at these while the larger, clumsier jays and starlings can't get a foothold. On the other hand, sparrows, grosbeaks and cardinals prefer to feed from a level area rather than a tube.

By offering certain kinds of bird food you can, to a great degree, fine tune your bird feeding so that you have all the birds you want, yet few if any of the birds you don't want. I don't buy the ready-mixes of wild bird food because it includes so much milo and, in my experience, milo is not as attractive to the birds I want to see as some of the other seeds.

Niger (thistle seed) is a must if you want to attract goldfinches and pine siskins—and who does not! It's expensive, even when you buy in larger amounts, but I consider it an almost necessary luxury. Put it in one of the special tube feeders made for niger—they have small holes plus perches so the birds can sit while picking out the seeds. There also are fabric mesh feeders for niger. Other birds, including chickadee, titmouse and junco may also enjoy niger seed, but the goldfinches and pine siskins are the most eager thistle feeders.

Black (oil-type) or striped sunflower seeds and hulled sun-flower seeds or seed chips, served singly or in combination, will attract a wide variety of marvelous winter birds, including the cardinal, chickadee, titmouse, sparrows, junco, purple and house finches. Serve peanut butter in a suspended jar lid and you will attract these as well as the Carolina wren and the woodpeckers.

A suet feeder will attract most of the woodpeckers. I like the ones that are made of woven wire coated with a rubbery plastic and comes in block shapes—they are easy to fill and hang. I've had downy and hairy woodpeckers feeding at my suet feeders at the same time—a good opportunity to compare these two similarly marked birds. The red-headed woodpecker is not such a constant feeder, but it is rarer; red-bellied woodpeckers are fairly common. In Arkansas and southern Missouri, you might see the yellow-bellied sapsucker at winter feeders—these birds migrate from summer homes in Illinois and northward. A couple of times I have seen a pileated woodpecker at the suet, but that is rare since these are shy birds and there are not many of them. Other birds that will come to suet feeders are wrens, nuthatches, chickadees, titmice, mockingbirds and starlings. Some report having seen eastern bluebirds, kinglets and brown creepers at suet feeders, but I have not been that fortunate.

Orange sections, pieces of apple, raisins and other fruit are likely to attract mockingbirds. Since mockers will chase other birds, you may want to place the fruit 10 feet or more away from the other feeders. Fruit also may attract the house finch, red-bellied wood-pecker, mourning dove, red-headed woodpecker and starling.

FEBRUARY

February Observations

7

Gulls Inland

You will find ring-billed and herring gulls all along the seacoast of the United States, right? Well, yes, but that's not the whole story. These gulls are year-round residents in the Great Lakes area, and Bonaparte's gull and the glaucous are winter visitors there. You also may find these gulls around large lakes. At times other gulls may drop in to our region, including the laughing gull, Franklin's gull and the greater black-backed gull. Ring-billed and herring gulls commonly winter throughout a large part of Illinois, Missouri and Arkansas. The ring-billed gull used to be considered the more common but, in recent years, the herring gull appears to have taken the population lead. The sight of thousands of these gulls at inland rivers and lakes is astounding to those of us who grew up associating gulls with seaside habitats.

The Thayer's gull, an occasional visitor to these interior states, is very similar to the herring gull. In fact, Thayer's gull used to be classed as a subspecies of the herring gull. Since Thayer's gull is so difficult to positively identify and there is a rumor (or is it a wish?) that the classification of this gull may return it to the status of a herring gull subspecies, I intend to ignore any further mention of it in this book.

It's much easier to identify gulls in the winter than in other seasons. Their plumage is fresh from the fall moult and so is not dingy and dull, a common summer condition. Further, the distinctions of the different ages is clearer at this time of year. Gulls can be very confusing since first-year gulls may look nothing like the adults. The plumage of second-year gulls also is confusing—it falls somewhere in between the first year and the adult coloring. The majority of gulls will change their plumage pattern gradually over at least their first two years. It takes three and a half years for herring gulls to reach adulthood which means that there are four distinct plumage patterns. This, combined with individual differences, makes it tough on birders. If you are just beginning to learn the gulls, you may wish to ignore the juveniles for a while and concentrate on identifying the mature birds.

Although the adults may have slightly different head and neck patterns in the winter and summer, there are enough reliable field marks that you can ignore those seasonal variations. Although the wing and tail feathers of gulls are molted only once a year, in late summer or early fall, the head and neck feathers are shed twice a year, in late winter and early spring as well as late summer or early fall.

Because the field marks are more obvious in flying birds, try to identify gulls in flight—when the wings are folded and gulls are resting, critical field marks may be difficult or impossible to see. Learn the shape of gulls. When you can do this, you often will be able to identify them at a glance, without checking the field marks. This will prove to be very handy when you learn the common gulls, the ring-billed and herring gulls in our territory, because then you will notice those that are not the usual sort. This way you will discover the rare accidentals that may appear.

Most gulls are fish eaters and also scavengers. As scavengers, they perform valuable services for us, picking up leftover food that careless people leave in parks and along shorelines. Where gulls are common, you will find them in great numbers, taking full advantage of the food in landfills. The old-fashioned town dump was a dandy gathering place for gulls.

The herring gull is a big bird about 2 feet in length with a wingspread of nearly 5 feet. This gull takes full advantage of landfill food. It also eats fish and other marine animals as well as the eggs and young of other birds. Indeed, the herring gull will eat just about anything. This bird has been able to compete so successfully with other gulls that it now is the most numerous gull we have. It is a permanent resident in some northern parts of our three-state region.

Field marks for the herring gull include the pale gray mantle, white belly and underparts, white head (streaked with brown in the winter), black tips on primary wing feathers, pink legs and feet and yellow bill with red spot. The red spot is curious in that it is tied to the feeding of young. When a herring gull chick pecks the red spot on its parent's bill, the parent regurgitates and feeds the chick. It takes four years for this gull to mature. This bird is a marvelous flyer, able to hover forward and backward as well as soar and fly forward strongly. It is a clever bird that has learned the trick of dropping shellfish on a hard surface to crack them open.

The ring-billed gull, which used to be far more numerous than the herring gull, is a smaller bird about 18 to 20 inches in length with a 4-foot wingspan. With its pale gray mantle, white head and underparts, it looks remarkably similar to the herring gull. Look closer and you will see an entirely different bird. The ring-billed gull has yellow legs and feet, and an obvious black ring around its bill. The black tips of its primary wing feathers have two white spots. This bird is a fish eater and scavenger but is also a great insect eater, particularly fond of grasshoppers. The ring-billed gull matures in three years.

The adult Bonaparte's gull, which matures in two years, has a gray mantle with small black tips on its primary wing feathers, red legs, black bill and white belly and underparts. During the breeding season it has a black hood; during the winter its head is white with a dark spot behind each eye. As I noted before, this gull winters on the Great Lakes where it is numerous during the cold season.

The glaucous gull as its Latin-Greek name indicates is a gleaming bird of pale gray and white. Another winter resident of the Great Lakes, it is 2 feet or more long with a wingspan of 5 feet. It takes four years to mature into a heavy-bodied adult with pink legs and a yellow bill that has a red spot like that of the herring gull. In winter months it has a pale gray mantle and translucent tips on the primary wing feathers. When it is at rest, its wings appear short, barely reaching beyond the end of its tail.

HOTSPOTS

Wherever there is a visitors' center or headquarters building at the parks and refuges that I'm recommending, take the time to stop there and chat with the staff. They often can provide daily updates on what animals and birds are in the area—they are well acquainted with the hotspots within large park and refuge areas.

In Arkansas, **Bull Shoals SP**, a top fishing and boating area, is also a good place to observe gulls. The park is located in the Ozark Mountains on the White River and Bull Shoals Lake, below the dam that confines the huge lake, and is a good place to start your search. Check out the tail waters first—gulls often hang out in such areas because the roiled water keeps fish moving. The trail map available at the visitors' center will get you oriented. To get there, take State Highway 5 6 miles north from Mountain Home, then take Arkansas State Highway 178 8 miles west to the park.

A top spot for viewing ring-billed gulls in Arkansas is the **Holla Bend NWR** near Russellville. From Russellville, take Arkansas Highway 7 south, across the Arkansas River, then 3 miles to Highway 154 and left for 2 miles to the entrance of the refuge.

Illinois Beach SP, approximately 4,160 acres that stretch along Lake Michigan for 6 1/2 miles, provides some good opportunities for seeing gulls during the winter. Regular birders note that it is a particularly good spot for studying both gulls and winter ducks as well as the spring and fall migrations of waterfowl. Headquarters for this waterside park is at Zion, Illinois, 6 miles north of Waukegan. Check there first to get a map and find out what gulls are in the area.

Crab Orchard NWR (see Chapter 1 for directions) near Carbondale in southern Illinois is a dandy spot for sighting ring-billed gulls in the winter, fall and spring. Herring gulls are also common in the winter. Bonaparte's gull, sometimes seen here in the winter, is more common in spring and fall.

The dam area of **Table Rock Lake** in **Table Rock SP** in southwestern Missouri is tops for gulls. With Branson, the country music entertainment capital nearby, it certainly is not a wilderness area, but the gulls don't seem to mind all the hustle and bustle. Actually, they benefit from all the fishing activity, as they can get the trimmings left by fishermen cleaning their catch. Table Rock SP is 7 miles southwest of Branson on Highway 165, just a mile south of Table Rock Dam. Among the absolutely best places to study gulls is **Riverland** (see Chapter 1 for directions). You will find the gulls all along the shoreline of the Mississippi River. They are usually found near the **Melvin Price Dam** of the Lock and Dam 26 complex because the water remains stirred up there and so the fishing is easier.

8

Amphibians of February Warm Spells

Here in these heartland states, the symphony of spring usually begins in February when the spring peepers and then the chorus frogs tune up during early warm spells of late winter. The trilling begins in the southern area and works its way north as the soil and water warm, allowing these small frogs to awaken from winter hibernation. These chorus frogs may be forced back into dormancy before spring truly arrives, but they give it their all whenever temperatures permit.

As spring approaches, other frogs and toads join in the music. The trilling songs of the American toad and Fowler's toad join during late February and March, the exact timing dependent upon the weather and the latitude. Northern spring peepers, pickerel frogs and leopard frogs join the group in March. Bullfrogs, green frogs, bronze frogs and gray tree frogs become part of the amphibian symphony later in the spring.

February may bring the most severe weather of winter. On the other hand, this month may offer warm spells with some of the first welcome signs of spring. Those first faint breeding calls of native frogs and toads during February and March will build as the weather warms. These animals are true amphibians that breed in water, though as adults they live in a wide variety of habitats.

The young hatch into tadpoles—also called polliwogs—from eggs laid in the water. They have true gills and live in the water for varying lengths of time. When the larval form is mature, it will metamorphose into the adult frog or toad. The hind legs appear first, then the front legs, one by one. The tail grows smaller, the mouth wider, the gills atrophy and, before long, an air-breathing, four-footed toad or frog climbs out of the water. Some, including the bullfrog, may take additional time to mature to full adult size after they become froglets.

Over two dozen of these amphibians are native to Illinois, Missouri and Arkansas. We will look at a few of the more common ones that we are likely to see and hear throughout most of the three states. Each has its own special call that is played over and over, especially during the breeding season. If you can become familiar with these calls, you can list the kinds of toads and frogs in the area without ever leaving the porch or campfire. The calls will help you find where these creatures live; they are shy and will stop calling if they see or hear you. For that reason, you may wish to sit quietly in a likely spot near water and see if you can hear and then see these elusive animals.

Some toads and frogs choose to breed in large ponds, the edges of lakes and quiet backwaters of rivers and streams. Others are just as pleased with the ephemeral puddles of spring or other small temporary bits of water. Naturally, those that breed in these latter places must mature quickly or their habitat will evaporate. Many species breed in very early spring while others breed in late spring or summer.

For many amphibians the rush to breed is competitive, with many males vying for each female, but once the toads and frogs have paired off, breeding commences in a peaceful fashion. The male clings to the female until she lays eggs, he fertilizes them, and both wander off to live out the warm season at the water's edge, in trees, woods or fields.

The tadpoles are primarily vegetarian, thriving on algae and other small plant life. The adults are carnivores, consuming amazing numbers of flying and crawling insects. Large frogs such as bullfrogs go after larger prey, including crayfish and, occasionally, vertebrates. When they see their prey they aim, then fire, with their folded sticky tongues that hit the prey animals and draw them back into the amphibian's mouth. This happens so fast that you may miss the action completely if you blink.

Scientists and, indeed, all those who appreciate nature, are concerned over the mysterious reduction in the numbers of amphibians throughout the world in recent years. The answers to this dilemma have not been found.

You will discover, if you are able to get audiotapes of toad and frog songs such as those available from the Missouri Department of Conservation, that some of the mysterious sounds of dark nights turn out to be such familiar creatures as the eastern American toad, Fowler's toad and the gray treefrog. Before I got the tapes I thought some of these toad and frog calls were made by birds unknown and unseen—I never would have guessed that the golden-eyed American and Fowler's toads sang so beautifully each evening. Nor would I have guessed that the trilling call that I was hearing both day and night was that of the gray treefrog.

The group of true toads includes the eastern American toad, found throughout Illinois and Missouri south to the level of the Missouri River, and its closely related subspecies, the dwarf American toad, found in Arkansas as well as the southern parts of Illinois and Missouri. The general color of the medium-sized (2 to 3 1/2 inches) eastern American toad may be from gray through tan to brown or reddish brown. The belly is white with gray mottling. The dark spots on the back encircle one to three of the raised "warts." (No—you can't get warts from handling a toad.) The dwarf American toad is reddish brown and there are fewer or no dark spots on the back. The belly is cream-colored and there are gray spots on the chest.

Fowler's toad and the Rocky Mountain or Woodhouse's toad, another pair of closely related subspecies (2 to 4 inches), are superficially similar to the American toads, but have three to six warts inside each black or dark brown spot over the base color of gray to greenish gray. The belly is white and may have a breast spot. The dark spots on the back of Woodhouse's toad are arranged in pairs and are usually larger and more similar in shape than those of Fowler's toad. Woodhouse's toad is found in west-central and northwestern Missouri while Fowler's toad is native to eastern and southern Missouri, the southern two-thirds of Illinois, northern and eastern Arkansas. Another subspecies, the eastern Texas toad, is found in southwestern Arkansas. It is dark breasted with many small black spots that may continue on the lower abdomen.

Specific identification is made more complex by the fact that these toads may interbreed in the common areas of their native territories. You may be satisfied to identify them merely as "one of the common toads."

Blanchard's cricket frog, northern spring peeper and gray treefrog are native throughout most of Illinois, Missouri and Arkansas. Blanchard's cricket frog is small, no more than 1 1/2 inches from stem to stern, stocky, and has a dark triangle on the top of its head between its eyes. This frog's color ranges from gray or tan to brown or almost black with a white belly. This frog does not climb.

The small (maximum to 1 1/4 inches), slim northern spring

peeper does climb. It lives in dense growth near ponds and streams. Its base color is from pinkish to tan or gray. This frog has a distinctive dark "X" on its back and the belly is plain and pale. This is one of the first to call in the spring.

The gray treefrog is larger (1 1/4 to 2 inches in body length) and has a warty skin with base color ranging from gray to greenish gray to brown with dark irregular spots on the back and a large white spot below each eye. The prominent adhesive pads on their toes make climbing a snap for this frog.

Most common of the true frogs throughout our three-state area are the leopard frog, green frog and bullfrog. Leopard frogs come in three kinds—the plains leopard frog, northern leopard frog and southern leopard frog. All are medium-sized (2 to nearly 4 inches in length) and have many dark roundish spots on a lighter base color. The plains frog has a pale tan base color and a wide, blunt head. The northern leopard frog is brown or green in its base color with white rings around the dark spots. The southern leopard frog lacks the prominent spot on top of the nose that both the plains and northern leopard frogs have. The southern leopard frog is generally green to greenish brown and, in addition to no dark spot on the nose, has a small white spot in the center of the tympanum (the round external ear drum on each side of the head). Look for the leopard frogs in a variety of aquatic habitats and temporarily wet sites as well as in insect-rich grassy areas during the summer.

The green frog and its southern cousin, the bronze frog, are both true frogs. They are medium-sized amphibians that may grow up to 3 to 4 inches in body length. Both subspecies are colored in hues of bright green and brown—the bronze frog obviously has a strong bronzy cast to its coloration. The green frog territory includes much of Illinois, Missouri and northwestern Arkansas, while the bronze frog is found in Missouri's Bootheel country as well as eastern and southern Arkansas. These quite solitary frogs like habitats that include small streams with deep pools.

The bullfrog is the region's largest frog with a body length that may reach 6 inches. This true frog is variable in color from brown or olive to green. Its bass notes are unmistakable. Being a primarily aquatic frog, it prefers to live near or in sites such as rivers, lakes, creeks, and permanent marshes or swamps. The bullfrog is easily alarmed during the day—it will leap into the water if you get too near. At night, however, it can be approached if you shine a flashlight at it—this will show you the locations of many frogs since their eyes reflect light in much the same way as the eyes of cats.

HOTSPOTS

Look and listen for some of our more common toads and frogs in swampy areas, near ponds, lakes, streams and rivers, especially where the water is quiet and insect life is abundant. Hear the songs and calls of frogs and toads, which in late winter and early spring may be more commonly heard in the evening, then walk slowly and as silently as you can toward the sound. With luck and a great deal of patience you may be able to sit quietly and observe these amphibians as they croak and trill their breeding songs.

Typical places that offer good opportunities to see toads and frogs include the wetlands of some of our big National Wildlife Refuges such as **Big Lake NWR** (see Chapter 1 for directions) and **Wapanocca NWR** (see Chapter 1 for directions) near Memphis in northeastern Arkansas, and **Felsenthal NWR** (see Chapter 2 for directions) in southern Arkansas.

In Illinois, **Crab Orchard NWR** (see Chapter 1 for directions) in the southern part of the state and the **Upper Mississippi River National Wildlife and Fish Refuge**, which encompasses thousands of acres of riverside and wetlands from Rock Island north to the state line and beyond, includes many good places to listen and look for toads and frogs. This 284-mile-long refuge is actually a complex of protected areas that reaches into Wisconsin. The Illinois office for the Savannah District (U.S. Post Office Building, PO Box #250, Savannah, IL 61074, (815) 273-2732) can furnish maps and other information—brochures, pool maps, and lists for amphibians as well as mammals, birds and reptiles.

Study amphibians at **Mingo NWR** near Puxico in southern Missouri or in the creeks and edges of the shallow lakes of **Swan Lake NWR**. You can get to Mingo by going north from Puxico on state Highway 51 for 1 1/2 miles—that takes you to the headquarters and an excellent visitors' center. To reach Swan Lake, take Swan Lake Drive a mile south of Sumner to the main gate. Note that Swan Lake closes for the winter—you need a special permit to enter between October 16 and March 1. (Call the Swan Lake refuge office at 816-856-3323 if you can't wait until March 1.)

9

Native Trees Bloom

A few of our native trees are harbingers of spring. Early warm spells and lengthening days—usually in February—result in tree sap rising into trunks, branches and twigs, and flower and leaf buds will begin to swell. Full flowering and leafing out probably won't occur until the end of the month or in March for those plants listed in this chapter, but there will be strong signs of the events to come. Buds will begin to swell as much as two to three weeks sooner in southern Arkansas than in northern Illinois. The order of buds, whether flowers or leaves come first or at the same time, is different in different plants. Some, like shadbush and dogwood, develop flowers first, then leaves later; others, like the oaks and ashes, develop leaves first, before the flowers bloom.

Most plants with showy flowers are pollinated by insects, birds and other creatures. Plants with inconspicuous flowers, including the grasses as well as many native trees, are pollinated by the wind blowing the pollen—they don't need to attract animal pollinators.

The silver maple of riverbottoms and banks is one of the first to show signs of swelling buds. Its greenish yellow or red flowers are among the earliest signs of spring. The male flowers may bloom on separate trees or on the same tree, in which case the flowers are bisexual. The flowers, which have no petals, grow in clusters—the female flowers are somewhat showier. The bark of the silver maple is gray and smooth on young trees, turning scaly with age. The bark of old trees forms long shaggy plates that peel away from the trunk easily. Silver maple twigs give off a rank odor when crushed or

Dogwood flowers that brighten the understory of the spring woods usually are of the purest white and appear just before tree leaves begin to appear.

broken. The leaf buds are opposite in pattern and are pointed. When the leaves open, you will see that the deeply cut, five-lobed simple shape is light green on the top surface and silvery underneath. The slightest breath of air will stir the leaves. An old tale says that when breezes turn the leaves so that they show their silver sides, a storm is coming.

If February brings a period of warm sunny days, this fast-growing maple will quickly get fat buds. Look for the silver maple in association with sycamores, elms, hackberries and cottonwoods. They are fast-growing trees with a comparatively short life span. The wood is brittle and so the trees are prone to storm and wind damage—ice storms can devastate these trees.

Red maples, known as scarlet or swamp maples, are also trees of bottomlands. The flowers, which have small petals, are usually red but sometimes yellow, with the female flower the showier of the two. Trees may have predominantly female or male flowers, or may include both sexes on the same tree. The red maple, a slower grower than the silver maple, has smooth gray bark with darker markings when young. The bark becomes dark brown and strongly fissured with age. Unlike the silver maple, its leaf buds, opposite in growth pattern, are rounded and the twigs do not smell rank when bruised or broken. The three- or five-lobed simple leaves are reddish at first, turning a medium to dark green as they mature. The undersides of the leaves are grayish.

Both silver and red maples can grow up to 100 feet. Both are known in the lumber trade as soft maples. Like all maples, the female flowers bear winged fruit called *samaras* that may helicopter their way quite far from the parent tree when the breezes blow.

The downy serviceberry or shadbush, a small tree that seldom grows more than 25 to 30 feet tall, is an understory tree of uplands

*Serviceberry trees, also known as shadbush, are among the earliest
bloomers in the spring woods. The flowers, shown here in close-up, have
petals with a raggedy look characteristic of this understory tree.*

near the edges of woods. It also can be found on dry, stony soils
where it grows in association with oaks and hickories. Its bright white
flowers are early and much showier than most trees, appearing well
before the wild cherry and dogwood. When seen at some distance,
its flash of white under taller trees in the woods is sometimes
mistaken for dogwood by people who are eager for spring. The
delicate flowers appear in clusters before the leaf buds unfurl. Each
flower is perfect—that is, it includes both sexes. Each flower has five
slightly wavy, strap-like petals that are a 1/2 inch or more in length.

The serviceberry is a member of the rose family, as are apples,
pears, plums and cherries. The fruit will ripen in June into dark red
to purple berries, juicy and sweet like their domestic relatives but
smaller, only 1/2 inch or less in diameter. You probably won't see
much serviceberry fruit because it is very popular with many kinds
of wildlife. The leaf buds are alternate in growth pattern. The bark is
light gray and very smooth on young trees, breaking up into ridges
with age.

All parts of spicebush, a member of the laurel family, are
fragrant when rubbed or broken. This 6- to 12-foot understory shrub
grows in rich, well-drained soils along with red oaks, white ashes,
tulip trees and sugar maples. Spicebush is dioecious, with male and

female flowers borne on different plants. The early greenish yellow flowers appear in numerous dense, flat-topped clusters before the leaves. The bright red fruits, under 1/2 inch in length, are persistent and appear quite showy after leaves drop in the fall. The small leaf buds are globular and grow alternately along twigs. The leaves themselves are simple and egg-shaped with long pointed tips. Edges of the leaves are smooth and give off a spicy aroma when crushed— these are good clues to the plant's identity. Twigs of the spicebush are slender and dark red.

Another small understory tree is the pawpaw, also called Missouri banana and custard apple, the only native member of the tropical custard apple family to be found in Illinois, Missouri and Arkansas. The insignificant 1-inch flowers have six petals that are green at first, then turn to brown and purple at maturity. They grow singly along the branches before or just as leaves begin to develop. Unless you're looking for these odd flowers, you'll probably miss them. The sweet edible fruits mature in mid- to late summer but you will rarely find any because raccoons, possums and other animals will beat you to them. The tree usually grows only 15 to 20 feet high and is often found in communal groups, which accounts for the song words "way down yonder in the pawpaw patch." Leaf buds are alternate and when the leaves develop, they are simple, entire and long, up to 1 foot in length and 3 to 5 inches in width. It is these large leaves that will grab your notice in rich bottomlands or wooded slopes along streams.

HOTSPOTS

For beginners, it's easier to study trees where they are labeled. You may wish to visit some of the places suggested in Chapter 4, including the **Memphis Botanic Garden**, **Morton Arboretum** in the Chicago area and **Washington Park Botanical Garden** in Springfield. The **Missouri Botanical Garden** in St. Louis and the garden area of **Powell Gardens** a bit east of Kansas City offer good places to study labeled trees in Missouri. (See Chapter 4 for directions to these parks and gardens.)

Learn to identify both native and introduced trees and shrubs when they are dormant, and they will be much easier to name during the growing season. Note the pattern of buds, whether they are alternate or opposite, the color and texture of the bark, and the general shape of the plant.

10

Winter Waterfowl

During the winter months, a dozen or more of our better-known waterfowl live in the parks and refuges of this three-state region. Their breeding grounds are in the treeless plains, prairies and tundras of the Dakotas and Canada all the way north to Hudson Bay and the Arctic Sea. Even though we get our share of frigid winter weather, this area is the sunny South to these migratory ducks and geese. I've listed and described the more common species, noting some of the better places to observe these handsome and varied birds. National Wildlife Refuges are large enough and have enough open water and food to attract large numbers of waterfowl during the cold season. Some state parks and other preserves also have the size and wetlands to take care of these winter residents.

Most common is the large Canada goose—with a body up to 45 inches long and wing span of up to 5 feet—that migrates in the recognized "V" pattern. Its brown body, dark wings and buff to dark breast are accented by the black head and neck. A white chin strap and white rump band are familiar to just about everybody since these geese have taken permanent residence in many city and town parks. A number of subspecies have been described, all varying in color and size. Wherever there is an ornamental pond or lake in an area with open woods or broad lawn areas, the Canada goose is likely to settle in for the duration of the cold weather and, perhaps, the rest of the year as well. If well-meaning souls feed the geese, their residence is guaranteed.

Although geese may become a nuisance at local parks, their

migration both day and night remains thrilling to see and hear. Canada geese have become year-round residents throughout much of our region, often nesting and raising their young near water and in close proximity to civilization. They are protective parents, which may create some springtime confrontations as the geese defend their goslings with hisses, head-pumping and other threats. An angered goose is not easy to face down!

Snow geese, which come in white and blue phases, continue to nest far north, in the arctic country of North America and Siberia. These birds are from 25 to 31 inches long and their call is not the familiar honk of the Canada goose, but a higher note that sounds more like a yelp. You will see snow geese in large flocks of hundreds or even thousands. Their flight formation is not the tight "V" of Canada geese, but rather a curved line that may take the shape of a "U." During the winter months they are likely to be found in coastal wetlands and near large lakes as well as in grain fields and grasslands.

Geese are a sociable bunch. They gab all the time so that you often hear a large flock before you see them. They talk while they fly and they talk while they feed. There's lots of room for the scientific study of goose language.

During winter months you are likely to see some of the surface-feeding ducks that dabble in shallow water, feeding primarily on vegetation but also insects, small fish and mollusks. These ducks, including the mallard, black duck, northern pintail, gadwall and American widgeon, are able to take off without a running start—they seem to spring straight up from the water.

The mallard is another familiar face in suburban parks although it's seen in greater numbers in preserves and refuges. Probably the most common and best known of all the wild ducks, the green-headed male with his yellow bill and chestnut breast is easy to identify. Both he and his brindled mate have white on the tail and underwings and a bright blue speculum bordered in white on each wing.

The American black duck, a bird primarily of eastern North America, is being replaced by the mallard duck. You can tell the black duck from the mallard by its darker color and the violet wing speculum that has only a thin line of white as a rear border. The pale head of the black duck is in high contrast to the dark body, which is not the case with the mallard. These are shy birds that often nest a distance from water. This species has similar male and female coloration—both male and female are of a brindled sooty brown color.

The northern pintail duck is a lovely swift and slender bird that has a distinctive needlelike tail. The male has a brown head, white neck stripe and primarily gray body with thin black tail feathers. The female is grayish brown and similarly slender, with a long neck and gray bill. This dabbler duck is fond of shallow ponds and potholes. Like the other dabblers, it tips its tail straight up as it paddles its feet and stretches its neck to hunt for food in the bottom mud. Dabblers eat grass, sedge and other pond weed seeds, as well as invertebrates such as snails, crayfish and any other shallow-water creatures that are small enough to catch and swallow.

The gadwall, another dabbling duck, though not a common bird, is often seen in the company of pintails and widgeons. This duck is best identified by its white wing patches. The male is mostly gray with a pale belly, black tail coverts and a pale chestnut color on the wings. The gadwall seems to be expanding its habitat eastward. Although this is a dabbler duck, it often dives.

The American widgeon is a dabbling duck that feeds on the foliage and seeds of aquatic plants as well as insects and some mollusks. It also steals favorite plants from diving ducks after they emerge with some tasty morsel. The male widgeon is easily identified by the large white patch on its forehead and crown and its green ear patch. The female is sandy brown and has a pale bluish gray bill similar to the bill of the male. White wing patches will distinguish both sexes of the American widgeon.

The ring-necked duck, one of the so-called diving or bay ducks, commonly spends winters in freshwater bays and woodland ponds. Field marks of the male are the black back and vertical white stripe on the side just in front of the wing. The female has a white eye ring and the top of the head is dark. Both sexes have a white ring around the bill. These diving ducks eat the seeds and foliage of water plants, insects and whatever crustaceans they can catch.

The lesser scaup is an agile diving duck that feeds on mollusks, fish and plants. This stocky duck, often seen in large flocks, shows a short white wing stripe in flight. The male has a purple head, steep forehead, light gray body and black rump and breast. The female is dark brown with a wide face ring just behind the bill. Both sexes have pale blue bills. The young are precocious, able to find their own food when only a few days old and dive deep into the water both for food and to escape danger.

Common mergansers are fish-eating ducks that have long thin bills with serrated edges, all the better to hold fish. They fly rapidly with their bodies held horizontally and have white wing patches. The male has a very dark green head and a crest. The female's head is chestnut with a larger crest than the male's. The throat is white with a distinct contrast between the white and the chestnut colors. They often band together in small flocks. Mergansers' diets include whatever animals they can catch, from fish and frogs to salamanders, mollusks and crustaceans.

HOTSPOTS

Look for these geese, ducks and other waterfowl wherever there is open water surrounded by open land or, in the case of larger bodies of water, woods.

Felsenthal NWR on U.S. Highway 82 between Crossett and Strong in southern Arkansas is an excellent place for studying waterfowl. The Saline and Oachita rivers flow through this refuge and, in addition, there are many sloughs, creeks and lakes—ideal for wintering geese and ducks. The other National Wildlife Refuges also are good places to look for waterfowl. These include **Holla Bend NWR** (see Chapter 7 for directions) west of Little Rock and **Wapanocca NWR** (see Chapter 1 for directions) in northeast Arkansas.

Millwood SP near Texarkana, Arkansas, has 824 acres located on Millwood Lake, a bass fishing hotspot known throughout the country. This is a good spot for observing a variety of ducks. From I-30 at Texarkana, take U.S. 71 19 miles north to Ashdown, then 9 miles east on Highway 32. The visitors' center will be on your left.

The waterfront of **Lincoln Park** in north Chicago, from Oak Street Beach to Foster Avenue, easily accessible from Lake Shore Drive, offers good birding for winter waterfowl as long as the water is not frozen. There are sheltered harbors and ponds, as well as Lake Michigan. Look for geese and ducks in Diversey, Belmont, and Montrose harbors. A major migration flyway along the western edge of Lake Michigan makes this a good place for seeing many migratory birds.

Chautauqua NWR on the Illinois River 10 miles north of Havana on the Manito Road (see Chapter 1 for directions) has some of the largest flocks of geese and ducks you will find in the region. Experts estimate that over forty thousand Canada and snow geese plus well over one hundred thousand ducks gather in this refuge each winter. Not surprisingly, mallards are the most common ducks but there is a good variety of others as well.

Crab Orchard NWR in southern Illinois (see Chapter 1 for directions) is another great place for seeing waterfowl at this time of year. This is primarily a waterfowl refuge, providing a resting and feeding place for Canada geese. You will find many duck species there as well.

The **Calhoun Lake** area of the **Brussels District of Mark Twain Refuge Complex** about 30 miles northwest of St. Louis (see Chapter 3 for directions) has riverbottom habitat with plenty of sloughs, lakes and backwaters. Visit the Brussels District office just off county route 754 about 4 miles southeast of Brussels in Calhoun County first, to get a map of the area and see what species are in the refuge.

In Missouri, **Mingo NWR** (see Chapter 1 for directions), **Squaw Creek NWR** (see Chapter 1 for directions), and **Swan Lake NWR** (see Chapter 8 for directions), located in southern, northwestern, and north central Missouri respectively, are loaded with waterfowl during the winter. Hundreds of thousands of ducks migrate through Mingo each year—many are winter residents and some remain for the breeding season. The snow goose population of Squaw Creek is estimated to reach two hundred thousand or more each winter. Swan Lake is the winter residence for over one hundred thousand Canada geese each year. Shallow lakes and land cultivated for the use of wildlife explain the high numbers of waterfowl in these preserves.

The **August A. Busch Memorial Wildlife Area** some 30 miles west of St. Louis has a number of lakes and nearby grainfields that make it ideal for waterfowl. To reach this Missouri Department of Conservation refuge, take Highway 40 (64) west from the city to Highway 94, shortly after you cross the Missouri River, then go left. The entrance to Busch Wildlife, as it is called, will be on your right just a short distance down the road. Be sure to get a map at the headquarters building so that you don't get confused by the several roads through the area. Ask also at which lake the ducks and geese are most likely to be. Chances are that the **Auden Knight Hampton Memorial Lake** near the headquarters may hold a good selection of winter waterfowl. There is a hiking trail around the lake.

Probably the best Missouri site for viewing geese and ducks at this time of year is **Riverlands**, the comparatively new refuge by the **Melvin Price Locks & Dam 26** on the Mississippi River slightly downstream from the Illinois town of Alton (see Chapter 1 for directions). There is a handy lookout tower on the road to the headquarters. Stop in at the headquarters for a chat to see what birds are around. There are wetlands, lakes and harbors here, all good havens for geese and ducks.

11

February Shorttakes

Killdeer

The sharp calls of these plovers announce their return to the northern parts of our three-state territory—they are resident in the more southern portions, usually from the level of the Missouri River southward. This is a brown and white bird with black trimming; the lower back and upper tail are orange. The adult killdeer has two neck bands while the young birds have one.

Woodcocks

Woodcocks begin their courtship flights on warm evenings at their traditional sites. This nocturnal bird of woodlands, thickets and swamps is seldom seen, though quite common. The courting flight involves spiraling upward and then swooping toward the ground while calling. Check with your local birders or Audubon club to learn where woodcock courtship grounds are located.

Robins

Large flocks return throughout the region. Theory has it that robins often migrate just a few hundred miles south, not all the way to Central America or South America, so what we have is a slide of the entire population southward in the fall and northward in the spring. Even during the harshest winter weather, you can often find robins and bluebirds in wooded valleys where they are protected from wind.

Cedar Waxwings

Listen for the high twittery sound of cedar waxwing flocks near cedar trees where they come to feed on their blue berries. They also feed on other berries, but the common red cedar is especially popular with this beautiful brown bird.

See also:

Chapter 68, Winter Birds: Finches, Sparrows and Grosbeaks. American goldfinches are shedding their drab winter coat and beginning to sport the bright yellow feathers of the warm season. They will come readily to bird feeders, especially if you offer them black thistle seed (niger).

12

Breakout:
Breeding Songs of Birds

When days begin to lengthen appreciably and gray days of winter are often lightened by periods of welcome sunlight, the first hesitant notes of the spring concert begin as resident birds sing their territorial songs. The hours of daylight activate birds' sexual hormones just as extra added light will make hens lay more eggs. The songs they sing are statements that declare they are in their territory and intend to defend their claim.

The breeding or territorial song is different from the other vocalizations of birds. The other calls usually are shorter and make up what we might call birds' conversational repertoire. These are scolding calls, flight calls, alarm calls, calls to announce a bird's whereabouts and whatever else birds need to convey to one another. They are likely to be short chips or buzzy notes. Thus, you can sometimes learn to recognize a bird's full vocabulary if you take the time to observe and listen carefully. The birdsong records and tapes that are so handy for recognizing territorial songs are of no help in identifying the rest of bird vocabulary—you will be pretty much on your own.

The territorial claim that is staked out by the male birds will differ in size from species to species. Some birds need more elbow room for nesting and raising their broods than others. The space needed may be a 1/2 acre or less, or may be much larger. Most bird territorial calls are species specific—for instance, a cardinal does not want other cardinals in his own backyard but will tolerate chickadees and titmice. Some birds, including the mockingbird, prefer to hold as much territory as they can just for themselves. The mockingbird likes to dictate who and what will come into its nesting area. They will dive at cats, dogs and people alike if they come too close to the nest. Being outweighed is no deterrent to this bird.

The chickadees are usually the first of our songbirds to sing their breeding season tunes in early February, and the cardinals are usually not far behind. Robins will soon join the chorus as they return from their southern winter residences. As the weeks roll on, listen for other migratory birds returning for the warm season or passing through to more northern climates.

I strongly believe that the way to learn more about bird territory and their breeding songs is to find a comfortable spot where there are likely to be lots of birds—a place where you can go early in the morning, when you'll hear the most bird songs. Dress warmly and move slowly so that you don't startle the birds. Settle in for an hour or two so that the birds get used to you.

When the birds sing their territorial songs, other birds in other territories may answer or seem to answer. This appears to be an "I'm here and you're there" sort of message. If strange birds try to enter a bird's territory, the home bird may chase it out or try to get rid of it by pecking and beating it with its wings. Territorial battles usually occur early in the season before actual nesting occurs. By the time the breeding pairs begin to build their nests, these boundary disagreements are all settled. Later in the season young birds are usually the ones who dispute territories and try to kick the old-timers out.

MARCH

March Observations

13

Woodland Wildflowers

This is the season when the forest floor under deciduous trees gets plenty of sunlight. Leaves of most trees are only beginning to come out so there will be plenty of time for the early flowers to burst from the humusy earth, flower and develop seeds before the foliage matures. Once the leaves have reached their full size there will be little sunlight reaching the forest floor, just a light dappling that does not linger but moves with the sun's passage across the sky. Photosynthesis, the process by which plants make simple carbohydrates, is powered by the sun—that's why woodland wildflowers have to rush through their growing period in very early spring. Many of these early flowering plants of woodlands are ephemeral, that is, they will die back to the ground later in the season after tree leaves are fully developed and you may see no sign of their foliage until early next spring.

The following spring wildflowers can be found throughout most of our three states, although they are less inclined to grow in the prairielands of the region. A wildflower book will help you with its illustrations and descriptions. Since wildflowers can be arranged in a number of valid ways, be sure to read the introduction so you will know how the guide is arranged and how to key the flowers.

Earliest of all the wildflowers is the one called harbinger of spring, a small (under 10 inches) parsley relative that has little florets in simple umbels. In southern parts of our region, it may bloom as early as January. The flowers are white with red anthers that gives rise to its other common name, pepper-and-salt. The fern-like basal leaves develop fully only after the flower blooms. The root is a round tuber.

Spring beauty is probably our most common early woodland flower, appearing in large colonies on moist woodland floors as well as under trees on suburban lawns. Some homeowners find spring beauty and violets in their lawns offensive; I think they are beautiful, certainly far more so than lawn grass. A member of the purslane family, it has a five-petaled pink flower that is actually white with bright pink veining. The plant grows to about 5 inches tall at flowering, and about twice that height after flowering. The root is a small round corm that American Indians used as food—experts say that the leaves and flowers are also edible.

Hepatica or liverleaf, a member of the buttercup or crowfoot family, has leaves that are thick with three deeply divided parts. The plant, often found on wooded slopes, grows to a height of about 6 inches. The flowers, occurring singly on hairy stems or scapes, come in shades of white to pink to mauve. Each flower has six to twelve petal-like sepals, many stamens and, under the sepals, three green bracts. After flowering, the leaves persist and through the warm season gradually become russet brown and leathery.

Two more members of the buttercup or crowfoot family that flower in the woods in very early spring are rue anemone and false rue anemone. Rue anemone has pink or white flowers about 3/4 inch wide that consist of five to ten petal-like sepals that surround the large number of yellowish stamens. The leaves of this 4- to 9-inch plant grow in a whorl under the flowers and have three lobes. Basal leaves appear after the flowers. This is a plant mainly of wooded hillsides.

False rue anemone grows primarily in wooded bottomlands or at the base of slopes. The white flowers that grow in small clusters are each about 1/2 inch in diameter and are notable for their five bright sepals. The compound leaves have three leaflets, each with two or three lobes.

Bloodroot, my favorite of all the spring wildflowers, is a member of the poppy family that grows in rich woodsy soil. The bone-white flowers are up to 1 1/2 inches wide and have eight to twelve or more petals surrounding yellow stamens. At the time of bloom the plant is rarely more than 6 inches high but it grows somewhat taller later in the season. The leaves, at first wrapped around the flower stem, are large, up to 6 inches or more in width when they unfurl. Unfortunately, each flower lasts only a day. The tuberous roots have red juice that was used as a dye by American Indians.

Rose verbena grows at the edge of woods, along rights of way and in glades. A member of the vervain family along with lantana and many tender verbenas, it spreads along the ground with runners that soon form their own roots. Seldom growing over a foot tall, the opposite, toothed leaves are divided into three parts. The plant is crowned by pink clusters of tubular flowers 2 inches or more wide.

Less conspicuous are the small clusters of yellow flowers on fragrant sumac that appear at the ends of terminal growth. Crush the leaves of this 2- to 4-foot plant and you will smell what I have always called "the smell of the woods in summer." The three-part compound leaves have wavy edges and look similar to their close relative, poison ivy. Fragrant sumac's young leaves are not as shiny as those of poison ivy. This is also called the lemonade bush because the fuzzy red berries taste like lemon when sucked. Pioneers are said to have soaked the berries in water to make a lemony drink—the berries were then discarded before drinking.

Pussy's toes is a small composite, a daisy relative, that is also called everlasting. Found on poor, rocky soils in woods and fields, it has small fuzzy clumps of flowers that, when they first appear, before the stem elongates, look like the bottom of cats' feet . The basal leaves are generally somewhat long and ovate in shape. Small thin leaves also appear on the flower stem. The whitish flowers lack the ray florets that daisies have circling their centers—they have disk florets only.

Dutchman's breeches has curious white to pale pink flowers with two spurs at the top of each, making the shape look strangely like pantaloons. They are in the fumitory family, a plant group sometimes lumped with poppies. The roots are small, scaly tubers. It has feathery divided leaves and seldom grows more than a foot tall, often less. This pretty little woodland plant is found in rich soils of hillsides and bottomlands.

HOTSPOTS

Look for the woodland wildflowers of spring wherever there are woods and forests that are protected. The National Wildlife Refuges offer such locations. So do state parks and other preserves.

In Arkansas, **White Oak SP** offers 725 acres known for a rich diversity of wildlife, including spring wildflowers. This park is in the wooded hills of southwestern Arkansas and has two nature trails that wander through a variety of habitats that range from bottomland marshes to beech-covered ridges. To get there, take I-30 from Prescott 20 miles west on Arkansas Highway 24 to Bluff City, then take Arkansas Highway 209 just 100 yards and turn onto Highway 387. The park is just 2.5 miles south.

Lake Poinsett SP in the rolling hills of northeastern Arkansas is another likely spot to look for wildflowers in early spring. Located on the area known as Crowley's Ridge, this park offers more than 7 miles of hiking trails with a variety of good wildflower habitats. From Harrisburg, go east one mile on Arkansas Highway 14, then take Arkansas Highway 163 south 3 miles to the park.

Pere Marquette SP in west central Illinois offers many trails and a varied wooded environment with a good variety of spring wildflowers. Largest of Illinois state parks, it is located at the confluence of the Mississippi and Illinois rivers on Illinois Highway 100, 2 miles west of Grafton and about 25 miles northwest of Alton.

Starved Rock SP in north central Illinois also is a good spot for woodland wildflowers. From the bottomland along the Illinois to the bluffland and sandstone cliffs, this park offers especially good opportunities on the slopes and in the gorges. It can be reached by going 10 miles west of Ottawa on I-80, then 5 miles south on Illinois Highway 178.

Missouri's **Roaring River SP**, one of Missouri's oldest state parks dating back to the 1920s, has rugged hills, open glades, limestone bluffs and a large cold spring. Look for spring wildflowers here in any of several habitats. Located in southwestern Missouri in the heart of the Ozarks, this park can be reached by taking Missouri Highway 112 south from Cassville for about 6 miles—watch for park signs. Cassville is about 17 miles south of Monett on Highway 37.

Cuivre River SP in east central Missouri is northwest of St. Louis and about 3 miles north of Troy on U.S. Highway 61. This park has rugged landscape, rich woodlands, limestone glades and rocks that are glacial erratics, since this park is in the glaciated portion of the state. There are plenty of trails that lace through the park's 6,200 acres that will take you to a variety of woodland wildflower sites.

14

Mourning Cloak and Spring Azure Butterflies

On the earliest warm days of the new spring, you may see mourning cloak butterflies flitting along woodland paths. Their dark puce wings (I rarely get to use this word that means purplish brown) are trimmed on the outer edges by a lacy border of pale creamy yellow that trims a row of small blue-purple spots. The drab undersides of the wings are beautifully camouflaged when the insect lands on tree bark. Their front legs are smaller than the other two pairs and are held against their body in such a way that they may appear to have four legs rather than the six legs typical of insects. In England, this butterfly is known as the Camberwell beauty and is greatly prized.

The larvae are black with small white spots and a row of red spots on their backs. Several rows of black bristles run down the back and they have rusty brown legs. After breeding, the female lays pale eggs in groups on or around twigs of favorite food trees. The eggs will hatch in one or two weeks after which the caterpillars can be found feeding in groups. They continue eating, growing and molting for about a month, until they are about 2 inches in length. Then each pupates in a sheltered spot, turning into a gray to tan chrysalis. Within about two weeks, the adult butterfly emerges, its soft wings slowly expanding as bodily fluid helps make them rigid. In the northern part of our region there probably will be only one brood a year, while in the southern regions there may be two or more.

These butterflies hibernate, overwintering in deep crevices of rocks or tree bark, as do their relatives the tortoiseshell butterflies. The mourning cloaks are large butterflies with a wing span of about

3 inches, whereas the tortoiseshells have an average wingspan of 2 inches or slightly less. Both the California tortoiseshell, a western species, and Milbert's tortoiseshell, a northern species, have been found in our region but the mourning cloak is, by far, more common.

The diet of mourning cloak larvae includes the foliage of willows, birch, poplar and elm. The adult can be found feeding on nectar from early-blooming plants such as willows, decaying fruit and tree sap—especially that of maples, and occasionally flowers. Look for mourning cloaks along paths through deciduous forests, especially in moist areas, on days when the temperature is above 60 degrees Fahrenheit. Look for sap on tree branches and trunks. When you see a butterfly flapping, then gliding, that is the pattern of flight for the mourning cloak, first butterfly of spring. There will be fewer of them later in the spring when most will have mated, laid eggs and died.

Watch for the mating dance of the mourning cloaks. They chase each other, then fly up in spirals that take them 30 feet or more in the air. Then one of them will drop to the earth while the other slowly glides down.

When the weather turns cooler again as it often does at this time of year, the mourning cloak butterflies will disappear, once more seeking the shelter of tree bark or cracks in rocks.

Another spring butterfly is the spring azure, one of the many small blue butterflies found in our region. With a wingspan of only about 1 inch, it is the earliest butterfly to emerge from its winter pupa. You may see freshly emerged spring azures before the dogwood blooms. They may have as many as four broods a year and, oddly, the later spring and summer forms of spring azure may be paler, almost white with small dark spots on the wings or with black-bordered wings. The later forms look to me like entirely different species.

Variably colored caterpillars hatch from tiny green eggs laid on a wide variety of flowering plants, including dogwoods, viburnums and meadowsweets. The rich brown pupae of the final summer broods will overwinter.

Look for this butterfly in some of the same places that you would find mourning cloaks: open deciduous woods and forests as well as along paths and in glades or clearings.

Whites, sulphurs and orange tips are butterflies that occur worldwide and are common throughout our region. They come in shades of white, yellow and orange with black markings. They usually have wingspans of about 1 1/2 inches. You may find large numbers of them gathering in damp places. The slender larvae are usually green and covered with fine short hairs.

The common cabbage butterfly is one of the better-known examples of this group and, indeed, many species are inordinately fond of members of the cabbage family, as any gardener will tell you. The clouded sulphur, a yellow butterfly with black trimming on its wing edges and a black spot of each front wing, is another well-known species. Some of these butterflies feed on tube flowers such as petunias and phlox.

Look for this group of butterflies in meadows or other lush places where there are plenty of plants in bloom. They will be particularly in evidence on warm sunny days when there is no wind. After these butterflies have mated, you will often see the female lazing about flowering plants to find some with the preferred taste for her young. When she finds suitable plants, watch carefully to see her touch the leaf with the end of her abdomen. In that brief moment she will have laid a small white egg on the underside of the leaf.

HOTSPOTS

Parks and refuges with open deciduous woods, wide hiking trails and open glades are ideal for seeking butterflies early in the season. In Arkansas, such places include parks and refuges like **Petit Jean SP** in central Arkansas between the Ozark and Ouachita mountains. The mountain setting has trails, woods, streams, springs and spectacular views. To get there, take Highway 9 (Exit 108) off I-40 at Morrilton 9 miles south to Oppelo. From there, take Highway 12 west for 10 miles to the park. Another likely place to look for butterflies in Arkansas in early spring is **Felsenthal NWR** in southern Arkansas (see Chapter 2 for directions).

In Illinois, likely places to look for spring butterflies include **Pere Marquette SP** in the west central part of the state (see Chapter 13 for directions). Trails through its deciduous woodsy hills and valleys should have spring butterfly activity on warm sunny days. Another good spot for hunting butterflies on pleasant spring days should be the trails at **Eagle Creek SP** on the shores of Lake Shelbyville, north of Shelbyville in central Illinois near the small town of Findley. Take Highway 128 north from Shelbyville about 12 miles toward Findley, then watch for park signs.

To look for early spring butterflies, try the bottomland hardwood forests of **Swan Lake NWR** in north central Missouri (see Chapter 8 for directions). **Lake of the Ozarks SP** is another place to look for butterflies. Located off Highway 42 from U.S. Highway 54, it has wild areas with trails as well as numerous other trails. This is Missouri's largest (17,000 acres) and most varied state park. Go to the visitors' center and get a brochure with trail map so you can find your way around.

15

Wild Turkeys

The sight of wild turkeys in woods and cropfields is no longer the rarity it once was. During the late 1920s and continuing through the 1940s, the wild turkey population declined drastically until, in 1952, Missouri studies showed that there were fewer than 2,500 of these birds in the entire state. A U.S. survey of the turkey population in 1948 indicated that turkeys occupied only 12 percent of their former range. This was a critical time for wild turkeys throughout the country.

Much of the success of the restoration of the wild turkey population belongs to John Lewis, upland wildlife research supervisor, who joined the Missouri Department of Conservation (DOC) in 1952. He developed the trapping technology and methods of capturing and releasing wild turkeys beginning in 1954 and 1955. He and his wild turkey team trapped and relocated some twenty-seven hundred turkeys to 154 sites in nine counties during the years between 1954 and 1979.

They used cannon-net traps in baited sites. Four-inch mortars were attached to the corners of the net and propelled by black powder. Lewis reported that the wild birds have "keen eyesight and memories that are unbelievable." Everything had to be camouflaged. When Lewis realized that and put greater effort into camouflaging even small bits of exposed wire, the team had greater success in trapping wild turkeys.

When Missouri communities heard about the program, they signed up to have turkeys released in their areas. About 80 percent of the birds were released on private land. Normal releases included twenty to twenty-four birds in a group, with a couple of hens to each tom. They trapped and moved turkeys between January and early March, choosing relocation sites that were at least 50 percent timber and taking into account that areas with corn and bean fields will support larger populations.

This project was one of Missouri DOC's greatest successes. Relocation helped restore the threatened wild turkey throughout the state. Presently, the department is trading turkeys for other animal species it wishes to restore. The river otter, a trade with Louisiana, is a good example of the trading program.

Wild turkeys, unlike their domestic counterparts that seem neither as athletic nor as bright, are good runners and are capable of sprintlike flights although they do seem to lack basic aerodynamic qualities. They can leap into flight from a standstill, much like the partridge.

The wild turkey looks much like a streamlined barnyard specimen, with rusty rather than pale tail feather tips. The body is both iridescent and bronze in color although it appears black in the distance and when not in sunlight. Both primary and secondary wing feathers are barred. The naked bluish head has warty red wattles. Both male and female are likely to develop hairy "beards" that hang like thin pendulums from their breasts. In the female, the beard is smaller and, indeed, the female is smaller and less iridescent than the big toms.

Wild turkeys strut, raise their feathers, beat their wings and leap into the air in elaborate courtship displays. The males initiate the breeding season by beginning to chase the females in mid-February. Big tom turkeys gobble and hoot, rushing at the sound of female calls with tails spread, wings depressed and feathers fluffed. Their wings quiver as they strut pompously, emitting a series of explosive puffs from their lungs as they woo available hens. Rivalry may result in bloodshed and even loss of life as stronger males strike the heads of weaker rivals. Each tom tries to gather a harem of several hens. The female turkey shows acceptance of the male by strutting near him, then suddenly spreading her wings and throwing herself on the ground before him. The turkey mating dances are as dramatic as anything you will find in nature.

Turkey hens build solitary secluded nests where the males can't find them, and take extraordinary pains to keep the locations secret by never approaching the same way twice. The toms are far better breeders than parents! During the egg-laying period, the hens return to the toms for a short time each day. The ovate to long, pointed eggs are from soft white to pale, buffy pink with reddish dots and a smooth matte surface. Incubation takes 28 days and the number of eggs ranges from eight to fifteen.

When the chicks hatch, usually in May, the hen is very attentive. She may return to the nest the first night, but then usually moves the brood to high, dry ground. When the chicks are in the fluffy-down stage of development, cold rains are a great threat to them; once the feathers develop, they are more able to tolerate inclement weather. A post-juvenile molt takes place in September after which the young birds look quite adult, although they will continue to gain in size and weight for their first several years.

Close observers have long noted that turkeys have a rather large vocabulary ranging from quiet motherly clucks to loud yelps and gobbles, querulous notes and irritated "quitquits."

Although wild turkeys are not migratory in the true sense, they often wander extensively in search of food, especially in fall and winter. Their usual means of locomotion is by foot rather than wing— flight is most often used in alarm or to cross a barrier. The long, powerful legs make it possible for the turkey to travel swiftly over long distances. In past centuries, they were known to outdistance both men and horses during hunts.

The turkey diet includes about 15 percent animal matter and about 85 percent plants. Insects and miscellaneous invertebrates including snails and spiders are among favorite turkey treats. The vegetable foods include grass and other foliage, fruit, mast (acorns) and other miscellaneous plant matters. During summer and fall, turkeys often show an inordinate fondness for grasshoppers and crickets.

The only time that turkeys may have trouble getting around the forest floor is when the snow is deep and soft. At such times they may remain in roost trees until conditions improve, subsisting on whatever buds, fruits, nuts and berries may have remained on the branches. In modern times, turkeys' foraging journeys often take them through cropfields as well as along roads and tracks where grain may have spilled.

Look for the large tracks and other signs of turkeys after rains soften dirt paths and roads. In the woods under oak trees you will see areas where the leafy layer has been thoroughly scuffed up by turkeys looking for mast. You will see signs of turkeys more often than the turkeys themselves for they are shy, always alert, quick to detect moving objects and have acute hearing. Mechanical turkey calls plus sitting quietly in a known turkey territory may bring toms within sight during the breeding season that includes this month.

HOTSPOTS

Among the best places to look for turkeys in Arkansas are the National Wildlife Refuges. Wild turkeys are common at **Felsenthal NWR** in southeastern Arkansas (see Chapter 2 for directions), **Wapanocca NWR** in northeastern Arkansas (see Chapter 1 for directions) and **White River NWR** in the east central part of the state. White River NWR, near the town of Dewitt, is open to the public from March 1 through October 31. You can get there by way of highways 1, 17, and 44. Because there often are flooded roads, check with refuge personnel prior to visiting. The phone number is (501) 946-1468.

In Illinois, wild turkeys are more unusual. They can be found occasionally at **Crab Orchard NWR** (see Chapter 1 for directions). Stop at the headquarters to ask for a map of the preserve and to learn if anyone has recently seen wild turkeys.

Another place in Illinois where you might see these large wild birds is in the remote areas of **Morton Arboretum** west of downtown Chicago (see Chapter 3 for directions). Again, it will pay to stop in at the headquarters building to see if turkeys have been recently sighted.

In Missouri, **Mingo NWR** is one of the best places for sighting wild turkeys (see Chapter 1 for directions). Although uncommon, wild turkeys do live in **Squaw Creek NWR** (see Chapter 1 for directions). Ask refuge personnel if any have been sighted and where you might successfully look.

16

Flowerless Plants: Lichens

Lichens are strange and complex organisms that represent a unique relationship between algae and fungi. Although lichens are scientifically classed as single species, each lichen represents an organic and symbiotic relationship between two entirely different life forms. The resulting organisms look little like either component. The fungi furnish support, moisture and nutrients in solution to the lichens. The fungi get those nutrients by decom-posing the organic or inorganic surface upon which the lichens grow. The algae provide simple sugars to both elements of the lichens through photosynthesis, the process whereby common earth elements are turned into carbohydrates in the presence of light.

The evolution of lichens suggests that the relationship began as parasitism and then developed into a mutually beneficial relationship. This is supported by the fact that the fungal cells actually penetrate the algal cells in some of the more primitive lichens, whereas the more advanced lichens are composed of fungal and algal cells living closely together but showing no signs of cell penetration by either partner. However the relationship began, clearly lichens are a successful and ancient form of life. They grow slowly and occupy some unusual niches in the natural world.

Another way of describing lichens is that they are flowerless plants that grow on rocks, trees and waste places throughout the world. They are well represented in our midwestern states of Illinois, Missouri and Arkansas. They grow in bottomlands and on mountaintops. Scientists have identified approximately fifteen thousand species of lichen.

These strange plants come in colors of yellow, brown, blue, green or black. Lichens have neither roots nor leaves, but are made up of layers of irregular extensions called *thalli*. Lichens multiply by means of special structures called fruiting bodies. When spores or fragments break away from the plants they may be carried by the wind quite a distance from the parent plant. Where they land, they may grow into a new lichen if conditions are favorable.

Since lichens don't require soil, they grow in many places where higher forms of plants cannot. The fungal partner in lichens produces acids that break up rock into little particles. These small particles of rock mixed with decaying lichens are one of the sources of soil.

Lichens are of commercial value in some parts of the world. Some lichens are used as dyes for wools as well as litmus that is used to assess acidity. Wools dyed with lichen colors are said to be resistant to moth damage. The so-called reindeer moss that is commonly found in our region is a valuable food for reindeer and caribou in more northern parts of the world. Icelandians use a lichen called Iceland moss to make a kind of bread.

There are three types of lichens, a classification that has been made according to their appearances. A *crustose* lichen is one pressed

Common foliose lichens appear on trees, fallen logs and rocks. They are especially prevalent on deciduous trees.

tightly to the surface on which it grows. It appears as tight as a coat of paint and has new little edges that rise above the growing surface. *Foliose* lichens are as their name indicates—they have leafy parts and fewer places of attachment than the crustose lichens. The final class of lichens is called *fruticose*—this form may appear bushy or may have branches or stalks that rise above the surface. In addition to these forms, there are many lichens that fall somewhere in between the three classes.

Lichens are the pioneer plants of the world, the first to grow on rock and begin the process of turning rock into soil. Mosses, which we'll look at in Chapter 32, are also essential in this role as a pioneer of life that, over tens of thousands of years, turns barren rock into fertile soil that will foster the growth of trees, grasses and all the other more advanced plants.

A common lichen you will see in your travels through our region is the reindeer moss. Upon close examination, its many gray-green stems look a little like minute reindeer antlers. This fruticose lichen also resembles a tiny winter forest of deciduous trees. Reindeer moss grows on the forest floor in little mats or rounded mounds. When it is moist, it's quite soft and even spongy as well as brighter green-gray, but when dry, it's crunchy underfoot, brittle and poorly attached to the poor soil on which it grows.

British soldiers is the descriptive name of several fruticose lichens that have crimson knobs at the tops of short stems. These red caps are fruiting bodies that appear on the tops of thin upright thalli. The upright yellow to gray-green thallus may be either smooth in texture or rough and covered by a grayish green crust. The British soldiers often grow on rotting wood, humus or soil in conjunction with other gray-green lichens that may make them more difficult to spot.

Brown caps appear very much like British soldiers except they have pale brown fruiting bodies rather than red ones. The erect thalli range from gray to pale grayish green and may be either branched or single. There are several similar species that have tan to brown fruiting bodies.

Rock tripe is the intriguing name of one of the foliose lichens. It may be leathery brown or whitish gray. The roundish thallus attaches to rocks or, more rarely, trees by means of a central cord. Although rock tripe feels leathery when moist, it becomes brittle when dry. The edges, which may split in places, will curl up when wet and lie flat when dry.

Shield lichens, commonly found on rocks and deciduous

trees, constitute the largest group of foliose lichens. The thalli have many large and small lobes that range from broad to narrow. These lichens are gray tinted with yellows, greens and browns. A good field mark for shield lichens is that their undersides are black. These lichens attach to rocks and trees by means of rootlike structures. Occasionally you may find large brown fruiting bodies on shield lichens.

Map lichen is one of many crustose lichens usually found on rocks. White, gray and brown with hints of green are among the colors worn by these lichens. They appear almost as if painted on rocks. The small fruiting bodies look like darker dots on the main color, and their shapes are irregular.

HOTSPOTS

Look for lichens in places that have both old rocks and deciduous trees. In Arkansas, try **Mount Nebo SP** north of Hot Springs—you will find its miles of trails enjoyable. The mountain itself rises 1,800 feet above the mountain valleys offering a great view of nearby **Lake Dardanelle**. Stop at the visitors' center for a trail map. To get there, take Exit 81 from I-40 and go south on Highway 7 through Russellville to Dardanelle, then turn right on Highway 22 west, then Highway 155 south up Mt. Nebo

Devil's Den SP in the Boston Mountains of northwestern Arkansas is another good place to look for a variety of lichens. Located at the bottom of a steep valley, this park features a clear mountain stream with a dam of native stone. In addition to plenty of rocks and deciduous trees, this park has some of the prettiest Ozark scenery in the state. Take U.S. Highway 71 8 miles south of Fayetteville. Then take State Highway 170 at West Fork and go 13 miles to the park.

In Illinois, **Starved Rock SP** (for directions, see Chapter 13) with its towering sandstone bluffs and deciduous forest offers good opportunities to study lichens. Check at the visitors' center or lodge for a trail map.

Giant City SP in southern Illinois is another place with lots of natural rock formations plus plenty of deciduous trees—a combination ideal for finding lichen of all sorts. Located in Shawnee National Forest, this park was inhabited by Native Americans roughly twelve thousand years ago. The park and its lodge were named for the unusual rock formations that are said to look very much like walls and streets of a mythical giant's town. To get there, take Illinois Highway 13 about 12 miles south of Carbondale, then take Giant City Road to the park.

The sunny rocky glades and woods of **Graham Cave SP** in east central Missouri offer good opportunities for studying lichens. The cave itself is an interesting geological formation that occurred where limestone and sandstone layers came together. To get to this park, go 2 miles west of Danville, off I-70 on Highway TT in Montgomery County.

Another likely place for seeking lichens is **Mastodon SP** 20 miles south of St. Louis near I-55 at Imperial. The visitors' center has brochures describing this and other parks. Exit at the Imperial ramp and follow signs to the park which is on the west outer road a mile or so north of the exit.

17

March
Shorttakes

Water Striders

When the days are warm, look for the overwintering insects called water striders. They look a bit like spiders but are true insects with three body parts and six legs. They take advantage of surface water tension to stride rapidly about, making dimples on the water as they run here and there in search of food.

Female Red-winged Blackbirds

Watch around marshes and swamps for the female red-winged blackbirds to arrive. You will recognize them by their brown striped feather patterns as they join the males and sit on cattails or low bushes and trees near wet places. The males arrive earlier—do the males stake out nesting sites or merely choose their territories? See if you can figure that out.

See also:

Chapter 8, Amphibians of February Warm Spells. March is the peak time to hear spring peepers and many other frogs.

18

Breakout: A Few Freshwater Fish

As the weather and water get warmer, take a little time to snoop around ponds, lakes and streams. You will be in luck if the water is clear and there are docks that shade the water. Look for the colors and general shapes of the fish in profile—are they long and slim like minnows or are they wider in the middle, sometimes almost oval like some members of the sunfish family?

Fish like to hang around docks where they can hide in the shade, along banks just under overhangs or behind the edges of shadows where they are less visible. Children beginning to fish learn this early and usually can catch sunfish by angling in the water below the edge of docks. (Some avid observers of water life use masks and snorkels to study fish. This method will be covered in Chapter 43.) With a little luck and a lot of patience, you might see some of the more common midwestern freshwater fish. There are well over two hundred species in our three-state region.

The minnow and sunfish families are well represented in our region. Although most are fairly small, they usually look long and lean. Their dorsal fins are triangular, like small sails that are set on the rear half of the spine. Both fish groups are usually highly iridescent.

The duskystripe shiner is one of several small minnows of the Ozarks. As its name suggests, it has a dark lengthwise stripe on a paler body. Another Ozark shiner is the bleeding shiner, which got its name from the red markings on its fins, tail, gills and face. Golden shiners found in prairie ponds and streams are excellent bait fish and easily raised commercially. This minnow is thicker in the middle than most minnows, but its triangular dorsal fin is the key to its family. It is pale golden-silver and may reach a length of nearly 8 inches. You may see the whitetail sucker, noted for the white areas near the base of the tail, in Ozark streams where it feeds on aquatic insects. The horny-head chub, another minnow, nests in gravel mounds of Ozark streams and may reach a length of 10 inches. Like trout, this big minnow may rise to artificial baits.

The members of the sunfish family are common throughout our region. The dorsal fin is the giveaway of this fish family. It is nearly double from front to rear with the front part consisting of six or more sharp spines connected by tissue. The rear part of the dorsal fin is rounder and softer—its spines are not stiff and sharp and do not stick out of the fin. The other key to the sunfish family is the tab on the rear of the gill cover. This is less conspicuous in the largemouth and smallmouth basses but very obvious in the several sunfish.

This group includes the esteemed game fish, largemouth bass and its cousin, the smallmouth bass as well as all those scrappy little fish known collectively as sunfish. The largemouth bass, largest member of this group, matures in about five years to well over a foot long and about 2 pounds in weight, though the trophy fish are considerably larger. You can tell these fish by their dark and irregular lateral stripe and the large mouth that reaches well behind the eye level of the head. These fish are found in slow-moving streams and lakes. These carnivores feed on insects and, as they grow larger, on other fish and crayfish. The smallmouth bass frequents clear moun-tain streams of the Ozark and Ouachita mountains. This fish has no conspicuous lateral stripe and its mouth reaches only to about the rear side of the eye. The smallmouth feeds on insects and their larvae until it's large enough to add fish and crayfish to its diet.

The long prominent gill cover tab or "ear flap" of the longear sunfish and distinctly round profile distinguishes this small sunfish of clear swift streams. Growing to 5 inches in as many years, the longear prefers streams with stony or sandy bottoms. The most common of the sunfishes is the large-mouthed, thick-bodied green sunfish that is found in streams throughout the region. Look for the somewhat greenish appearance of this fish and its plain dark ear flap. The common bluegill of ponds and lakes is another deep-bodied sunfish that thrives on its diet of insects and their larvae. They have small mouths and a dark ear flap, and reach 6 inches at maturity. The redear sunfish of the southern parts of our region is larger, reaching nearly a foot in length at maturity, and has a prominent orange or red spot on its dark ear flap and a small mouth. Some people call it the shellcracker for its practice of eating snails. The sunfishes will rise to artificial lures or baits and are very scrappy fish for the sport fisherman.

Rock bass also is a sunfish family member. Its ear flap is dark but not as prominent as that of sunfish. It's heavy-bodied with a large mouth, is darker on top than on the belly, and has distinct but irregular horizontal lines on the body. The general impression is one of a dark, rather yellowish green to brown fish. The white crappie, which may reach 15 inches, is another favorite of sport fishermen. This sunfish family member is silvery, slab sided and deep bodied. Common in rivers, lakes and reservoirs, it feeds on aquatic insects as well as other fish and crustaceans. Less common is the black crappie with its darker markings and dorsal fin that has seven or eight spines as opposed to the five or six found in the white crappie.

In the spring when water has warmed and days are longer, you may see round, cleared places on the pebbly bottoms of lakes, ponds and quiet waters of streams. These usually are the nesting beds prepared by male sunfishes who become extremely territorial during the breeding season. They will drive other fish away at the same time that they attempt to lure gravid females to the bed. Once they attract the females and the eggs are laid and fertilized, the males continue to protect the eggs from other fish. It is at this time of year that the males, edgy and aggressive, will bite on just about anything an angler uses as bait or lure.

APRIL

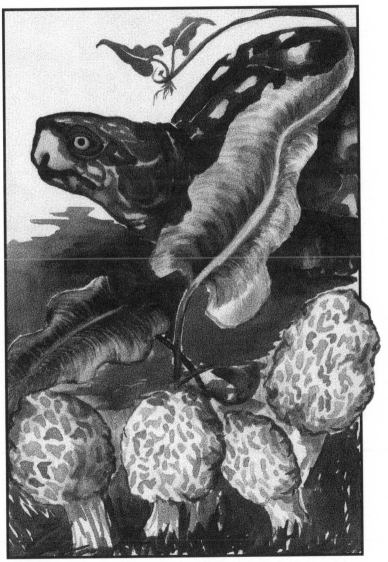

April Observations

19

Morels and Other Spring Fungi

You can find fungi just about any place, but you will have the most success if you choose places that are shady and moist. Spring rains and warming soil will trigger the development of many of those fungal fruiting bodies we call mushrooms and toadstools. They are called fleshy fungi, a group that also includes puffballs, shelf fungi and morels. These fruiting bodies are the more visible parts of strange plants that have no chlorophyll, and thus do not have photosynthesis as part of their repertoire.

Most scientists include fungi as part of the plant kingdom, but there are those who argue convincingly that, since fungi do not manufacture carbohydrates, they should be classified as a separate kingdom. The vegetable body of a fungus is called *mycelium* and consists of a multitude of *hyphae*, tiny branched tubes that grow in and around food sources, including decaying plants and dung. Each microscopic hypha produces digestive enzymes that reduce food sources to absorbable molecules. You can see what mycelium looks like by studying the inside of the bark of hardwood trees that have died and begun to decay—the many-branched hyphae intertwine making a complex network.

Some fungi grow in close association with the roots of certain green plants, an association that benefits both. The green plant is better able to take up soluble nutrients and the fungus is close to available food in the form of tree roots, both live and dead. In helping decay dead tissue, the fungi play an important role in the environment.

The mycelium produces those familiar fruiting bodies when it has achieved sufficient growth and conditions are right. The highly structured mushrooms and other fungal fruiting bodies are made up of modified hyphae that produce and disperse reproductive cells called spores.

The two basic types of fleshy fungi are Ascomycetes or sac fungi and Basidiomycetes or club fungi. A third kind of fungus often seen in woods and fields includes the slime molds which have the proper name of Myxomycetes. The root for part of the names and terms for different fungi is *mykes*, a Greek word for mushroom.

The sac fungi also are called cup- or disc-fungi because of the shape of the fruiting body. When the spores ripen, they shoot from the saclike structures that hold them and are carried off on wind currents. The sac fungi of spring include the black urn, scarlet elf cup and the morels, including false morel and black morel, the latter a culinary delicacy.

The small black urn fungus, about 1 to 3 inches wide, is dark brown to black and blends in so well with the forest floor that you may never see it. One of the first mushrooms of the season, it is usually found under deciduous trees. The scarlet elf cup, another small early mushroom, can be found in woodsy moist places where it often grows on the dead twigs of deciduous trees. Its scarlet cup, the spore bearing layer, is white on the outside.

The morels have distinctive ridges and folds, looking quite a bit like brain coral of the sea. True morels all are edible and both cap and stem are hollow. They have a single chamber within their peculiar pyramidal heads—there are several delectable species. False morels, which may be poisonous, have hollow heads with several chambers.

Many mushroom hunters are out simply to enjoy finding and identifying different species in different seasons—mushrooming is as good an excuse to get outdoors as any. Others hunt for edibles, of which there are many. Since there also are many species that are very poisonous, it pays to learn mushroom identification well if you plan to eat wild mushrooms. Look for a mycological society that you can join and learn from; going with experienced mushroomers will sharpen your eye and get you started on identification.

Some poisonous mushrooms look very much like some delicious and safe mushrooms. For that reason, many people prefer not to eat the wild ones. If you do, it is wise to eat only one species at a time and to keep one aside in case you should get sick—you can take it to the emergency room with you. One of our region's most experienced mycologists only eats mushrooms from the grocery store.

The club fungi group, Basidiomycetes, includes most of the common fleshy fungi that you will see in your travels through the woods and fields. Gilled mushrooms, puffballs, boletes, polypores and parchment fungi all belong to this group. Since field identification of mushrooms is not always conclusive, we are giving you just a few suggestions of the types of club fungi you may see in the spring.

Agarics or true mushrooms are colorful and abundant, growing in woods and forests as well as lawns and other open areas. These are soft-gilled fungi that swiftly disappear after the spores are shed. They are identifiable by spore print and by spore conformation under a microscope as well as by the gross appearance of the fruiting bodies. The way the gills are shaped and attached to the stem is one key to identification. Other keys are the presence or absence of the cup at the base of the stem, the stem itself and the presence or absence of a ring where the gills were originally attached to the stem.

Most of the agarics are more common in summer and fall but a few are readily discovered in the spring, including those of the mycena group. The peaked cap mycena and orange mycena are common throughout the growing season. Both are found on hardwood logs in gregarious clusters. Oyster mushrooms appear whenever there has been lots of rain. Growing on the dead stumps and logs of deciduous trees, the fan-shape cap is nearly white with a brown or grayish cast and white gills. Some have a slight and offset stalk but most do not.

Puffballs are agarics of summer and fall so we will take a closer look at them and the boletes, fleshy pore mushrooms in Chapter 49.

The slime molds of the Myxomycetes group begin their short life moving like amoebae to surround their food which consists of bacteria and small organic bits. They occur during wet weather and their entire life cycle may take only a day. As their surroundings begin to dry out, they stop moving and produce small fruiting bodies called *sporangia*. These contain the spores that are released and spread by the wind.

Polypores are mushrooms that don't have gills but do have many small openings on the undersurfaces of their caps. Most are woody and tough—many are perennial. Polypores have no stalk and usually grow on wood, on the trunks of trees and on fallen logs. Other polypores have stalks and grow on the ground. The common bracket or shelf fungi are polypores. One of the shelf fungi 1- to 4-inch fungus has overlapping semicircular layers that have stripes of different colors reminiscent of the bands on turkeys' tails. The shelf fungi group includes some of our largest mushrooms. The artist's fungus, the one with the soft white undersurface that you can decorate with a sharp twig and keep as a memento, is one of the many common polypores.

You will see parchment fungi all over the woods where they grow on dead deciduous wood. These are stalkless, thin and woody or leathery with their spore-bearing surfaces concealed on the undersides. They grow in the summer and fall but last a long time and so may be seen frequently. These fungi sometimes look almost like a coat of paint, especially when they are dry.

You are usually allowed to collect mushrooms and other fungal fruiting bodies for your own use in most public parks and refuges. Protected natural areas discourage the collection of anything; because these rules are made to protect rare and endangered species, it is wise to respect those wishes. Ask at the headquarters or visitors' center of any park or refuge before you pick anything.

HOTSPOTS

For early success, look for fungi primarily in deciduous woods after rains have fallen. Since the spores are carried throughout the world on currents of air, you can find fungi wherever the conditions are right for given species.

In Arkansas, the bottomland deciduous forests of **White River NWR** (see Chapter 15 for directions) promise a good selection of spring fungi for you to find and study. **Petit Jean SP** (see Chapter 14 for directions) between the Ozark and Ouachita mountains in west central Arkansas offers not only opportunities for mushrooming but also woods, springs, streams, and ravines of great beauty.

The forests of the bottomlands along the Illinois River are likely places to look for fungi in **Chautauqua NWR** (see Chapter 1 for directions) in west central Illinois. **Trail of Tears State Forest** in the Shawnee Hill country of southern Illinois is another good spot to look for mushrooms during the spring. To get there, take Highway 127 5 miles northwest of Jonesboro.

One thousand acres of bottomland deciduous forest in **Swan Lake NWR** (see Chapter 8 for directions) in north central Missouri offer plenty of opportunity for seeking out spring fungi. In the southeastern part of the state, **Lake Wappapello SP** offers plenty of good Ozark terrain for hunting down mushrooms and other fungi. To get there, go 16 miles north of Poplar Bluff on U.S. Highway 67, then 9 miles east on Highway 172 to the park.

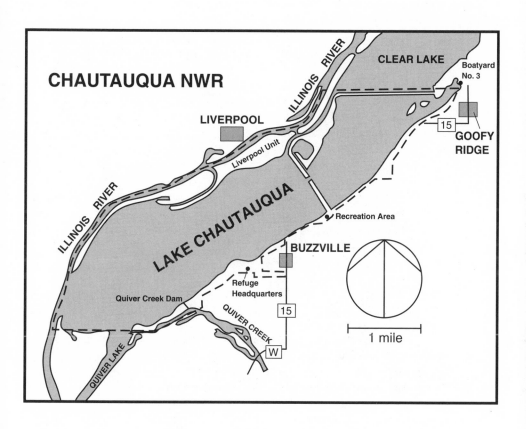

20

Ruby-throated Hummingbirds

Late April, after the threat of hard freezes is past, marks the arrival of the ruby-throated hummingbird in Arkansas. This is the only hummingbird seen throughout most of the eastern half of the United States. It breeds and spends its summers throughout much of Illinois, Missouri and Arkansas. It also is the most wide-ranging of all the North American hummingbirds.

Looking only for hummingbirds probably would be an unrewarding quest—look for them secondarily on your naturalist outings (or put out a feeder). Favorite places for these acrobatic birds are deciduous woods, the edges of woods and orchards. They are among the wild birds that have adapted well to suburbia.

In the sunlight, the ruby-throated hummingbird is one of the most brilliant of our wild birds. The iridescent emerald of its back and wing tops is in high contrast to the ruby red of the male's throat. The female's throat is whitish. Both sexes are pale cream to white with hints of gray underneath. The female has white tips on its tail feathers. Immature birds and some females may show a golden cast to their upper parts. Young males will begin to get their ruby throats by fall of the year in which they are fledged.

Hummingbirds are well adapted to taking nectar from flowers. The long bill, about a fifth of the length of the body, will reach into the deepest of flowers and the tubular tongue makes it easy for the bird to suck up the nectar. They are especially attracted to red and orange flowers. Although nectar is a main component of their diet, hummingbirds also eat small insects they take from flowers and spider webs. Spiders also are a favorite food. The end of the tongue has small hairs that allow the bird to pick up tiny insects, which are sometimes captured and eaten while in flight.

Hummingbird nests are constructed on limbs usually between 5 and 25 feet up in the trees. The small cuplike nest is made of an assortment of materials like spider web, lichens, small bits of grass and bark and cattail fluff. These materials blend so well into the surroundings that it's rare to see the nest—it looks more like a natural lump or branch stub on the limb.

Ruby-throated hummingbirds are less than 4 inches long as adults. Newly hatched hummingbirds, born naked and blind, are so small that several would fit into a teaspoon. The nest itself is only as big as a walnut and holds two tiny eggs about the size of navy beans. The female incubates the eggs for about twenty days. After they hatch the young grow quickly, and are ready to leave the nest in about three weeks. During the breeding season the male ruby-throated hummingbird is extremely territorial and bold. He will drive much larger enemies from his territory and may make a variety of chattering sounds.

Hummingbirds are highly athletic, able to fly rapidly backward, forward, up and down. They also can hover in one spot, making it easy for them to go from flower to flower seeking nectar. Their wings move so fast that they appear to be a blur, making the humming sound that gives them their common name. It is said that the wings beat sixty to seventy times each second, but who can count? Their call is soft, short, and slightly nasal—you often can hear it as they feed or perch near food supplies.

HOTSPOTS

Hummingbirds regularly spend the warm months and breeding season in the woodlands of **Felsenthal NWR** (see Chapter 2 for directions) and **White River NWR** (see Chapter 15 for directions) in Arkansas.

In Illinois, ruby-throated hummingbirds spend the breeding season at the **Gardner** (see Chapter 3 for directions) and **Brussels** (see Chapter 3 for directions) divisions of the **Mark Twain NWR Complex** along the Mississippi River. Look for them in deciduous woods of the bottomlands. Since the Gardner Division is only accessible by boat, you may have to scratch it from your list.

The **Annada District** (see Chapter 3 for directions) of the Mark Twain NWR in Missouri is known to have hummingbirds during the breeding season. So is **Mingo NWR** (see Chapter 1 for directions) in the southeastern part of the state.

21

Native Ferns

Ferns are found in many environments, although we may think of them most often in association with cool, moist woodsy areas. Some ferns can live on dry, exposed limestone outcroppings and others at the wet bases of those outcroppings. Some ferns live on exposed sandstone, some in open woods and glades. The greatest numbers of ferns or *pteridophytes* appear to live in shaded sandstone areas. Rich wooded soils and moist valleys are top habitats for a number of ferns. You also will find ferns along stream banks, in river bottom-lands and in swamps.

Like the flowering plants, ferns have stems, roots and leaves but there the similarity stops, since the fern method of reproduction is not at all the same. Reproduction for ferns is a two step process. Mature ferns develop spores, which then develop into *prothalli*. The prothalli in turn develop eggs and sperm, which require moisture for fertilization to take place. The resulting embryo develops into the plants we know as ferns.

Terminology is also a bit different in the case of ferns. The fern frond consists of the stipe or *petiole*, the stem, and the blade, the main part of the leaf. The stipe part that goes through the middle of the blade is called the *rachis*. The *pinnae* are the segments of the fronds. The underground portion of the stems are often perennial rhizomes and are referred to as rootstocks on which the wiry roots grow.

Fern blades come in a variety of shapes and patterns. They may be a simple feather or pinnate shape or they may be further divided. The shapes of the blades offer simple identification clues that are further enhanced by the placement and patterns of the spore-bearing parts called *sporangia*. An aggregation of sporangia is called a *sorus*.

The family of ferns called adder's tongues includes both grape ferns and adder's tongue ferns. The sporangia of these ferns grow separately from the blades on a fertile spike. The blades of the grape fern types are triangular, deeply divided, and may be in three sections, as is the case with the rattlesnake fern. They usually grow 10 to 12 inches tall. Rich moist woodlands and valleys are their favorite habitats.

The true adder's tongue ferns have thick oval blades that do not look at all like regular ferns. These are ferns of limestone glades and ledges. Some are very small while others grow 6 to 7 inches tall.

The royal fern family includes cinnamon, royal and inter-rupted ferns, all of which grow to 3 feet in height. Cinnamon ferns have sporangia borne on separate fertile fronds that are narrower, compressed and appear woolly, like cinnamon. The sterile fronds are deeply lobed and shaped like long feathers. Interrupted ferns have an area of fertile sporangia located part way up the frond. There are sterile frond parts both above and below the fertile area. Royal ferns have dense greenish brown sporangia at the top end of the frond.

The true fern family includes many familiar native ferns of our region. The rare hay-scented fern smells like fresh hay and grows tall, to 3 or more feet; the finely cut fronds are graceful and arching. Small round spots called *sori* develop near the blade margins at the ends of veins and produce the spores. Hay-scented ferns grow near shady moist sandstone bluffs and valleys.

The maidenhair ferns also are true ferns as are the brackens. Maidenhair ferns, growing in wet limestone ledges and the rich soil of moist valleys, have alternate branches on the rachis and develop spores in marginal sori along the outer edges of the leaves. Maidenhairs grow only a foot or so in height. Bracken fern is large, up to 3 feet tall, with fronds that appear to be in three different parts. Sori develop along the edges of leaf margins. Bracken occurs on roadsides, in dry open woods and in fields.

Purple cliffbrake, about 10 inches tall, has a dark purple-brown stipe and rachis and grows in glades, on ledges and around dry cliffs. The side parts of the fronds are nearly at right angles to the rachis. Sori develop along the leaf margins of both the purple cliffbrake and the smooth cliffbrake. The smooth cliffbrake has blue-green blades and brown to reddish brown stipe and rachis. This fern grows on limestone bluffs and ledges.

Common polypody has arching green fronds that persist into winter. The fronds have smooth margins and grow up to 12 inches tall. Polypody ferns grow in shady sandstone areas, often on northern and eastern slopes. Christmas ferns, so-called because of their evergreen growth, grow in thick clumps, often to well over a foot in height. The stipe has a fuzzy surface and is brown toward the base, green toward the blade. Christmas ferns commonly grow in fertile moist valleys and on shaded wooded slopes.

Sensitive fern grows in swamps, near springs, along river margins and in wet woodlands. The spores develop on a separate fertile frond. The sterile blades are triangular and not deeply divided. Common wood fern is a plant of most shaded sandstone areas and swampy woods. This fern grows to 3 feet in height and has a slightly arching pattern of growth. The blades are narrow triangles and deeply toothed. Sori develop on undersides of leaves between the midrib and the margin.

Broad beech ferns of wooded valleys and ravines have triangular fronds with the first pair of pinnae angled downward. The small round sori develop on either side of the midrib on the undersides of pinnae. Marginal shield ferns of sandstone and granite rocky areas are under 3 feet in height and quite evergreen. The leaflets of the feather-shaped blades may be smooth or have shallow teeth. Ebony spleenwort, which may grow to a foot in height, has a shiny purple stipe and rachis. The long slim blades may be sterile or have elongated sori on the undersides. It grows in woodlands and at the edges of glades.

Walking ferns have short stipes and simple, entire blades. They often have small plantlets developing at the tips of their mature fronds. Elongated sori develop irregularly on the undersides of fronds. This fern grows on moss-covered limestone and moist ledges.

Common horsetail, although not a true fern, usually is lumped in with ferns for convenience and because they are considered allied families of the ferns. Found along streams, the stems may grow 3 feet tall and have segments with teeth along the upper edge of the segment sheath. Fertile spore-bearing organs appear like buds at the end of stems. The stems grow without branching.

HOTSPOTS

Lake Ouachita SP in central Arkansas, located around Arkansas' largest man-made lake, has trails that offer good opportunities for studying ferns. For instance, the Caddo Bend Trail wanders for about four miles through the woods and along the lake shore of Point 50

Peninsula. (To get there, go 3 miles west from Hot Springs on U.S. Route 270, then 12 miles north on Highway 227 to the park.)

Cypress swamps, wild pecan trees and a horseshoe lake that formerly was a channel of the Mississippi River are features of **Lake Chicot SP** in southeastern Arkansas. Look for native ferns along the trails around Arkansas' largest natural lake. To get there, take Highway 144 from U.S. Route 65 at Lake Village and drive 8 miles northeast to the park.

Starved Rock SP in north central Illinois is a likely spot for seeking native ferns. The park has a narrow strip of wooded bluffs with sandstone cliffs that rise over 100 feet above the Illinois River. Vegetation is luxuriant on the slopes and in the ravines where you are likely to find ferns. (See Chapter 13 for directions.)

Pere Marquette SP in west central Illinois is another place that should be pretty good for studying native ferns. Look for the trails that will take you through the rainshed valleys of the park. (See Chapter 13 for directions.)

Hawn SP in east central Missouri is a grand place to find many ferns (see Chapter 4 for directions). This park has mixed pine and hardwood forest and an unusual variety of rare plants, including at least eighteen species of ferns.

Roaring River SP in southwestern Missouri is another beautiful spot ideal for studying ferns (see Chapter 13 for directions). Where water rises out of the earth at the base of a shady dolomite cliff, it also flows from above into the blue pool making this an ideal spot for the ferns and mosses that thrive there.

22

Spring
Wood Warblers

Small, fast and inclined to hide behind the smallest leaflet or twig—
that's one way to describe spring wood warblers. For those of us who
have less than perfect eyesight, finding these small warblers is more
than a little challenging. They are only about 5 inches long. To give
you some idea of the many species of warblers, over four dozen are
listed in most birding guides. Identifying warblers in the spring may
be demanding but at least then the males are in their bright breeding
plumage, which is flashier and easier to identify than the duller fall
plumage.

In the fall, many warblers wear the drab plumage that has
given rise to the term "confusing fall warblers." Young birds still in
their juvenile plumage and all of the adults molt in late summer just
before they leave the breeding range, and again before migrating
north in the spring.

Although some of these birds spend their winters in the
southern United States, many warblers migrate to Central America
and South America. Some spend the warm season in our region,
while we only see others as they migrate through our area on their
way to northern breeding grounds. Looking for warblers in the
deciduous trees where they search for insects, spiders and berries will
be easier before the trees are in full leaf. Some warblers are totally
insectivorous while others enjoy a mixed diet of animal and plant life.
Most of the northward-migrating warblers traveling to or through our
region will be seen during April and May.

In our region, lying as it does on the great Mississippi Flyway, the most commonly seen warblers are the yellow-rumped warbler, Tennessee warbler and Nashville warbler. The yellow-rumped warbler, known in the East as the myrtle warbler and in the West as Audubon's warbler, is one of our better-known songbirds.

The western birds have a yellow throat while the eastern ones have a white throat. The eastern version of this bird also has white markings around the eye. Both the myrtle and the Audubon's warblers have four prominent patches of yellow on the crown, the rump and each side. The winter range of these birds includes southern Missouri and Illinois as well as much of Arkansas. These are among the earliest warblers to appear as they migrate northward. The summer range is in the evergreen forests of the Rocky Mountains, the northern United States and Canada.

You will see the Tennessee warbler as it migrates through our region from its winter home in Central America and South America to summer breeding grounds in forests and bogs of Canada. The male is olive green with a gray crown, white eyebrow and a darker line going through the eye area. The female is very similar but duller. The rising song of the Tennessee warbler will help you know when it is in the area. The nest is built on the ground and made of plant rootlets, grasses and sphagnum moss.

The Nashville warbler winters along the coast of Mexico and farther south, then migrates through our region to its summer home in northeastern United States and southeastern Canada. This bird's breeding range also includes the Rocky Mountains. This bird has a gray head and olive-green wings, back and tail. The throat and belly are bright yellow and it has a conspicuous white eye-ring. The female is somewhat muted in color as compared to the male. This is a common bird of second-growth woods, brush and the spruce bogs where it nests. The nest itself is a small cup placed at ground level in brushy or grassy places and constructed of grass, plant stems, moss and fur.

There are a number of other wood warblers that migrate through our region in somewhat lesser numbers on their way to breeding grounds in more northern realms, some going as far as Alaska and Labrador. One of the most traveled birds is the blackpoll warbler that spends winters in the rain forests of South America and summers in the North, more than 10,000 miles away. The male blackpoll has a black cap and white cheek plus black and white streaking on the body and two bold wing bars. In the spruce forests where it nests, it uses twigs, bark, grass and plant stems to make its nest in the lower branches of small trees. The blackpoll comes through our region in the later part of the migrating season, usually appearing in mid-April to late May.

The chestnut-sided warbler is another late migrant that comes through our region later in the season in its passage from South American rain forests to northern regions. This species nests in the northeast quadrant of North America in areas with scrubby brush, woodlands and pastures. It builds its nest of plant materials—bark, stems, seed down and other fibrous stuff. The male in its breeding plumage has a bright yellow crown, chestnut stripe along the side of the breast, a black whiskerlike stripe and two wing bars. The female is similar but muted.

The black-throated green warbler migrates thousands of miles each spring and fall to its winter grounds in Central America and South America, then to its breeding grounds in evergreen and mixed forests of the Appalachian Mountains and much of northeastern North America. The nest, usually high in conifers at a limb crotch, is made of grass, bark strips and other plant parts. The black throat of this greenish bird wraps around the sides of the breast. This, plus the yellow face and two white wing bars, are its field marks. The female looks much the same but duller and with less contrast. This is one of the warblers that stays high in the trees, making it a particularly exasperating bird to identify.

The palm warbler winters along our Gulf Coast and down into Mexico and Central America. It spends the breeding season through-out much of Canada where it nests in spruce bogs—its favorite habitat is in bushes and weedy fields. This is a ground-dwelling warbler often seen on golf courses where it casts about for insects and berries. The palm warbler male has a chestnut-colored cap, brown upper parts, yellow throat and eyebrow and gray underparts. This is one of the first warblers of spring, usually even earlier than the yellow-rumped warbler. Its manner of walking is distinctive—it flips its tail up and down as it walks while most warblers hop.

Here at last is a warbler that includes our region in its breeding ground—the American redstart spends its winters in Central America and South America but summers in much of the eastern United States and southern Canada. This flashy bird is noted for the coloration of the male—it is mainly black with bright orange patches on the wings, tail and sides of the breast. The common Latin American name for this bird is "little torch." The female and juveniles are a less brilliant version of the same pattern with yellow wing, tail and breast patches on an olive-gray base color. The colorful patches are usually easy to see because of the way these birds often fan their tails and spread their wings. These warblers live in deciduous thickets and forests where they build their nests of lichens, grass and other plant fibers above the ground.

The magnolia warbler is another species that winters in Central America or South America, and spends the breeding season primarily in the coniferous forests of Canada, the Appalachian Mountains and parts of our northern states. They build their nests of grass and twigs and anchor them to the top of level evergreen branches. The male in his breeding plumage has a yellow rump, wide white tail patches, black on his back and the sides of his head and an obvious white eyebrow. The female is duller and has less white on her wings.

In recent years, scientists and others interested in the wild songbirds have wondered at the diminishing numbers of many species, including a number of warblers. No one has been able to pinpoint any single cause for this—it is likely that the reduced numbers of songbirds are due to a number of factors. The Central and South American tropical forests where many of these birds spend the winter are being cleared at an alarming rate. In our country, countless swamps and other wetlands were drained before the advent of protective legislation, which drastically changed thousands of acres of once prime songbird territory.

Similarly, the forests of this country are no longer contiguous stretches of trees but now consist mostly of fragments. Scientists have theorized that fragmented forest, combined with the spread of cow-birds, has diminished the numbers of songbirds—cowbirds frequent forest edges and parasitize the nests of other birds in larger numbers every year. Undoubtedly, pesticides used unwisely have had an effect on our wildlife since World War II, especially those that are dependent upon insects for their diet. The move toward wiser policies on making and using pesticides of all sorts is only too welcome.

Migrating songbirds often travel at night. They may become confused by fog, lights, tall buildings and other tall structures that are not a natural part of the landscape. There have been occasions during the migrating season when hundreds of birds have been killed by flying into television towers, tall buildings with reflective glass and other objects, including the Statue of Liberty in New York Harbor.

Whatever the reasons for the diminishing numbers of song-birds, it has become increasingly important for us to gain better knowledge of these small feathered jewels. Breeding bird censuses as well as Christmas Bird Counts and other studies of our songbird population are more important than ever before. We have to have knowledge before we can figure out what to do.

HOTSPOTS

Looking for wood warblers during April and May is the crowning joy of many birders and the ultimate frustration of others. During the height of the migrating season, you probably will see warblers flitting through the brush and trees almost any place you settle for a little while.

Wapanocca NWR (see Chapter 1 for directions) in northeast Arkansas is a good spot to visit if you want to see spring warblers. In southeastern Arkansas, **Felsenthal NWR** is a great place for seeking migratory songbirds, including wood warblers (see Chapter 2 for directions). Look in the treetops of the bottomland forests for a variety of warblers. **Hot Springs National Park** in west central Arkansas is almost completely surrounded by the city of Hot Springs and has a good collection of birds, including some of the warblers, and is typical of upland country with many hot springs as well. The park visitors' center is in the Fordyce Bathhouse in the middle of Bathhouse Row in the heart of town. This is a fairly big park so you would be wise to go there first to get a map and advice on the specific hotspots of the moment. You can reach Hot Springs on U.S. Highway 270 and 70 or via Arkansas Route 7.

Starved Rock SP in north central Illinois is well known for the heavy migratory traffic that passes by each spring. The park is along 5 miles of Illinois River shoreline (see Chapter 13 for directions). The entire **Mark Twain NWR Complex** (see Chapter 3 for directions) that lies along some 250 miles of the Mississippi and Illinois rivers in Illinois, Iowa and Missouri is good for seeking warblers since its three districts are directly on one of the world's greatest flyways. The **Calhoun Division** is particularly well known for its spring warblers.

Big Oak Tree SP, about 24 miles south of Charleston in southeast Missouri, is a likely place to find spring warblers. Take the boardwalk through the park to get a good view of birds and the remnants of the vast swampy forest that once covered the Missouri Bootheel country. You can get there by taking Highway 102 14 miles south of East Prairie in Mississippi County. Spring warblers are likely to pass through **Meramec SP** in east central Missouri during late April. To get there, take I-44 west of St. Louis to Sullivan and follow the signs to the park, which is 4 miles east of Sullivan on Highway 185.

23

April
Shorttakes

Migratory Birds

Many summer residents arrive this month, including house wrens, orioles, indigo buntings, catbirds and ruby-throated hummingbirds.

Killing Frosts

The average date of last killing frosts will occur this month, sooner in more southern areas than in northern Illinois. Note that since cold air is heavier than warm air, micro-environments can occur where there is frost in valleys and not on nearby slopes and hilltops.

Canada Geese and Kingfishers

If you have a chance to visit wetland areas, look for the goslings of Canada geese, which hatch this month. Listen for the rattling calls of kingfishers along streams—they prefer to nest in tunnels excavated from high stream banks.

See also:

Chapter 13, Woodland Wildflowers. Many flowers begin blooming this month.

Chapter 15, Wild Turkeys. Listen for their gobbling during their continued breeding season.

Chapter 24, Box Turtles on the Roads. This is the season when box turtles begin to cross roads and highways—be a good Samaritan and carry them the rest of the way across the road if traffic allows.

24

Breakout:
Box Turtles on the Roads

Several species of box turtles are found throughout our region. These North American turtles live primarily in the eastern half of the United States and in Mexico, and may live 30 years or more. Depending on the species they hibernate under the soil and leaves of the forest floor or open land; during very hot weather, they may hole up under rotting leaves and logs or in mud. Extreme cold may take its toll on turtles if caught unaware in a place where they cannot dig themselves into a more protected situation. They are omnivorous animals, eating insects or meat and also fruits, berries and other plant materials. When spring weather arrives along with their breeding season, these land turtles are often seen crossing roads—too often they meet with a violent death, crushed under car and truck wheels.

Box turtles have high domed shells and broad hinges on the *plastron* or underneath part of the shell that allow the turtles to protect themselves by closing up when danger threatens. Eastern box turtles, common throughout the southern half of Illinois, have varied coloration that may include markings of yellow, orange, or gray-green on base colors of dark brown to almost black. Females often have flat or slightly convex plastrons and their eyes usually are brown. The plastrons of males tend to be slightly concave and their eyes often are red. Blanding's turtle, a similar subspecies with a hinge across the plastron, is common in northern Illinois and northeastern Missouri. It has a slightly flatter shell than other box turtles, many light spots and a shell hinge that will not close completely. This turtle is somewhat aquatic and hibernates in the mud of marshes. Blanding's turtle is listed as endangered because of the destruction of so much marshy habitat.

The three-toed box turtle, found throughout Arkansas and Missouri, often has plain khaki or pale brown areas on the upper shell and orange to yellow spots on the front legs and head. The ornate box turtle, which ranges through most of Missouri, part of southern Illinois and northwestern Arkansas, is a similar species with a flatter top shell surface and a fairly constant pattern of yellow rays over much of the shell. Habitat will help you tell the difference here. The three-toed box turtle tends to live in woods, forests, and thickets while the ornate turtle lives in open plains areas.

Never fear if you can't decide which species of box turtle you are looking at—the different species often interbreed so that it might take a chromosomal study to give you the exact species or combination of species. Don't go by the number of toes on the hind feet because that is not a consistent trait either. Note that there are many biomes in the box turtle world, places where territories meet and overlap, and where interspecies breeding is the rule. Generally speaking, east of the Mississippi River you will find the eastern box turtle and west of the river you will find the three-toed or ornate box turtles.

Mating of box turtles takes place from April through June or early July. The female digs a hole in loose soil or sand, lays the eggs, and covers them up. Two to eight eggs are in each clutch—they will hatch in eight to twelve weeks. Turtle eggs are a favorite treat for raccoons and skunks.

A day in the life of box turtles begins with foraging for insects, earthworms and, as the turtles mature, increasing amounts of fruits, berries, plant buds, grasses and even mushrooms. During midmornings, turtles find an open area where they can enjoy the sun. Toward nightfall they look for a protected spot to spend the night, often scuffling under dead foliage or branches.

From 1965 to 1983, Elizabeth and Charles Schwartz studied the home ranges, movements and populations of three-toed box turtles in central Missouri, with the help of their keen-nosed Labrador retrievers that became experts at retrieving turtles. They captured 1,568 turtles in a 55-acre study area. Some of these turtles were caught many times for a grand total of 6,789 records of individual captures.

The Schwartzes' work as naturalists with the Missouri Department of Conservation plus their unique collecting technique combined to bring them success in these territorial and population studies. This was the first time that scientists had studied a wild

vertebrate population over so long a period. Radio-equipped trans-
mitters and trailing devices helped them learn where the turtles were
going and how far they ranged—the average turtle's home range is
about 12.8 acres.

The Schwartzes' territory, deciduous woodlands and their
borders, is ideal habitat for three-toed box turtles. The open oak-
hickory wood has large trees and enough sunlight for turtles to bask
and allow the healthy growth of the plants and animals upon which
they feed. The soil and decaying vegetation is soft enough to allow
turtles to dig for hibernation and food.

They learned that turtle population remained fairly stable as
to age and sex as well as total numbers, appearing to fluctuate
between four hundred and six hundred turtles in the 55-acre area.
The box turtle population includes transients as well as permanent
residents. Some turtles just seem to be travelers, which may serve to
ensure the transfer of genes from one fairly sedentary population to
another.

MAY

May Observations

25

Bats in the Belfries and Other Places

Perhaps it's partly the fear of the unknown that makes so many people wary of bats. To be sure, bats are strange creatures, seldom seen and rarely understood. Bats hang out in caves and other mysterious places and they are most active at night. Their little faces with sharp fangs look demonic to many people—certainly you can't say that bats are pretty in the usual sense. Bats often are credited for things that just aren't true. For instance, they will not get tangled in your hair. Quite the opposite, they will go to great lengths to avoid getting near one of their greatest natural enemies—humans.

Take a closer look at bats and you will see soft, beautiful fur, large delicate ears and long delicate wing bones covered with a soft membranous skin. Study the life of bats and you will discover a sociable creature that carefully cares for its young. Bats have unusually acute hearing that, like sonar, can detect echoes bouncing off objects. They make continuous ultrasonic cries when flying— these calls combined with their excellent hearing allow them to navigate effortlessly through complex surroundings such as woods. This is how they find their way around, how they find their prey at night and how they avoid running into objects.

The bat families comprise the world's only flying mammals. There are animals like flying squirrels that glide on modified skin membranes, but bats are the only mammals that truly fly. Their wings are highly modified, having specialized hands with skin membrane stretched between the fingers, forearms, sides of the body and hind legs. Most bats also have skin membrane connecting the hind legs and the tail. Those few that don't are called freetail bats. Their hind legs are also highly modified to allow bats to land and hang upside down by their toes.

Bats can lower their metabolism and body temperature when they are hibernating or resting, allowing them to conserve energy. During the warm season, bats find shelter in a variety of places such as caves, mines, buildings, trees or rock crevices.

Young bats are born in the spring, usually during May or June. Most of the bats native to our region have just one offspring each year but some species produce two young bats per year. The female feeds its young on milk until it is able to fly and hunt on its own. Bats usually live in communal nursery colonies while they are bearing and raising young. When disturbed at this season, many deaths can occur when the females panic and drop their babies. These colonies break up during summer, usually July or August, when the bats begin moving to their hibernation sites. Bats store up fat—like bears—when they begin to get ready for hibernation. They pick places that are well-protected from the vagaries of weather for their winter sleep—mines or caves, hollow trees and buildings.

The bats native to our region are entirely insectivorous. In fact, they are one of our great allies in controlling agricultural pests as well as simply annoying nocturnal insects. Unfortunately, bats of all species seem to be declining in numbers. Part of this is due to pesticides and part due to the loss of natural habitat. In some places, defor-estation and urbanization have deprived bats of natural habitats. In other places, the commercialization of caves and the construction of reservoirs have destroyed their roosting places.

Some bats native to our region roost in trees while others roost in caves. The most commonly seen bat is probably the tree-roasting red bat, which is a solitary bat of woods and forests. As its name suggests, it is a rusty-red bat that has white tips on its hair. The females are a lighter red than the males. A similar solitary bat of the forests is the hoary bat, with white-tipped pale to mahogany-brown fur and a yellow throat. These bats hang upside down in trees during the daylight hours. The hoary bat with its 15-inch wingspread is our largest bat. The silver-haired bat is native to forests throughout our region with the exception of southern and western Arkansas. The silver-haired bat is dark brownish black with silver tips on the fur along the middle of its back. These bats spend the day hours secluded in crevices under tree bark.

The three endangered species of bats—gray bats, Indiana bats and Ozark big-eared bats—all are cave bats with the habit of gathering in large numbers in just a few caves. These colonies of many thousands of bats are very sensitive to disturbances and so are threatened by human contact or destruction of their roosting sites.

Gray bats are grayish brown, native to northern Arkansas and southern Illinois and Missouri, and live in caves year-round. Their presence is easily known by the piles of bat guano and the noisy chirping of the colony. Since these bats panic easily, it's wise to retreat from the cave and observe them as they leave the cave in early evening or return just before the sun rises.

Indiana bats spend their summers in small colonies that usually roost under tree bark. They are seldom seen and little is known about their everyday life. They are worth mentioning as natives because we all need to understand how important it is to protect their winter roosting places. During the winter they hibernate by clustering in thick colonies on the ceilings and near the entrances of a few cold caves in the Ozark Mountains. Their locations make them vulnerable to human cave explorers who may not realize how skittish these animals are.

You may recognize both the eastern and the endangered Ozark large-eared bats simply by their outsized ears that are over an inch high. These are cave bats that are found in small numbers in southern Missouri and most of Arkansas.

The little brown bat, gray bat, Keen's bat and Indiana bat are members of the *Myotis* genus of cave bats, which has the largest number of species and the widest distribution of any group of bats. These bats come in various shades of brown, are fairly small, have plain noses and a long, pointed tragus in each ear. The tragus is a projection that rises from the middle of the internal base of the external ear. Little brown bats spend their summer days roosting in barns and attics where they may gather in communal groups, but they spend their winters in cave roosts. They have glossy brown fur and blackish ears. Keen's bat also is glossy brown but has longer ears than the little brown bat.

Eastern pipistrelle bats are a pale brown color and are the smallest of our cave bats. They winter singly in caves and hang under building eaves or in crevices during summer days. Their erratic flight is distinctive as is their early arrival in the evening, often well before sundown.

Big brown bats are dark brown with dark ears and wing membranes. These noisy bats are among our most common species. They take shelter in buildings and hollow trees during the summer, then spend the winter as singles or small groups near the entrances of caves.

Sit outdoors with your binoculars at dusk and you will usually see some species of native bat flitting after insects along with night hawks, chimney swifts, purple martins and swallows, all of whom appreciate the heightened activities of insects at sundown. Do not disturb roosting bats or colonies of cave bats.

HOTSPOTS

Dusk is the best time to study bats. Look for them as they emerge from their resting places and swoop about in their typical fluttery way. It is highly unlikely that you will be able to identify the different species in the field. Still, it is important to realize the number of species that live in Illinois, Missouri and Arkansas. Consider you have done well if you can distinguish the tree bats from the cave bats. I think it is enough to be able to watch bats hunting insects on the wing, using their echo-locating system. Near water or swampy sites are good places to look for bats because of their high insect populations.

Devil's Den SP in northwestern Arkansas, located in an Ozark valley, has a stream, a small lake, cliffs, rock crevices and caves, all of which add up to making it a likely place to look for bats (see Chapter 16 for directions). This park has 2,000 acres of the most spectacular scenery in Arkansas. There are miles of trails in this park—check with the visitors' center for a trail map and information on good sites for checking out the local wildlife.

Holla Bend NWR with its shallow water impoundments is a good spot to look for bats. (See Chapter 7 for directions.) Get the area brochure and try the wildlife trail or the observation tower at dusk—it would make a good site for finding bats.

In Illinois, try **Cave-in-Rock SP** for bat watching. This park is on the Ohio River and has a 55-foot-wide cave that served as headquarters for outlaws during the eighteenth and nineteenth centuries. To get there, take I-57 approximately 55 miles southeast of Marion, then Illinois Route 13 southeast to Illinois Route 1 and south to the park.

Swan Lake NWR (see Chapter 8 for directions) in north central Missouri provides a variety of habitats ranging from lakes and wetlands to bottomland hardwood forests. With its high potential for insect life, this refuge should provide a good habitat for bats as well.

Roaring River SP in southwestern Missouri (see Chapter 13 for directions) has rugged Ozark Mountain terrain with an assortment of environments that native bats should find appealing. Glades and bluffs, forests and cold springs all make this park a treat for both residents and visitors.

26

Prairie Plants of Spring

Summer to fall is when the prairies are in their best flowering season, but that does not mean there is no flowering action earlier in the season. In fact, the month of May brings a couple of dozen flowering prairie plants to their peak display. First a few words about prairies, then we'll take a look at some of the early flowers of prairielands.

Prairies are lands of grasses and forbs—the term used for wild flowering plants. The word prairie comes from a French word that means extensive meadow. Prairies usually occupy fertile land lying 300 to 1,500 feet above sea level and feature low, rolling hills and shallow river valleys.

Prairies have no trees. The great prairies of America were created by fire and maintained by fire. Lightning and Native Americans started fires which kept trees from growing, destroyed shallow-rooted weeds and encouraged the growth of grasses and flowers. Fires also helped to recycle plant nutrients back into the soil. Weed control is one of the most difficult tasks in maintaining a prairie.

Intentional fires are important tools of managing prairies. Prairie managers have learned that carefully controlled fires each year will keep the prairie healthy and thriving. Spring fires tend to encourage grasses and legumes over other flowers, while burning in the fall after the main round of bloom tends to favor such plants as goldenrods and asters. There are few remaining virgin prairies, but there are several replicated and restored prairies in Missouri and Illinois. In recent years there has been growing interest in preserving our environmental heritage.

This replicated prairie includes many forbs (flowering plants) as well as well-known prairie grasses.

Replicated prairies strive to imitate the original prairieland that covered much of the western part of our region. Deep-rooted grasses and forbs are carefully planted and controlled fires are used where possible to encourage the native plants. Where fire is not possible because of inherent dangers in a particular location, mowing makes a reasonable substitute. Where mowing is used as the management tool, the mowed materials are removed to allow the sun to get to the soil—prairie plants thrive on summer heat.

Prairie soils range from dry and sandy to fairly heavy and moist with the full array of stages in between. Most of the attractive flowers of the prairie thrive on medium soils that are well-draining sandy to clay loams with medium fertility. Once established, prairie plants will tolerate the extremes of midwestern climate that is cold in the winter, hot in the summer and includes of drought and flood.

Carolina larkspur and prairie larkspur bloom during May and June. The flowers, looking much like garden delphiniums, grow on stalks up to 3 feet in height. The Carolina delphineum has flowers of blue, purple, pink or white while the prairie larkspur has white to greenish white flowers with a hint of purple or blue.

White false indigo, cream false indigo and blue false indigo are spring flowers you may find in prairies. The flowers and leaves show these plants to be in the legume family. Handsome blue flowers shaped like sweet peas grow on upright stalks up to 3 feet in height. The white false indigo, also called wild white indigo, is taller, up to 5 feet in height, with pure white pea-like flowers. The cream false indigo is a smaller plant that grows only about a foot tall and bears handsome cream to yellow flowers in the spring.

Yellow star grass, a member of the amaryllis family, blooms from April to May in spring prairies. Six yellow flower parts, three petals and three sepals, make the blooms stand out even though they are borne fairly close to the ground on plants not much over a foot tall. The leaves of yellow star grass are spear shaped and have the parallel veining typical of this plant family.

Spiderwort is the common name of this prairie plant that grows up to 3 feet tall and bears flowers that usually are blue but may also be in rose, purple or white. The flowers appear in boat-shaped bracts and have three petals and prominent yellow stamens. The long lance-shaped leaves have parallel veining.

Smooth sumac, a shrubby plant of upland prairies, begins to bloom in May and has tiny greenish flowers that develop in large, tight pyramidal clusters up to 6 or 7 inches in length on terminal growth. The clusters will turn red later in the summer. The long compound leaves have anywhere from nine to twenty-seven leaflets. The pithy branches are smooth, unlike the staghorn sumac with its fuzzy bark.

Wild onion has spring flowers that range from almost white through pinks to nearly purple. Its relatives, the bulbous alliums of spring gardens, are pretty garden plants and I think the wild onion is handsome also. This plant with its long hollow leaves and parallel veining, grows up to a foot in height and colonizes nicely.

Meadow parsnip, a 2 1/2-foot tall plant, has flat umbels of florets that are usually a rich yellow but may on occasion come in a purplish shade. The basal leaves are entire or in only two parts, but the leaves on the stems divide into three oval, finely-toothed leaflets. Look for meadow parsnip in the prairies from April through June.

Common milkweed and purple milkweed herald spring in prairielands. You can recognize these milkweeds by their big ovate, pointed leaves that grow up to 6 inches long and by the large umbels of small florets that develop on terminal growth. Another way to identify milkweed is that if you break any part of the plant, you will see a sticky, milky sap oozing from the break. Common milkweed has pink flowers and purple milkweed's flowers are a deep magenta.

Tickseed coreopsis begins blooming in the prairies in April and continues into June. It has daisylike flowers signaling its membership in the composite family and undivided lance-shaped leaves. The flowers grow atop the multiple stems of this 2-foot plant. The golden ray florets at the center of each flower are surrounded by a single circle of bright yellow ray flowers.

Both the purple coneflower and its close relative, the pale purple coneflower begin blooming in prairielands in May and continue flowering through much of the summer. You can tell the two apart by the paler pinkish or sometimes nearly white thin petals of the pale purple coneflower. The central disk flowers form a cone-shaped brownish knob on the pale purple coneflower and a flatter, purplish center on the purple coneflower. Both plants grow to nearly 3 feet in height and have coarse, lanceolate leaves.

The shooting star, an unusual member of the primrose family, grows about 2 feet tall in prairies and glades. The pink or white flowers grow in umbels on tall stems, each with five petal-like lobes that curve upward. The petals surround a brown and yellow center. The pistil and stamens protrude downward from the petal tube, making the flower look remotely like a shooting star. The leaves, which often have a reddish midrib, grow in a basal rosette and are long and slightly oval.

New Jersey tea is an upland prairie shrub that blooms in May with many tiny white florets that develop in round panicles somewhat like lilac flowers. A member of the buckthorn family, this plant has alternate, finely-toothed leaves that are broadly ovate in shape. The plant usually reaches a height of about 3 feet.

Beardtongue or penstamon, a relative of snapdragons, has elegant white flowers that are borne in loose clusters. It usually grows to be 2 to 3 feet tall but may reach 4 feet in ideal conditions. Each irregular flower, a field mark of the snapdragon family, has a two-lobed upper lip and a three-lobed lower lip.

One final spring-blooming prairie flower is the prairie violet found in western Missouri and Illinois. The leaves of this violet are divided in a palmate fashion. The flowers are typically blue-violet, larger than many other violets, and grow on longish stems so that they stand slightly above the foliage.

HOTSPOTS

Railroad Prairie State Natural Area and **Warren Prairie** are both joint projects of The Nature Conservancy, Arkansas Field Office, and the Arkansas Natural Heritage Commission. Contact the field office for maps and plant lists. (The Nature Conservancy address and phone number are in the Appendix.) Railroad Prairie is east of

Little Rock on the north side of U.S. Highway 70 between Lonoke and Hazen, and on the east side of Hazen toward DeValls Bluff. Watch for signs. Warren Prairie—in truth, a salt barren that has plants in common with true prairies—is in south central Arkansas. Take Highway 4/8 east from Warren until you cross the Saline River bridge. At next intersection, take right (south) on Highway 8 for three miles. Watch for signs.

Markham Prairie in the Chicago area includes about 300 acres of native grassland and wetland. This preserve, a National Landmark, comes under the umbrella of The Nature Conservancy, Illinois Field Office, and is managed by Northeastern Illinois University and is the largest remaining tall-grass prairie of top quality in Illinois. To get there, take I-94 about 20 miles south from the Loop in Chicago to I-57, and go south on I-57 to 159th Street. Go east to Whipple Street where you turn left (north) and drive to the end. You will usually find a preserve manager at the site. The managers ask that you stay on the trails when visiting.

Nachusa Grasslands, located approximately 80 miles west of Chicago, is also under the wing of The Nature Conservancy. Managed by Western Illinois University, it is just west of Rochelle and north of Franklin Grove, between Ashton and Dixon on the Lowden Road. Here you will find the rolling topography of several hundred acres of prairie hillsides. It would be wise to contact the Illinois Field Office of The Nature Conservancy before visiting either of these prairies to get brochures and trail guides and inquire about their guided tours. (The address and phone number of the office are in the Appendix.)

Squaw Creek NWR (see Chapter 1 for directions) in northwestern Missouri includes some upland prairie that offers spring wildflowers. There are auto tour routes as well as hiking trails at this refuge. In central Missouri, **Pershing SP** offers a rare example of bottomland wet prairie that used to be far more common in broad river valleys. To get there, go west from Laclede 2 miles on U.S. Highway 36, then turn south on Missouri Highway 130 for 2 more miles—the park will be on your right.

The **Missouri Botanical Garden's Shaw Arboretum** at Gray Summit, west of St. Louis, has an impressive replicated prairie area that includes spring wildflowers. Stop at the gatehouse to get a brochure telling you how to get to the prairie. (For directions, see Chapter 2.)

27

Peregrines, Nighthawks and Swifts in Cities

We usually think of birding as an activity of the countryside; the conventional wisdom is to pack up and go out to forests and fields, far from city streets. As is often the case, the conventional wisdom is not always right. In our region there are a number of cities and towns where you can go birding with great expectations within the city limits.

Sometimes you will see nothing but common birds like pigeons, starlings and English sparrows, but occasionally you may achieve a real find such as a peregrine falcon—ornithologists having seen fledging peregrines in a number of cities, including St. Louis. This effort is bringing the peregrine falcon back from near extinction. These falcons will nest high on building ledges in the middle of cities. This large bird is nearly 1 1/2 feet or more long—the female is larger than the male. The peregrine hunts birds in flight as well as large insects and small mammals. In cities, they are adept at hunting pigeons and English sparrows.

The common nighthawk's nasal call is often heard above city streets. Look up and you will see the bird with its slim white-banded wings foraging for moths and other insects in its flitty way. The nighthawk's short but wide mouth is fringed with bristles that help it scoop insects out of the air. Look for nighthawks near the outdoor lights of night activities—baseball parks and shopping malls are likely places to hear and see this bird. Nighthawks "nest" on rooftops in the city, though they do not make nests but simply lay eggs on the surface of the roof.

Listen for the twitter of chimney swifts, also common evening birds of urban places. The term "flying cigar" will help you identify these small birds on the wing. These little birds are hardy migrators, spending their winters as far south as Peru. Like the woodpeckers, they have stiff tail feathers to help them brace themselves as they cling to the inside of chimneys and similar places where they nest. Like the nighthawk, it has a tiny bill with a wide mouth to help it scoop insects out of the air as they skitter around in their jerky flight pattern.

In city parks, expect to see a full range of the migrating warblers. They will be flitting around in the foliage of tall trees so you will more often hear them than see them. Look also for vireos and a number of the flycatchers. It's not unusual to see migrating waterfowl and shorebirds if a city park has the right kind of habitat—and many of them do. In Swope Park, Kansas City, you can even hear whip-poor-wills if you are there in the evening when they begin to tune up.

Washington Park in Springfield, Illinois, has a number of waterfowl traveling through at this time of year, including buffle-heads and ring-necked ducks. Carolina wrens, tufted titmice, red-headed woodpeckers and red-bellied woodpeckers are year-round residents here. The beautiful songs of wood thrushes can be heard here each spring when the birds return in April for their breeding season—they remain in the park until October. Swainson's thrush, a bird that nests farther north, also can be seen along wooded paths in the spring and again in the fall. Look for spring warblers, including the prothonotary, black-throated green and blackpoll at this time of year. The woods and West Pond are the best hotspots.

You are apt to see kestrels in wooded city parks. These small raptors are about the size of blue jays and often perch on phone wires or at the tops of dead trees. Their silhouette is more compact and vertical than other birds you would see in those places. Kestrels are masters of the hunt, capturing all sorts of small animals from insects to mice to lizards. This little falcon is reddish brown and the male has blue-gray wings. Both sexes have two vertical black stripes that bracket the eye. The wings are long and pointed. For three years, I had a family of kestrels nesting in an old woodpecker hole in a dead tree about 75 yards from my porch, and so was able to observe them over an extended period. I soon learned to recognize its soft but harsh cry. They are devoted parents who work hard to provide the growing chicks with enough meat. Kestrels are permanent residents through-out our region.

The Carolina wren is another permanent resident with the exception of northern Illinois. You can find this bird in city parks throughout the region. During the breeding season the Carolina wren is imaginative, building its nest in such odd spots as in a mailbox, on top of boat cushions hung on a shed wall or inside a cow skull hung on a porch wall. This deep rusty brown bird is buff on its belly and has a white throat plus a conspicuous white eye stripe. Many birders say that its loud song is *cheery cheery cheery* and that describes it as well as one can, though some insist that this bird says *wheat eater, wheat eater, wheat eater*. Take your pick—whatever it says this is a delightful bird to watch with its perky manner and amusing ways.

HOTSPOTS

Hot Springs National Park, headquartered right on Bathhouse Row in the old Fordyce Bathhouse should count as an urban birding place. Hot Springs itself does not come under park jurisdiction, but the city nearly surrounds the park. Get trail maps from the park office. (For directions, see Chapter 22.) In Little Rock, in central Arkansas, there are a half dozen city parks that make good birding sites during the spring migration season.

Chicago's **Lincoln Park** on the north side and **Jackson Park** on the south side are both marvelous places for urban birding. Lincoln Park, accessible from Lake Shore Drive, is on a migratory flyway on the western shore of Lake Michigan and includes many varied habitats—open lake, coves, shoreline, lawns and open forests. Jackson Park is located at 63rd Street about two blocks east of Stoney Island Avenue and one block west of the large statue of Columbus. The two bridges to Stoney Island offer the best birding in this park because you can see both the woodsy areas and the lagoons.

In Springfield, Illinois, **Washington Park** with its south entrance only four blocks west of the intersection of South Grand Avenue and MacArthur Boulevard is another good urban birding spot. The park includes about 120 acres of hilly land with large mature oaks and hickories and some evergreens. The central area of the park offers the best opportunities, especially around the pond toward the west. Lots of warblers, waterfowl and other migratory songbirds come through this area in the spring.

The **Missouri Botanical Garden** and **Tower Grove Park**, both in the City of St. Louis, are excellent urban birding locations. You can get a booklet on the birds of the two sites at the botanical garden's gift shop. Birding is especially exciting at these places during the spring migration season when all the warblers are coming through, plus many other birds as well. From I-44 follow the signs to Missouri Botanical Garden at the Kings Highway Exit a few miles west of the downtown area. To get to Tower Grove Park, take this same exit and follow Kings Highway south to Magnolia Avenue about a .5 mile. Tower Grove Park is located just south and east of this intersection and has entrances off Magnolia, Kings Highway, Arsenal and Grand. Missouri Botanical Garden is next to Tower Grove Park on the northwestern quadrant of Magnolia Avenue and Tower Grove Boulevard.

In Kansas City, the grounds of **Swope Park** in the southeastern part of the city is a good site for spring birding. The park includes over 1,000 acres of oak-hickory forest as well as bottomland along the Blue River. Though not exactly on a major flyway, you will nonetheless see migratory birds arriving and passing through. At this time of year you might see as many as twenty species of warblers. You can get to Swope Park by exiting off I-435 at Gregory Boulevard and proceeding west. Stop at the nature center just a mile down the road where there are park staff who can suggest where you might see the most birds.

28

The Green Lull

The woodland wildflowers have had their day and are quietly fading away on the forest floor. Many of them will disappear above the ground in the same way that tulips, daffodils and other spring bulbs die back after blooming. The roots, tubers and bulb-lets of the spring wildflowers have stored up the nutrients they need for next season's growth, bloom and seed development. Before the tree leaves emerge, the wildflowers of the hardwood forest floor rush to expand their foliage so that by means of photosynthesis they can manufacture the simple carbohydrates they need for their existence.

Deciduous trees have finished blooming and are setting their seeds. This is the time in the woods that is often called the green lull—the time when the leaves of deciduous trees become fully developed and the light dappled shade of early spring is replaced by the denser shade of summer. The direct light that does reach the forest floor at this time is sparse and lasts only a short time in any single spot. It is far easier to identify the region's native trees now, during the growing season, than when they are dormant.

Oaks are the most common trees of the woods in our region; the white oak is the most plentiful. Often called monarchs of the forest, white oaks grow to an impressive size, often crowding out other trees. The oak family includes the white oak and the red oak tribes. You can tell them apart because all the oaks in the white oak tribe have rounded lobes on alternate leaves while those in the red oak tribe have a sharp bristle at the end of each alternate leaf or leaf lobe. White oaks usually have lighter gray bark than the red oaks.

This close-up of the bark of a white oak, a common tree throughout our region, will help you identify the tree. Look also for the leaves of the white oak, with their many rounded lobes.

The bur oak, a member of the white oak tribe, has the largest leaves and acorns of all the oaks. The leaves grow up to 10 inches. The acorn, 1 1/2 inches or more in diameter, grows in a deep cup with a hairy fringe around the rim. The largest bur oak ever found was in Big Oak State Park in Missouri. This old giant was over 140 feet tall and had a circumference of over 21 feet.

Post oaks are easy to identify because of their crosslike leaves—the middle lobe is wide and extends beyond the other smaller lobes. Chinquapin oaks, also in the white oak tribe, have leaves with coarsely-toothed edges and acorns that are long, ovate and dark, with caps enclosing only about one-third to half of the nut.

The red oak tribe includes the well-known pin oak of our suburban landscapes, a tree of heavy moist soils of bottomlands. It has alternate leaves with five to seven narrow, forked lobes that are bristled on the ends, and small, often striped acorns that are a favorite food of waterfowl and turkeys. The northern red oak, a treasured timber species, has oval leaves with the broadest point above the middle and sharply tipped lobes that point upward toward the ends of the leaves. Its acorns are an inch long and reddish in color. A few other members of the red oak tribe are the scarlet, shumard, black, southern red, blackjack and shingle oaks.

Hickories are another common tree of our region. Although there are seven different hickory species here, the easiest one to identify is the shagbark hickory. Hickories thrive in the rich soils of bottomlands but they also grow on drier slopes and hilly sites. Hickory leaves are compound with five or more leaflets. The shagbark hickory has five leaflets, each one of which will grow up to 6 inches long. The entire compound leaf is usually about 9 to 14 inches long. The key to recognizing the shagbark hickory is, obviously, its bark. Although smooth and gray on young trees, the bark of older trees comes loose in long strips that are attached at the middle and curve away from the tree at both ends.

A very similar tree is the shellbark hickory that has the largest leaves and nuts of all the hickories. Its bark also tends to separate into long thin plates that are loose at both ends. The way you can tell the shellbark from the shagbark is that its leaves grow up to 2 feet long and each compound leaf has seven or nine leaflets. Each leaflet is large, up to 9 inches long and about half as wide. The end leaflet is considerably larger than the others. The shellbark hickory is a giant of a tree, reaching its greatest size in the bottomlands of northeast Arkansas and southeast Missouri. One grew to be the largest of its kind in the world in Big Oak State Park in southeast Missouri, reaching a height of 122 feet with a circumference of nearly 13 feet.

To my mind, these are the most impressive hickories and easiest to identify. With a field guide, you will also be able to find and identify the other hickories: the mockernut, pignut, black and bitternut varieties.

Beech trees, native in the acid soils of sandy uplands throughout our three-state region, have coarsely toothed, oval alternate leaves and thin smooth bark that is a pale blue-gray. To thrive, beeches need deep soils that are well-draining and moist. You will find beeches aplenty in Arkansas' White Oak Lake State Park.

Sugar maples are a major component of the climax forest in the northern part of our region and where there is rich, moist loamy soil. Their palmate, simple opposite leaves with five lobes are 4 to 5 inches across and typically turn beautiful shades of gold, orange and red in the fall. In moist bottomlands, you will find the soft or silver maple with its deeply cut palmate leaves. The undersides of the leaves are silvery green and often in a wind will all turn so that the tree itself has a silvery look. In our region there are other maples as well, including the black and red maples with opposite palmate leaves and the boxelder with its compound, un-maplelike leaves that usually have three to five leaflets.

In the understory of the woods smaller trees thrive under the protection of the predominant oaks, hickories and maples. The dogwood, redwood and shadbush also finished blooming earlier in the spring when the wildflowers were at their peak. Now the pealike pods of the redbud, a legume, and also the berries of the dogwood and the shadbush are ripening. Birds will grab the sweet, soft shadbush fruit as soon as it begins to ripen. These tasty berries make an excellent jam—if you can beat the birds to them. The berries of the dogwood will persist into fall and even winter before the birds eat them—I would guess that birds eat dogwood berries only when there are few other foods available.

By the time of the green lull, the singing of birds has diminished. Migratory birds of more northern climes have passed through and the local residents have paired up, established their territories, built their nests and started to raise their families. Bird watching now is more challenging—not only is the foliage fresh, thick and green, but nesting birds are warier of intruders.

Listen and look for insects in the tender young foliage of deciduous trees. The larval caterpillars of many butterflies and moths have hatched and are doing their best to eat just about every kind of leaf in the forest. You may see insectivorous birds hunting an easy meal wherever there are many caterpillars.

HOTSPOTS

White Oak Lake SP in southwestern Arkansas is a haven for nature lovers since it represents the rich diversity of flora and fauna typical of the area known as the western Gulf Coastal Plain. (See Chapter 13 for directions.) The trails meander from bottomlands to ridges covered with beech, hickory and white oak trees. Go to the park visitors' center and get the self-guided brochures for the Spring Branch and Beech Ridge trails.

Pinnacle Mountain SP, located just 12 miles west of the State Capitol in Little Rock, is Arkansas' first state park adjoining a major city. This 1,700-acre park is a great place for seeing native deciduous trees of the region because the area is being developed as the Arkansas Arboretum. Check with the visitors' center for trail guides and to see what programs are available while you are there. To get there, take Exit 9 off I-430 to Highway 10, go 7 miles west to Highway 300, then turn right and go 2 miles to the park. You can also get there by taking Pinnacle Valley Road north off Highway 10 just 3 miles west of I-430.

Morton Arboretum in northern Illinois west of Chicago is ideal for studying deciduous trees during spring's green lull. (For directions, see Chapter 3.) The eastern part includes native climax forests of oaks and sugar maples with hillsides and deep ravines offering wildflowers earlier in the season and even into early May. By the time the tree leaves have fully developed, the peak of the wildflower season is well past. Be sure to visit the Thornhill Building where you can get trail guides and other information.

The 4,000-acre wilderness area of **Crab Orchard NWR** in southern Illinois (see Chapter 1 for directions) offers plenty of opportunity to study deciduous forests. Crab Orchard NWR is rich in a variety of habitats and so has a large mix of native plants and animals. Be sure to get the area brochure at the visitors' center so that you can find your way on the nature trail.

Big Oak Tree SP in southeast Missouri is a must for those wanting to see the best of deciduous forests during the green lull of spring. (For directions, see Chapter 22.) Although it includes only 1,000 acres, it is unique in that it contains a magnificent remnant of the original forest that used to extend all the way through Louisiana, throughout the area known as the Mississippi Embayment. Most was destroyed by logging and agriculture. During the 1960s Big Oak SP had nine of the American Forestry Association's Big Trees, largest known representatives of their species. Now, in the early 1990s, it has the national champion persimmon plus eight or more state champion trees. Clearly, this is a great place for appreciating deciduous trees.

In southwestern Missouri, **Roaring River SP** offers several types of forest in a spectacular setting of Ozark hills with springs, small caves, savannas and dolomitic glades. (See Chapter 13 for directions.) You will find the beautiful yellowwood tree, a member of the pea family, and also the Ozark chinquapin oak. You also will see plants and animals more usually associated with states farther west and south, including armadillos and roadrunners.

29

May Shorttakes

Virburnums

Blackhaw viburnums are in bloom during May—look for them along the edges of woods. Viburnum leaves grow in an opposite pattern, a good clue to identifying this plant.

Lightning Bugs

Watch for lightning bugs on warm evenings. Note that there are early-evening species that you will see near the ground and later species that appear higher up in trees. The flashing lights of these insects remain somewhat of a mystery to scientists. The bugs flash their cold greenish yellow lights to attract potential mates, but it is not known exactly how the mechanism works—one of many common things in nature that is not yet understood.

Missouri Primroses

These large handsome flowers on low rambling plants begin to bloom in May. Watch for them on glades and along the edges of Ozark roads.

Chiggers

Naturalists, both professional and amateur, should note that this month marks the beginning of chigger season. These minute mites will cause misery to those who become hosts. They burrow in the skin to suck blood and, at the same time, inject their victims with a very itchy substance. Scratching causes increased itching and inflamed sores. Those who spend extensive periods outdoors should protect themselves with powdered sulfur or other non-deet repellents.

See also:

Chapter 18, Breakout: A Few Freshwater Fish. Look for circular or oval gravelly places on the bottom of streams and lakes—these are the spawning grounds of bluegills and sunfish.

Chapter 56, Waterfowl Migration. Migratory shorebirds stop to rest on shallow wetlands and mudflats this month on their flight to northern breeding grounds.

30

Breakout:
Evening and Night Sounds

Mysterious sounds at the end of the day make late spring and summer evenings both curious and captivating. After the sun goes down listen for a variety of calls and songs especially around water at this time of year. Birds, insects, frogs and toads are the maestros of the evening throughout our region, especially in areas less touched by civilization. Sit quietly and listen carefully. With luck and a warm night, you will hear a half dozen or more of these wild creatures tuning up and practicing their evening repertoire.

Common nighthawks, whip-poor-wills and chuck-will's-widow are part of the evening symphony throughout most of our region. Chuck-will's-widow is a summer resident of Arkansas, southern Missouri and the southern half of Illinois. These summer residents are members of the nightjar family, birds that fly at night, catching their insect prey on the wing with their wide gaping mouths that are fringed with modified feathers that expand the physical "net" that catches the insects. You will rarely see these well-camouflaged birds even though they are fairly common in our region, but you will hear their calls and songs.

The call of the common nighthawk is a nasal *peet* quite similar to the woodcock's call. See this bird with its long narrow wings, wing patches and shallowly forked tail as it flies above treetops and houses. Although most of us have seen flying nighthawks, few people ever see them at rest. They perch lengthwise on tree limbs and, with their barklike coloration, picking them out with the eye is difficult. If you should see a stocky brownish bird with a big head perching diagonally on a wire, that would be a nighthawk, a sighting that deserves bonus points.

Whip-poor-wills and chuck-will's-widow are even more difficult to spot since they do not fly in open areas at dusk making distinctive calls as do the nighthawks. All of these nocturnal members of the nightjar family are beautifully camouflaged. They fly with wide bill agape, gathering insects, beetles and even small birds into their capacious mouths, hunting most effectively on moonlit nights. Listen for the calls of *whip-poor-will* and *chuck-will's-widow* in the early evening when they are most vocal—their songs pronounce their names and are repeated over and over.

In the woods where they usually live, these birds use shallow depressions on the forest floor as nests, laying two pale, often spotted eggs. The female incubates the eggs although the male nighthawk occasionally helps with this task. After twenty days, the young hatch and in their pale grayish brown fluff are as well camouflaged as their parents. They will fledge in less than three weeks.

Crickets and katydids are the stars of the insect chorus at night. We mention them as part of the night symphony now but, in reality, you will probably not hear these insects in any great numbers until a bit later in the season. The hotter the night, the more rapidly they will chirp. So reliable is the cricket's reaction to heat that you can figure out the approximate Fahrenheit temperature by counting the number of calls in fifteen seconds and adding that number to thirty-seven. Crickets and katydids have similar life cycles. Most of them go through the winter as eggs, then hatch when warm weather arrives and go through several molts in the nymph stage until they attain adulthood in about two months. The nymphs do not have wings but the adults have two pairs of wings, one thin tough pair that covers the second pleated pair. Common field crickets are black, the male with two extensions from the rear, the female with three.

Katydids, also called long-horned grasshoppers, are a lovely pale green and have antennae that are much longer than their bodies. Cricket wings lie flat on their bodies while katydids carry their wings in a tented position. Katydid and cricket males are the songmakers— the females of the species are mute.

They make the chirping sounds by rubbing the bases of their front wings together; tiny ridges on the wings make the rasping sound. Even when you know how they do it, it's hard to believe that small insects can make such loud noises—on some hot summer nights when the night symphony is at its crescendo, you can hardly hear yourself think.

The night songs are like bird songs in that they are both for territorial and breeding purposes. The songs help the insects identify and defend their small territories, and also help the male and female find each other. Crickets and katydids, unlike the more widely traveled short-horned grasshoppers, are homebodies that stay pretty much in one spot.

Two of the most impressive night voices are the sweet trill of the American toad and the lusty chugs of bullfrogs. The medium sized toad has kidney-shaped parotid glands behind its golden eyes and brown or black spots that usually include one to three warts. This toad usually lives at the edges of woods and is most active at night when it feeds on insects and earthworms. The males begin their mating calls as early as March, depending on the weather. They find small ponds or slow streams and settle there to trill their musical song to attract the females.

Bullfrogs, the largest frog of our region, are quite aquatic in their habits and live in and near permanent bodies of water, especially large ponds, lakes, streams and rivers. More active at night, this large green to brown frog eats a wide variety of insects, crustaceans, fish, small mammals and even birds. The males are extremely territorial during the May to July breeding season. The chorusing of several bullfrogs is as impressive as a tuba band concert

Big Lake National Wildlife Refuge offers ideal habitat for a variety of amphibians.

as the males announce their presence to each other and to the females.

If you are in an area where gray treefrogs are in residence, you may have thought their birdlike calls were from a group of rare birds. Occasionally you will hear their trills during the day but they really tune up in the evening. The frequency increases with the heat. The breeding season, April to June, brings male treefrogs to the ponds and swamps where they begin calling to attract the females. The rest of the time is spent in forest trees as well as around farms and homes where they may hide in cracks and crevices of decks and eaves. These treefrogs have sticky footpads that let them climb vertical surfaces. They have slightly warty skin and range in color from gray to greenish gray to brownish gray and have dark irregular spots on their backs.

Spring peepers are another major component of the night chorus throughout our region. The high-pitched, clear breeding calls of groups of male peepers is one of the first harbingers of spring and continues throughout the breeding season well into May. Woodland ponds and slow streams are favorite breeding places for peepers. These small brown to gray frogs have a dark "X" on their backs and a dark line across the top of their heads between the eyes, and sticky pads on their toes. The *peep* comes about once a second and has a rise at the end—a welcome forest melody.

In recent years there have been fewer amphibians in the world and no one knows exactly why. Perhaps some reduction in numbers is due to land development, some to drainage of wetlands and some to water or air pollution. I hope that some way can be found to begin restoring these marvelous amphibians to their former numbers—we all would be a lot poorer if we could not look forward to their night choruses.

JUNE

June Observations

31

Nonpoisonous Snakes

Snakes are shy, retiring creatures that go out of their way to avoid contact with people. When one sees you, chances are that it will retreat into the brush or the first handy hole. I suggest that you be aware of snakes so that when you happen to see them, you will be able to identify them and know a little about their life and habits. When you go birding and botanizing you are sure to find some species, but when you want to study snakes, not only are there fewer of them but they are protected by their camouflaged coloration as well as by hasty retreats into more secluded spots.

Snakes are reptiles, a group of animals that also includes lizards, turtles, alligators and crocodiles. A snake's spine has hundreds of vertebrae, usually two to four hundred, and is extremely flexible. Another interesting anatomical fact about snakes is that most have elongated right lungs and either a rudimentary left lung or no left lung at all. Some snakes move by inching along expanding and contracting their ribs—they are, in a sense, walking on their ribs. Other snakes move by undulating along in a side-to-side motion. Snakes can swim either on top of the water or under its surface.

Many people are repulsed by snakes, though I don't understand why. Perhaps it's the sinuous way that they move. Look at that motion from a different point of view and they are graceful animals. Perhaps it's the way they stick out their long forked tongue when you are near. That is not a stinger, as some people believe—the tongue is sensitive to heat and smell and the snake uses it to check its prey and enemies. The tongue takes odors from the air and transfers them to olfactory sense organs located in the roof of the snake's mouth. Perhaps it's their habit of appearing to sneak around, then suddenly appearing in the middle of a path or in a tree. In actuality, that effect is a result of the camouflage and shy behavior of snakes. What happens is that all of a sudden the snake may move and then you can see it against what may be a similarly-colored background. As long as snakes don't move, you will see very few of them.

I can understand being highly respectful of poisonous snakes, but the great majority are harmless, although some would like you to think otherwise. King snakes and rat snakes will make a great production of striking, but their bite is nothing to worry about. Many snakes will strike and try to frighten you if cornered. If you find what you think is a poisonous snake, leave it alone and it will go away if given a chance. Wise gardeners and farmers appreciate the help that snakes give them in controlling varmints, especially rodents.

Snakes are not slimy. They are soft to the touch and stay at about the temperature of their surroundings. Their scale-covered skin is actually handsome and often quite colorful, especially after they have shed. Sometimes you will find the molted skin of a snake. Take a close look at it and you will see that it is inverted in the same way that you can turn a sweater inside out as you take it off. Even the outside of the eye is shed along with the full length of the body. The eye itself is covered by a clear scale. Just before they shed their skins, snakes are inclined to be irritable and comparatively dull in color. Adult snakes may shed their skins every two months or so during the warm season, while young snakes may outgrow their skins every month.

The eating habits of snakes are unusual. They eat just about anything they can swallow, including insects and insect larvae, small rodents, crayfish, birds and bird eggs, fish, frogs, lizards and other snakes. Some snakes, including garter snakes and the water snakes, grab their prey then swallow it alive, head first. Others kill their prey through constriction and then eat them dead. Constrictors such as rat snakes and king snakes bite their prey and while holding it with their teeth, immediately wrap a few coils around its body and squeeze it until it can't breathe and dies of asphyxiation. The small teeth on snakes' jaws curve backward and the jaws unhinge so that they are able to swallow larger prey than you might imagine. It looks almost as if they are crawling around their food. The venomous snakes such as the copperhead and timber rattlesnake kill their food with a venomous bite before eating it.

The snakes of our region breed in the spring. About half of the species, like the black rat snake, lay eggs and the other half, like the garter snake, bear live young. The eggs of snakes, which hatch in late summer or fall, are long ovals and are covered by strong membranes. Females generally lay their eggs in protected places like under leaves or rotten logs. Like birds, each young snake has an egg tooth on top of its nose that helps it break out of the egg membrane—the horny tooth drops off a few days after hatching. Snakes giving birth to live young generally deliver their broods in the summer. Snakes do not provide any form of parental care to the young—they are on their own from the moment they are born or hatch.

Northern red-bellied snakes are found throughout our region with the exception of part of northwestern Missouri and a small part of northeastern Illinois. This is a small snake, only 8 to 10 inches in length, that is bright red or orange on its belly and gray to brown on the back, often with a pale stripe down the back. The red belly and lighter spots on the back of the head are the field marks for this breed. The red-bellied snake, a very shy animal, lives in or near open woods, under rocks or logs. This snake eats slugs, earthworms and a few insects.

Our region includes the meeting ground for the midland brown snake and the Texas brown snake that often hybridize when they occupy the same land in western Arkansas, Illinois and Missouri. They are very similar and I believe it's good enough to iden-tify both subspecies as simply brown snakes. These are in the same genus as the red-bellied snake. They also are fairly small in size, growing only 9 to 12 inches long. These snakes range in color from light yellowish brown to dark reddish brown with a paler tan dorsal stripe. These reptiles prefer to live in moist woods, swamps and marshes where they may be found under boards, rocks or logs. Like their red-bellied cousins, they eat earthworms, slugs and an occasional soft-bodied insect.

There are a number of garter snakes in our region—western and eastern plains garter snakes, red-sided garter snakes and eastern garter snakes. Most have light lateral and/or dorsal stripes that run the entire length of their bodies. The precise location of those stripes is a clue to which garter snake is which. A reptile field guide will help you if you are interested in those details. Garter snakes eat just about any live prey they can handle including salamander, toads, frogs, earthworms, small fish and tadpoles. Most are fairly tame but some will react strongly to being approached or handled by striking and biting. When captured, they emit an unpleasant heavy odor from glands at the base of their tails. Garter snakes usually reach a length of 1 1/2 to 2 1/2 feet. Snakes may become nocturnal in very hot weather.

The eastern garter snake is most common in our region. In color this snake ranges from green to dark brown, nearly black. Normally it has a dorsal and two lateral yellowish stripes plus often a double row of dark spots between the stripes. Either spots or stripes can dominate. In western Missouri live the easternmost representatives of the red-sided garter snakes, easy to recognize with the orange to red bars on their sides. The western ribbon snake is a colorful member of the garter snake group. This snake has a yellow to orange dorsal stripe flanked by two black stripes, then two narrow yellow stripes.

There are a number of water snakes, all in the same genus, in our region. These are harmless snakes that you often will see basking on tree limbs or logs. They are skillful swimmers and drop into the water at the slightest cause for alarm. Because many are stout, strong-looking reptiles and have dark, mottled patterns, and because they will strike and bite hard when threatened, they are often mistaken for poisonous snakes and maimed or killed. Their bite is harmless.

Water snakes get most of their food near or in the water—frogs, toads, tadpoles, fish, crayfish and salamanders. Contrary to the common belief of many fishermen that water snakes catch game fish, wildlife management experts consider water snakes beneficial. These big serpents weed out weak and sick fish and also thin overcrowded ponds, thus keeping the fish from becoming stunted.

The diamondback water snake is native throughout Arkansas, the southern half of Illinois and most of Missouri except for the northwestern corner. This is the largest snake, reaching 4 feet in length. It has a yellow belly and large chainlike pattern in shades of brown to dull ocher on the back. When threatened, diamondback water snakes give off a foul-smelling musk from glands near the base of the tail.

The most common water snake throughout much of our region is the northern water snake. It has dark blotchy crossbands on a background of brown to gray. This snake also is large, often growing to over 3 feet in length. These snakes, like most of the others, are usually active from early April until October, depending on the weather.

The rough green snake is common throughout the Ozarks and much of our region with the exception of northern Illinois and northern Missouri. Often reaching a length of 2 feet or more, this slender bright green snake is active during the day and most often found in trees and bushes near bodies of water. I recently saw one in a small redbud tree at Johnson's Shut-Ins State Park in southern Missouri, but I wouldn't have seen it if it didn't move—green snakes blend in with the foliage very successfully. These snakes eat crickets, grasshoppers, spiders, caterpillars and other soft insects. These excellent climbers spend their nights coiled around the ends of leafy branches in deciduous trees and bushes. In northern Missouri and northern Illinois, you may find a similar species, the western smooth green snake. It is similar in coloration but not as big as the rough green snake, usually reaching a length of 20 inches or so.

One of my favorites is the eastern hognose snake, a comical actor when threatened. If its hissing cobralike stance, coiled with head and neck spread into a hood and strike doesn't scare an enemy, the hognose will thrash about, open its mouth, turn over on its back and play dead. If you turn it back on its stomach, it will turn over on its back again and not move, as if to say, "No. I'm dead—can't you tell?" Its coloring is highly variable, usually spotted and ranging from yellow and brown through gray and olive. The upturned end of its nose is the easily identified field mark of this snake.

King snakes and milk snakes all are members of the same genus. They are shiny snakes, all powerful constrictors that feed mainly on mice, smaller snakes and lizards. They are not against eating their own relatives which is why two or more shouldn't be kept together in captivity. King snakes are basically dark brown or black with light spots on their scales that vary in size and spacing among the species. King snakes hiss and strike when threatened, but tame down quickly when captured. Milk snakes are handsome creatures that come in a variety of colored blotches of red or brown, black, and white or yellow. Milk snakes will hiss and strike when threatened but do not become tame when captured.

Most striking of the king snakes is the speckled king snake or salt-and-pepper snake, a black snake up to 4 feet long that has a white or pale yellow spot in the center of each scale. This species is found throughout Arkansas and Missouri and in the southwestern quadrant of Illinois.

The red milk snake is a beauty with orange to red markings bordered with black against a pale tan background. It is native to northern Arkansas, southern Illinois and all of Missouri. In southern Arkansas you will find the Louisiana milk snake, another beauty with broad red bands bordered with black and separated by pale tan rings. In northern Illinois lives the eastern milk snake, somewhat less colorful, with large dorsal reddish brown blotches that alternate with smaller lateral blotches—it has a distinctive "X" or "Y" on the back of its head.

The rat snakes are an interesting group of reptiles easily recognized by their body shape that, in cross section, is like a loaf of bread. When first hatched, they are marked with bold blotches that may or may not disappear with age. When cornered or threatened, rat snakes will fight back, rearing up, vibrating their tails as if they were rattlers, and opening their mouths wide then hissing as they strike—a scary sight, but harmless. They also release an unpleasant-smelling substance when disturbed. Rat snakes all are good climbers, able to climb trees and scale bluffs. Their prey includes mice, rats, birds, frogs—including tree frogs—and lizards that they kill by constriction before eating.

The black rat snake is common throughout most of our area except the Missouri Bootheel and the eastern third of Arkansas. There, the gray rat snake, a subspecies, is native. This is a snake of brushy woods next to bodies of water. These big snakes, up to 6 feet long, have black or brown splotches on gray when they hatch, but the gray background color fades to black as they mature. The gray rat snake holds the blotchy color of hatchlings and otherwise is like the black rat snake.

This will give you a good overview of some of the more common nonpoisonous snakes of our region. I'll introduce you to the poisonous snakes of our region in Chapter 38. Remember that during hot spells, most snakes become nocturnal and you need sharp eyes because they are so well camouflaged. Plan your trip around some other group of plants or animals, but keep a sharp eye out for the snakes you may happen to see.

HOTSPOTS

You can visit almost any of the spots mentioned throughout this book and, with luck, see one or more species of snakes as an added bonus. A visit to **Cossatot River SP and Natural Area** in west central Arkansas, a 4,300-acre preserve, provides some beautiful and interesting areas for exploring nature and possibly finding reptiles. There are maps available for the hiking trails through one of the state's most scenic parks. Get there by taking Arkansas Route 246 north between Vandervoort and Athens or by taking Arkansas Route 4 south between Wickes and Umpire. Another Arkansas place where you might find snakes is the watery wilderness of **Big Lake NWR** near Blytheville. (See Chapter 1 for directions.)

In Illinois, the mixed bottomlands and wilderness of **Crab**

Orchard NWR in the southern part of the state would be a good spot for naturalists—and you might just find a snake or two if you look sharp. (See Chapter 1 for directions.) You might also want to try to find snakes while you're birding or botanizing at **Morton Arboretum** in northern Illinois. (See Chapter 3 for directions.)

Mingo NWR in southern Missouri is a likely place to see snakes while you're mushrooming or birding. (See Chapter 1 for directions.) **Dr. Edmund A. Babler Memorial SP** in St. Louis County is another possibility. At the visitors' center you will find trail maps as well as a naturalist who can point you to trails where you might find snakes as well as other interesting plants and animals. This park is located 20 miles west of St. Louis. Take I-44 west to Highway 109 and go north, beyond Highway 100—the park is between Highway 100 and U.S. Highway 40 (I-64).

32

Mosses

True mosses are soft and green, growing so closely together that they often give the appearance of an emerald carpet or a small jade pillow. Examine them closely and they look somewhat like little trees or tiny ferns. A single moss plant has minute leaves growing around a stem and a small bit of hairlike rootlets. Mosses and liverworts are small nonflowering plants that both belong to the plant division known as *Bryophyta*, a name that comes from the Latin words meaning "moss plant." They reproduce, not by means of seeds as do the higher plants, but by means of spores.

The small plants are called *rhizoids*. In scientific terms, this common part of the moss plant, along with its stalk and tiny leaves, is called the *gametophyte*. This is the part that looks very much like some of our flowering plants. The other part of the moss plant, the slender upright stalk that is topped by the oval pointed capsule in which spores develop, is called the *sporophyte*.

Some mosses grow in or near shallow water while some grow on damp rocks, trees and stream banks, and yet others grow in places that are dry and warm. Scientists have theorized that mosses were among the first plants to live on land in ancient times when the earth was young.

Mosses are soil makers. When land is bare as a result of grading, mining or anything else, mosses and also lichens are the first troops on the scene to begin establishing life—the stripped area will eventually become forest again. Mosses slowly break up the rock and wood on which they grow, bit by bit. As parts of the plants die, they decompose

This moss is growing in the shade of deciduous woods in a fairly dry location. It is found mostly on rocks. Although moss identification is not positive unless you can study the fruiting bodies, this is quite likely silver beard moss.

and add to the organic matter of the soil, making it healthy and nutritious for other plants. You can see why mosses are an important part of biological succession. Mosses hold water well, tempering the extremes of drought and flood. In some places, sphagnum mosses grow so luxuriently that they eventually form partially decomposed layers called peat moss. This is a useful material for gardeners as an organic additive for their garden soils. In times gone by, Native Americans used soft mosses like reindeer moss to line their babies' cradles and in other places where soft sturdy materials were needed.

Mosses, like the ferns discussed in Chapter 21, have a two-stage developmental cycle. The sexual part of the cycle in mosses occurs when the male and female cells formed in two different organs growing at the top of the plant unite, growing together and developing into a stalk with a capsule or spore case at the top.

The asexual part of the moss developmental cycle now takes place within the capsule. Special cells divide and form tiny seedlike spores. Once these spores are ripe, the lid of the capsule opens and falls off, allowing the spores to fall to the ground. There they develop into thready growth from which buds sprout and become the moss plants we know so well. Wind, water and other agents may scatter spores far from the parent plants.

There are two main types of mosses. *Pleurocarpus* mosses have creeping stems that branch and produce sporophytes at the ends of special short branches. *Acrocarpus* mosses grow with single erect branches that develop sporophytes at the ends of those branches. To a great degree you can identify mosses by their environment, so take notice of where they are growing and what the conditions are.

Now we will discuss some of the *Acrocarpus* mosses. You will find twisted moss near the bases of tree trunks and also on rocks and decaying wood. This moss is bright green with slender leaves, and its individual plants are erect and short. Although it is more likely to grow on the cooler, shadier north sides of trees, this is not necessarily so. The sporophytes are green and appear in May.

You have seen the juniper hairy cap moss in many places though you may not have known its name. This moss, common in upland open woods, is the largest of the mosses you will see. The thick rhizoids grow to a height of nearly 4 1/2 inches and look very much like a pine forest. Where it finds the right habitat, this hairy cap moss will cover areas of several square feet or even yards. The leaves are long and stiff with pointed brown tips. The sporophytes have reddish stalks and a white jacket or *calyptera* covers the capsule. This is one of the few mosses eaten by wild creatures—rodents enjoy eating the large capsules.

The dense yellowish to bluish green tufts of pincushion moss grow on rocks and dry soil, producing spores in the spring. When the leaves of this moss dry, they curl up into tight ringlets. Look closely and you will see that the edges of the leaves are rolled. The capsules of this moss are ovate, upright and plump at first, but become wrinkled with time.

If you are in dry woods along roads or on ridges with poor soil and see small, rounded moss tufts that remind you of cat's paws, you are seeing ditrichum, a light green moss with long slender leaves that give it a furry appearance. Look closely to see the spring spores with very long, nearly translucent stems and green capsules.

The moss that grows in miniature hummocks between bricks or similar places with disturbed soils is known as *Bryum argenteum*— I don't have a common name for this one. You can find this moss at home in cities as well as fields and forests. This moss with its short nappy plants grows densely, looking like plush or velvet. The sporophytes are red when ripe and the capsules are plump and nodding.

Straight hair tree moss grows on tree trunks as its name implies. This dark green to brownish green moss has thin pointed leaves that are erect and dense. It grows just about everywhere except large cities. You have to look very closely to see the small, erect, yellow-capped green capsules that barely peak above the plants when they develop in spring.

Aquatic apple moss thrives in wet soils and on moist rocks such as are found near cold springs. This lush-looking lime-green moss has long stems with short small leaves placed sparsely on the stems, giving it a loose appearance. The sporophytes mature in late spring and have reddish capsules on long stalks.

And now for a few of the branching *Pleurocarpus* mosses. Look for campylium mosses growing on rotting wood or bark as well as rocks and soil. This soft yellowish green moss grows in attractive mats that are loose-looking and spreading. Its long graceful leaves attach to the stem at a 45-degree angle, then curve back to a right angle. The much-branched and creeping stems and leaves remind some of small pale foxtails.

In and around cold springs and quiet pools, you may find *leptodictyum* moss—sorry, no common English name. This native of wet environments has tapered leaves attached at right angles loosely arranged on long stems that form loose mats. They develop spores in the spring in long green capsules that turn red-brown when mature.

Glossy moss is often found on logs and bark as well as soil and rocks. Its large silvery-green mats consist of broad, glossy leaves growing tightly against the stems almost like scales. This moss may cover dry boulders and logs. It stays green and active during the winter which makes it easier to see then. It develops spores in fall.

Fern moss is a much-branched plant growing in loose mats on rocks and soil whose stems and leaves combine in shapes that look amazingly similar to branches of the common tree known as arbor vitae. This is a lovely moss often found in moist shady places—in those sites, fern moss thrives. Its sporophytes appear at various times.

Finally, sphagnum moss, also called peat moss, grows along sandy creek banks, on wet rocky outcroppings and in bogs. Moisture and high humidity are a must for this moss to thrive. You'll undoubtedly recognize the loosely-branched shaggy growth. This light to bright green moss has many branches growing in spirals on the stems.

HOTSPOTS

When looking for mosses, keep a few rules in mind. Do not collect them unless you have a very good reason such as research or teaching, and then don't collect more than you need. If you can, put the mosses back where you got them when you are through using them. Don't collect on either private or public lands or preserves unless you have been given permission.

In Arkansas an ideal place to study mosses is **Mammoth Spring SP**. Nine million gallons of cold clear water flow hourly from Mammoth Spring, the largest in Arkansas. It is the source of the Spring River, one of our region's great floating streams. Here you will find the moist and wet environments that are conducive to many healthy mosses and other water-loving plants. The visitors' center has trail maps and suggestions where to find mosses. The park is on the eastern edge of the city of Mammoth Springs off U.S. Highway 63, 2 miles south of Thayer and 16 miles north of Hardy.

Lake Catherine SP in the Ouachita Mountains of central Arkansas is another good place to study mosses. Get a map and information at the visitors' center. There are a number of good trails to find native mosses, including Falls Branch and Horseshoe Mountain trails. Get there by taking Exit 97 from I-30 and going north 12 miles on Highway 171, which dead ends at the park.

The rocks, ravines and sandstone buttes of 2,000-acre **Castle Rock SP** in northwestern Illinois promise some good mosses. Stop at the headquarters for information and to get a brochure that will tell you the best direction to head if you want to see area bryophytes. To get there, go 3 miles south of Oregon on Illinois Highway 2.

The trails through the ravines and hills of **Pere Marquette SP** in west central Illinois will take you past a number of good areas for mosses. Watch for mosses on trees and rocks as well as in low places where it remains moist and humid. (See Chapter 13 for directions.)

Just 9 miles northwest of Mammoth Spring is Missouri's **Grand Gulf SP**, a source of Mammoth Spring's water. Here is another one of those idyllic spots with a spectacular landscape—springs, rocky canyons, caves and a rocky natural bridge. Often called the Little Grand Canyon, the gulf resulted from the collapse of a gigantic cave. The cliffs are festooned with mosses, ferns and other moisture-loving plants. To get there, go 6 miles west of Thayer on County Highway W in Oregon County.

Elephant Rocks SP's granite outcroppings provide a perfect setting for mosses and lichens on the hillsides. This park in southeastern Missouri has well marked, evenly paved trails. You can find park brochures in the shelter near the entrance of the trails. The pink granite of this area is a billion years old—part of the St. Francois Mountain uplift caused by ancient volcanoes. This park is located on Highway 21 at the northwest edge of Graniteville in Iron County.

33

The Mimic
Thrushes

You can tell the voices of the three mimic thrushes—northern mockingbird, brown thrasher and gray catbird—in the following way. The mockingbird repeats each unit of its songs three times or more. The brown thrasher repeats each part usually two, sometimes three times, and the catbird repeats each part just once. Other than that, they all have fine singing voices of similar quality. All of these birds have tails considerably longer than the average bird. All of these birds eat berries, seeds and insects.

The mockingbird is a resident in all but the most northern part of our region and spends the breeding season throughout the area. It is a gray bird with a lighter underbelly, white outer tail feathers and conspicuous white wing patches. You often see a mockingbird sitting at the top of a tree or telephone pole as it sings. You'll also see it in bushes or running along the ground. Mockingbirds, those incomparable imitators of other birds and even people, sing lustily throughout the warm season. Only the male sings in the spring, but in the fall, both sexes may sing. Males often sing at night, especially when the moon is full.

Nesting birds find prime sites in just about any place you can think of. Some prime birding habitat exists at the edges of forests, in heavy brush and in glades, fields and meadows. Different species choose different types of nest sites and also choose different elevations. Ideal nesting sites exist where the birds are able to find food in the form of seeds, berries or insects, and where they have protection from predators, such as hawks. By now, almost all of the

A fledgling mockingbird hides in a clump of coneflowers where it is very difficult to see unless you know what you're looking for. It was spotted only because of the aggressive behavior of the parents who will take on any foe when their young appear threatened.

migrating birds that summer farther north have passed through our region. Those that remain include residents and those migrants that spend their breeding seasons with us. Let's take a look at the breeding habits of the mimic thrushes, three common birds that are nesting in our region at this time of year.

These birds claim not only breeding territory but feeding territory as well. They will energetically and forcefully attack other birds and animals, even people, who come too close to their nests after eggs are laid and when the young are still in the nest. Mockingbirds have an extensive language in addition to their imitative songs. They also have a number of interesting behavior patterns, including tail flicks, looping flights, drooped wings and wing flashes.

Both male and female mockingbirds build the nest, usually in trees or shrubs at a height of between 4 and 10 feet. Everything from leaves, twigs and small pieces of bark to rootlets and pieces of plastic go into a mockingbird nest that often has a lining of tiny rootlets in its 3-inch cup. You can usually find these nests by first noting where the birds are active, then moving around this territory and noting the birds' reactions as you do. The closer you get to the nest, the more disturbed they will be. Once you identify the site, retreat and watch from a distance so that you don't disturb the mockingbirds. The female incubates an average of four eggs until they hatch twelve days later, then both parents feed the young. Baby mockers fledge about twelve days after hatching and the young are fed by their parents for another month after they leave the nest.

The brown thrasher breeds throughout our region but spends the winter from Arkansas and the Missouri Bootheel south. This reddish brown bird has a heavily streaked breast and belly. You will see these thrashers low in brush, running under brush and at the edges of woods. In the spring when he is trying to attract a female, the male thrasher sings his songs loudly from the treetops. Later in the season, he sings muted versions from within bushes and brush. The repertoire of the brown thrasher is not as large as those of the mockingbird and catbird—they seem to sing unlimited variations of countless themes—and the female brown thrasher doesn't sing at all.

Both sexes build the nest which is similar to that of the mockingbirds. The bulky nest with its rootlet lining may be anywhere from almost on the ground to 15 feet up in dense growth or brush. Both sexes incubate an average of four or five eggs for nearly two weeks; after the eggs hatch, both work hard feeding their brood in the nest for almost two weeks. They continue feeding the young birds for another few weeks after they leave the nest. Find the nest location by watching the male to get an idea of the extent of his territory, then watch for the pair carrying pieces of nesting materials or listen for the male who often softly sings near the nest. Then retreat from the nest area and observe from a distance so that the birds don't abandon their nest.

The gray catbird spends its breeding season in our region but winters in the far southern United States and Mexico to Panama. This bird is predominantly gray with a dark cap and a rust-colored patch under its tail. The wings and tail are darker than the body. In addition to songs, it has a call that sounds like a harsh *miaow* as well as a collection of noises—squawks, whistles and shrieks. When trying to attract a female, the gray catbird male sings loudly from a prominent perch. Gray catbirds frequent thickets, tangles of shrubs and dense deciduous woods.

Neither the brown thrasher nor the gray catbird is as aggressive in defending its territory as the mockingbird, who is a real bruiser with intruders. The catbird is quite tolerant of other species, sometimes even nesting in the same small area as a pair of robins or other species. Find the nest by observing the pair as they carry nesting materials, follow them as they take food to the young or check in areas where you notice the parent birds have been flicking their wings.

The female incubates three or four eggs for just under two weeks after which both parents care for the young until they fledge in about eleven days. They continue feeding the babies for another two weeks before they strike out on their own. When mimic thrushes are feeding their babies after they've fledged and are away from the nest, you often can find the babies by noticing the parents' protective or alarm behavior.

The toilet habits of these birds are interesting. Mockingbird babies defecate over the side of the nest as soon as they are able. When the young are first hatched, the parents of the mimic thrushes eat the fecal matter of the young. After a few days, the parent mockingbirds, brown thrashers and gray catbirds remove any fecal sacks that are in the nest.

The mimic thrushes are attractive songbirds with enough similarities to make their close relationship obvious, although their behavioral patterns differ enough to provide interest to observers.

HOTSPOTS

Felthensal NWR (see Chapter 2 for directions) in southeastern Arkansas is a great place for these birds. They are common in the hardwood forests that surround the Ouachita and Saline rivers as well as in a number of sloughs, creeks and horseshoe lakes. Another good place to look for these birds is **Wapanocca NWR** in northeast Arkansas. (See Chapter 1 for directions.) **Mount Nebo SP** in west central Arkansas is another place to look for the fascinating mimic thrushes. (See Chapter 16 for directions.) There are some spectacular trails in this park that will take you through the lush vegetation that attracts these birds.

Crab Orchard NWR in southern Illinois is one of the places in that state where mockingbirds, brown thrashers and gray catbirds are commonly found. (See Chapter 1 for directions.) Check out the thickets and dense woods of this preserve. Get a flier on the area at the visitors' center and ask for likely places to see these birds. Another good place to look for mimic thrushes is **Starved Rock SP** in north

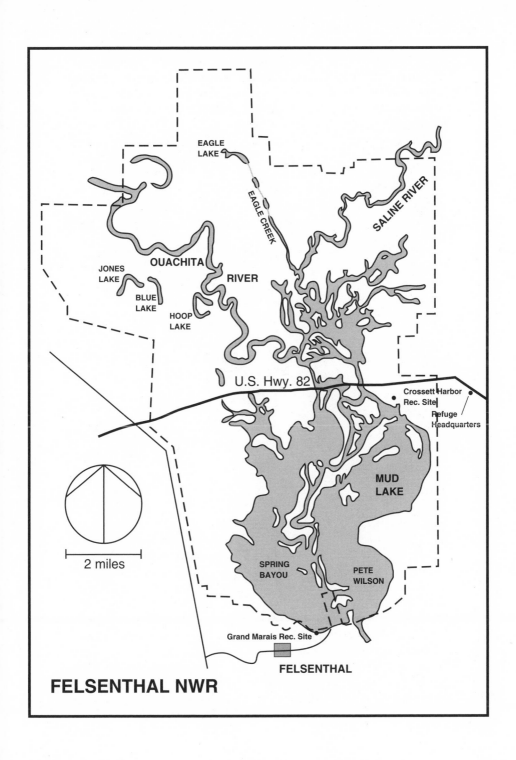

EAGLE
LAKE

EAGLE CREEK

SALINE RIVER

JONES
LAKE

OUACHITA

RIVER

BLUE
LAKE

HOOP
LAKE

U.S. Hwy. 82

Crossett Harbor
Rec. Site

Refuge
Headquarters

MUD
LAKE

2 miles

SPRING
BAYOU

PETE
WILSON

Grand Marais Rec. Site

FELSENTHAL

FELSENTHAL NWR

central Illinois. (See Chapter 13 for directions.) Here you will find a number of well-marked trails—get a map at the park's visitors' center. Nearby **Matthiessen SP** is another likely spot for these birds. To get there, take Exit 81 (Illinois Route 178) south for 6 miles, 3 miles south of Starved Rock SP.

Look for all three mimic thrushes at **Mingo NWR** in southeastern Missouri. (See Chapter 1 for directions.) The deciduous woods and forests of bottomlands and hillsides offer excellent habitat for these wild birds. Near St. Louis in east central Missouri is **Busch Wildlife Area**. (See Chapter 10 for directions.) Stop at the visitors' center for a map—this is one of the best birding spots in the St. Louis area.

34

Plants of the Edges of Woods

Wildflowers growing at the edges of woods and glades are numerous during June. As spring progresses, the blooms of wildflowers no longer appear on the forest floor—where they grow in early spring before the trees leafed out—but now bloom on the open environment at the edges of woods or glades where they can receive several hours of sun each day.

Representatives of a number of different plant families are in bloom in June. Earlier in the spring, the buttercup family was heavily represented in woodsy wildflowers. During summer and fall, members of the daisy family will be most visible in the wildflower world.

If you see wildflowers that look very much like flowering plants that you have seen in gardens, it is not surprising. A large percentage of our garden favorites have arisen from the native plant pool of North America. Plants that grow in our region with its climate of extremes are, as you might expect, tolerant of a wide variety of environmental conditions, which means that plant breeders have often been quick to take advantage of this strength. Many of our native plants were taken to Europe where they were bred into a variety of colors, forms and sizes, then sent back here where gardeners grab them up as "new" plants.

Both the prairie rose and the pasture rose are flowering along roadsides, in open woods, in fence rows and at the edges of woods during June. Both species have single pink, sometimes white roses with prominent yellow stamens—the flowers are delicate, sweet, fragrant and tough. The best way to tell the difference between these two native roses is that the pasture rose is a common low-growing rose whereas the prairie rose has much longer canes that climb or grow into loose thickets. The rose family is one of the most useful as it includes apples, cherries, peaches, pears and the brambles—blackberries and raspberries. Once you know that, learn to recognize the look of family members—complete flowers with five petals, prominent stamens and alternate leaves, to name the easiest. Complete flowers are those that include both sexes, the female pistil and the male stamens. Roses and the bramble berries have compound leaves and thorns while the fruit trees have simple leaves and no thorns.

Beardtongue, also called penstemon, blooms in June in moist soils at the edges of woods and glades as well as along roadsides and in prairies. These wildflowers are in the figwort family and so are cousins of snapdragons—look for the similarity in flower shapes. There are several penstemons, all fairly similar, so I'll describe a common one called white or foxglove beardtongue. Other species may have flowers that are off-white, lavender, or purple. The white flowers grow in a loose cluster at the top of the plant's single tall stem that usually grows 1 to 2 feet but may reach 4 feet. Each flower is trumpet-shaped and irregular with two-lobed upper lips and three-lobed lower lips. The opposite leaves are lance-shaped and widely spaced with finely notched edges. Penstemons are increasingly popular garden plants.

Look for spiderwort and its close relative, the dayflower, along roadsides, edges of woods and prairies. The flowers of the spiderwort family have three petals and long thin leaves with parallel veining. The leaves clasp the stems. These perennial plants grow up to 3 feet or more. Spiderworts usually have purple or blue flowers, sometimes pink or even white. The spiderwort has become a popular plant of the garden where it often develops into husky clumps over 3 feet tall. Spiderwort flowers develop in clusters with leafy bracts below the flowers. Only one flower is open at a time and each one may be up to 1 1/2 inches across. The dayflower has bright blue flowers up to 1 inch in diameter, each with three parts—the lower petal is smaller than the other two. The flower grows from a heart-shaped sheath. Dayflowers are shorter than spiderworts, growing to a height of only about 2 feet.

Deptford pinks are flowers you might overlook because they are so retiring compared to their larger neighbors. Look for these small delicate-looking relatives of carnations and chickweed along sunny paths, at the edges of woods, roadsides, fields and pastures.

The deep pink flowers are up to 1/2 inch wide, dotted with white, and have five petals that frequently are notched. This plant originally grew in Europe and probably came to this country in hay or straw. This annual plant is narrow and erect with similarly narrow erect leaves that grow in an opposite pattern. Under optimum conditions, these pinks form large colonies.

A relative of the Deptford pink is bouncing Bet or soapwort, another European immigrant that often grows in large colonies on gravel bars, roadsides and the edges of woods. The opposite leaves are oval, pointed on the ends, and large, up to 8 inches long; clusters of pink or white flowers grow on top of the stiff erect stems. Each flower is up to an inch in diameter and each petal has a curved notch on its outer edge. This plant is called soapwort (wort means plant) because its thick sap will lather up with water.

Black-eyed Susans begin blooming in May and continue displaying their sturdy, handsome black and yellow flowers through summer and much of fall. These daisylike plants are classic members of the composite family with flowers that consist of a cluster of central ray flowers surrounded by a corona of ray flowers. The central disk of the black-eyed Susan is of such a dark brown as to appear black. The ray flowers are a strong yellow. These plants grow in colonies in many places ranging from roadsides and the edges of woods to open woods and prairies. The alternate leaves are lance-shaped, hairy and slightly toothed.

HOTSPOTS

Many places are ideal for finding these flowers of late spring and early summer. Look for places with both woods and open fields, and along roadsides and fields. The following places offer the kind of habitats likely for finding a good selection of wildflowers.

The wooded rolling hills of **White Oak Lake SP** (see Chapter 13 for directions) in southwestern Arkansas offers some good opportunities for finding wildflowers. This park is in the region known as the western Gulf Coastal Plain and has a rich diversity of plants and animals. Check out the visitors' center for trail guides. The gravel road that goes northeast from the visitors' center looks promising for wildflowers at this time of year. Another good spot would be **Big Lake NWR** in northern Arkansas. (See Chapter 1 for directions.) Take the road along the lake and look for wildflowers as you go.

In the Chicago area, **Goose Lake Prairie State Natural Area** is a good spot for hunting wildflowers. This 2,380-acre preserve is the largest remnant of prairie left in Illinois and has prairie grasses as well as wildflowers common in and around the area. It contains dry, mesic (moist) and wet prairies and potholes. The Tallgrass Trail is a good one to take through the marshy land. To get there, go southwest from Chicago on I-55 and, about 15 miles southwest of Joliet, exit right at Lorenzo Road. Go west about 3 miles to Jugtown Road, then right for three-quarters of a mile to the park entrance.

Crab Orchard NWR's roads and nature trails in southern Illinois are good places to check out for wildflowers in June. (For directions, see Chapter 1.) Crab Orchard is a gigantic preserve with some 43,000 acres that includes a 4,000-acre wilderness, 5,000 acres of agricultural land and twelve natural areas. Check at the refuge office first to get a map of the area and perhaps a suggestion as to the current good spot to look for wildflowers.

Prairie SP in southwestern Missouri is ideal for finding wildflowers this time of year—you will find the flowers mentioned as well as many others. To get there, go 25 miles north of Joplin on Highway 43, then take Highway P from Highway K in Barton County.

Another good spot for botanizing in Missouri at this time of year is the **Missouri Botanical Garden's Shaw Arboretum** in Gray Summit, southwest of St. Louis off I-44. (See Chapter 2 for directions.) Here you will find replicated prairie, roadsides and edges of woods— all the good environments for June wildflowers.

Butterfly weed, common in prairie lands, lives up to its name by attracting countless butterflies.

35

June Shorttakes

Tulip Trees

These handsome large trees of bottomlands are in bloom early—look for orange and yellowish green flowers. Although a couple of inches in diameter, they may be hard to see since they are painted in pale pastels that blend in with the bright green foliage. Native tulip trees grow in the Missouri Bootheel, nearby southern Illinois and the moist lowlands of Arkansas. They are related to magnolias.

Nesting Bird

Watch for parents carrying food to newly hatched young. Many birds try to approach their nests in secretive or circuitous ways, so be patient.

Trumpet Creeper

The flowers of the trumpet vine begin to bloom this month. One constant visitor will be the ruby-throated hummingbird. The orange to orange-red flowers are trumpet-shaped with a long tube. The compound leaves average six to ten lance-shaped leaflets.

Butterflies and Butterfly Weed

Late this month, the butterfly weed, a milkweed, will begin blooming along roadsides and in prairies and fields. The flowers range from bright orange through hot red and attract many butterflies. The hairy lance-shaped leaves, narrow and very dark green, grow on numerous short stems that are topped by bright umbels of flowers.

36

Breakout: Starry Nights of Summer

Choose any moonless night when there is low humidity in a place away from city lights for the best star-watching you can imagine. Even if you don't have ideal conditions you can see many of the major star groups. Lie on a bench or a blanket on the ground to avoid getting a crick in your neck. It will take a few minutes for your eyes to adjust to the dark if you've been in a lighted room.

In the right spot, you will imagine yourself in the midst of the Milky Way, it will look so close. You may wish to get some star charts or a guide to help you learn. Experts estimate that, with the naked eye, you can see only about two to four thousand stars, even if conditions are excellent—that may be, but it sure looks like more than that to me.

When you see star charts, you may feel intimidated by the large number of named stars and constellations but, in reality, there are only about thirty major stars and only eighty-eight named constellations—we can see about sixty at our latitudes (between 33.0 and 42.5 degrees), though not all at the same time. If you were to learn half of those, you would know your way around the night skies with ease. When studying star charts, you will see that north is up on the page but, unlike terrestrial maps, east is to the left and west is to the right. That is because the star charts show you what is overhead—hold a star map over your head and look at it to understand how this works.

In identifying the different constellations, stars and planets, remember that the stars appear to move around the North Star each night. You will have to find a few easy constellations to get yourself oriented. A number of distinctive constellations are visible. Probably the best way to begin star-watching is to find the Big Dipper, the prominent seven stars that are part of the Great Bear constellation. The Big Dipper is a star group that is easily identified. The other major group known to just about everyone is Orion, the hunter, of winter skies.

Once you find the Big Dipper, look for the front of the bowl—those two stars point toward Polaris, the North Star. Polaris in turn is the last star in the handle of the Little Dipper. The dippers help form the constellations known as the Great Bear, Ursa Major, and the Little Bear, Ursa Minor. Polaris, an important navigational star in the Northern Hemisphere, does indicate true North as it is almost exactly at the pole of the sky. Polaris appears to be in the same spot all the time, about halfway up in the northern sky in our region. Another thing to remember is that, if you are farther north, Polaris will be higher in the sky and vice versa. If you face Polaris, then south will be at your back and you will have east and west on your right and left sides. Learn to find the North Star, Polaris, to orient yourself on earthly directions as well as the starry sky.

The constellations remain in the same relationship to one another as they circle in the sky. Think of the sky as a big umbrella with Polaris at its middle, then think of the way it turns and you will see the relationship of the circling stars to Polaris.

Now that you have found the Big Dipper and Little Dipper, look between the two for the tail of Draco, the dragon. Draco's head is an irregular four-star shape about the size of the Little Dipper's cup and beyond the Little Dipper from the Big Dipper. Look for the long, sinuous tail of the dragon that winds from its head around the Little Dipper almost to the Big Dipper.

Cassiopeia is an easy constellation to find because five of its stars form a clear "W" in the sky. If you take a line from the star that lies at the junction of the Big Dipper's handle and cup through the North Star and beyond, it will point to Cassiopeia. Her husband, Cepheus, is next to her, a constellation that looks like a triangle atop a rectangle. Take the pointer stars of the end of the Big Dipper through the North Star and beyond—that line points to the top of Cepheus' pointed cap. The couple for whom this galactic pair was named were an ancient king and queen of Ethiopia in Greek mythology.

See if you can figure out the entire Great Bear constellation of which the Big Dipper is a major part. The dipper's handle forms the bear's neck and top of his head with the final star in the handle being the bear's nose. The cup of the dipper is like a saddle on the shoulder of the bear—follow its top line through two stars to reach the bear's rear. From the bear's nose and rear, follow down toward his legs and note three pairs of stars that make up the bear's feet.

If you take the two stars that make up the side of the Big Dipper next to the handle and follow their line down beyond the Great Bear, you will see Leo, the lion, a large constellation with three bright stars. The line will go through the lion's shoulder star first and then to Regulus, the bright star that represents one of the lion's front paws. Leo is one of the zodiac constellations, a belt of twelve star groups representing different times of year and forming the basis for astrology. The sun, moon, and planets all appear to travel through the constellations of the zodiac in regular sequence through the year.

Another part of a circle in the sky is the Milky Way, that thick bright belt of stars that spans the night skies. Looking at the Milky Way is like looking at a cross-section of our galaxy, which includes all the stars of the constellations. Experts say that the Milky Way galaxy includes about three hundred billion stars.

Once you have learned to recognize major star groupings such as the Big Dipper and Great Bear plus Cassiopeia and, in the winter skies, Orion, the hunter, you will be able to follow the star charts through the sky and identify other constellations. At any given time, you will see at least two of these star groups in the sky. Various parts of the Big Dipper, as you have seen, serve as pointers to other star groups.

Meteors, small bits of stone or metal from space that glow when they enter Earth's atmosphere, are called meteorites if they reach Earth before they burn up. Many meteors are fragments of comets no bigger than a bit of sand. Meteor showers regularly occur each year. Those closest to June are the Eta Aquarid in early May and the Delta Aquarid in late July.

JULY

July Observations

37

The Cowbird Story

In the days when buffaloes roamed the land, brown-headed cowbirds followed the herds over the plains and prairies, feeding upon the buffalos' ticks and insects as well as grass seeds and berries. As buffaloes became scarcer, cowbirds switched their allegiances to cattle, continuing to drift with the herds. Today, look for them on lawn areas and short-cropped fields where they wander about in bold groups as they search for food.

Since nomadic life made it difficult for cowbirds to have their own nesting sites, they developed the habit of parasitizing other birds' nests. They lay their larger eggs in other birds' nests and, soon after hatching, often pitch their unrelated nestmates out of the nest. Cowbirds are the only brood parasites of the New World and have been known to parasitize over two hundred species of birds.

Brown-headed cowbirds are part of the same family of birds as blackbirds, bobolinks, meadow larks, grackles and orioles. They grow 6 to 8 inches long and are stocky with a sparrowlike bill. The male is a sleek greenish black color with glossy brown head and the female is grayish brown all over. The male's thick feathers on the back of his neck give him a hunchbacked appearance. The female cowbird is grayish brown from head to tail. Their flight is not light and graceful but rather ponderous and determined. Their calls are nondescript gurgles, whistles, rattles and squeaks. They walk rather than hop and their wide stance gives them a waddling gait that's easy to recognize.

Watch groups of feeding cowbirds and see if you can identify the one designated to act as sentinal to warn the others of possible danger. They favor areas with short plant growth where it's easier to identify approaching predators. They are at home in grain fields, along highways and in the suburbs. Brown-headed cowbirds seem to prefer living near the edges of woods and forest fragments and so are more common in the small woods of southern Illinois than in the forests of the Ozarks.

Toward the end of summer and fall, you may find large flocks of mixed blackbirds in harvested grain fields. Look for red-winged blackbirds, starlings and grackles, as well as brown-headed cowbirds.

Cowbirds lay up to twelve eggs per year, placing each one in a different bird's nest. The eggs hatch in about twelve days and the young cowbirds fledge in about ten days. Since the host birds, often warblers, finches, flycatchers or vireos, are usually smaller than the cowbirds, the cowbird hatchling dominates the nest, outcompeting its nestmates for food and space. The stepparents work overtime to find enough food to satisfy their large foundlings. How do the young cowbirds know they are cowbirds and end up back with their own kind? That's one of the many behavioral mysteries of our natural world.

Cowbirds are blamed by some experts for the disappearance of many birds, but research studies also are focusing on crows and blue jays, birds that are notorious for raiding songbird nests and eating eggs and babies. A number of researchers are sure that brown-headed cowbirds have eliminated Kirtland's warbler, a rare bird that occasionally used to migrate through our territory from its winter residence in the Bahamas to its summer residence in Michigan.

If cowbirds are a major factor in reduced populations of songbirds, then why are cowbird populations lower in our region in recent years after a rise in numbers from 1900 to 1980? Perhaps cowbirds are not as villainous as some experts thought they were. Other environmental factors undoubtedly have a great bearing on whether songbird populations fall or rise.

Cowbird predation of songbirds has increased as man has altered the land, creating more cleared land in previously forested areas. Predicaments such as the reduction in songbird populations should make us appreciative of the vast acreages of national forests, refuges and parklands throughout our region and country. In any case, the cowbird is a creature with curious breeding habits. When searching for cowbirds, look for open land that is near woods. Cowbirds feed on the open land and parasitize the nests of birds that live at the edges of and a few yards into the woods.

HOTSPOTS

Cowbirds are abundant in **Felsenthal NWR** in southeastern Arkansas (see Chapter 2 for directions), and **Wapanocca NWR** in the northeastern part of the state (see Chapter 1 for directions).

In Illinois, cowbirds are common throughout the year at **Crab Orchard NWR** in southern Illinois (see Chapter 1 for directions) and during the spring and summer breeding season at the **Brussels** and **Gardner divisions** of the **Mark Twain NWR Complex** (see Chapter 3 for directions).

In Missouri, brown-headed cowbirds are common throughout the breeding season at **Mingo NWR** in the southeast part of the state (see Chapter 1 for directions). At **Squaw Creek NWR** in northwestern Missouri, cowbirds are abundant at this time of year (see Chapter 1 for directions).

38

Poisonous Snakes

The important thing about poisonous snakes is to learn to recognize them—many people react strongly to snakes and assume that some of our most valuable snakes are poisonous. Too often, king snakes, water snakes and others are wrongly identified as rattlers, copperheads or cottonmouths and are destroyed.

It is wise to steer clear of areas known to have concentrations of poisonous snakes and give them a wide berth when you happen upon them in the wild. When you do go into areas where poisonous snakes are common, wear thick leather or rubber boots. Look before putting your hands on or under rocky ledges or logs, and look before you step or sit. If you are in a canoe or other boat and a snake drops into it, use the paddle to lift the snake over the side into the water—do not try to kill the snake in the boat.

Remember that snakes, even the poisonous ones, are shy animals that would prefer to avoid you. Their first defense against intruders is to remain motionless, a ploy that makes them nearly invisible as their camouflaged coloring blends into the background. They will not bite unless cornered or stepped on. Our native poisonous snakes are inclined to be more active during the evening and night, especially if the weather is very hot—be especially observant then. Your local American Red Cross office can provide instructions on snakebite procedures to follow. If you should get bitten, the most important thing to do is to stay calm and get to the nearest emergency room or physician as soon as possible. Beware of handling poisonous snakes even when they are dead because their reflexive action may be strong.

All of the poisonous snakes in our region are pit vipers with the exception of coral snakes, which have been found in southern Arkansas. Coral snakes, members of the cobra family, are dangerously poisonous, and are native from here to Argentina. They are in their northernmost territory in Arkansas. Fortunately, they have small mouths and small fangs so their bite is restricted to small appendages like fingers or toes. With their bright black, yellow and red coloring, they look much like the harmless scarlet snake and scarlet king snake. The key to identification of this small, 20- to 30-inch, poisonous snake is to remember that red touches yellow on the coral snake—that is not the case with the look-alike. Coral snakes, usually most active in the cool of the morning, hunt frogs, lizards and other snakes. Their favorite habitats are jungly growth known as hammocks in the South, edges of ponds and lakes and pine woods.

Copperheads, rattlesnakes and cottonmouths are all pit vipers. Pit vipers have a sensory pit, an open depression, on each side of the head between the eye and the nostril. This pit detects heat and so helps these snakes find their warm-blooded prey. Pit vipers also have broad heads and generally stocky bodies. They give birth to live young. They have a pair of retractable hollow fangs attached at the front of the mouth, and grow new fangs if they lose the old ones. Rattlesnakes, considered the most highly developed snakes from a scientific point of view, have tail scales modified into hollow segments that are loosely connected and vibrate when shaken, giving off the characteristic buzzing noise of a threatened rattlesnake.

Copperheads of rocky bluffs and cottonmouths of watery lowlands are in the same family. Both northern and southern copperheads, snakes that grow 2 to 3 feet long, are native to our region. The northern is most common from southern Illinois south through most of Missouri and the southwestern corner of Arkansas. The southern copperhead is found through most of Arkansas as well as the southern thirds of Missouri and Illinois. The northern copperhead has reddish brown bands against a paler ground color—the bands are wide on the sides of the body, narrower on top. The southern copperhead is paler with a tannish ground color and bands that may fail to meet on the top if its back. Their prey consists mostly of mice although they also eat insects, frogs, lizards and even small birds. Favorite hangouts for northern copperheads are rocky, wooded hillsides and brushy areas beside streams. Southern copperheads are more likely to be found along lowlands and in swamps.

The gregarious copperheads may spend their winters in communal dens.

The western cottonmouth is native to all of Arkansas and southern Illinois and Missouri. This thick-bodied dark, almost black snake with a dark brown or black belly is large, up to 3 1/2 feet in length. Both copperheads and cottonmouths vibrate their tails like rattlesnakes when alarmed which may make noise in dry leaves and brush. Cottonmouths open their mouths wide when threatened, showing off the white lining of their mouth from which the name comes. They eat fish, frogs, lizards, rodents, small birds and other snakes. They live in swamps and around lowland lakes, and also along the rocky streams and rivers of the Ozarks and Ouachita mountains—in these higher places, this snake is particularly secretive and nocturnal.

Rattlesnakes are known by their rattles, which make buzzy noises similar to the breeding songs of summer cicadas. The precise sound of that rattle depends upon the species of rattlesnake, larger snakes making respectively louder buzzes. Rodents and birds are the primary components of rattlesnake diets, but they also eat lizards, frogs and other small animals.

The timber rattlesnake is the most widely distributed and largest of our region's poisonous snakes, growing up to well over 4 feet long. Its territory includes the southern half of Illinois, all of Missouri except the Bootheel, and the northwestern quadrant of Arkansas. Dark brown crossbands that may break up into spots along the sides are in high contrast to background colors ranging from yellow to brownish gray to gray. A dark wide stripe goes from the eye to the rear of the jaw. The rattles on the tail are prominent and paler than the body. Timber rattlers live in wooded, rocky, hilly areas, especially in second-growth woods where rodents are likely to be common. In the northern part of its territory, these snakes are likely to gather together in the fall on warm, south-facing rocky slopes where they can overwinter in dens.

The territory of the canebrake rattlesnake meets that of the timber rattlesnake in Arkansas, southern Illinois and southern Missouri. These two snakes are actually subspecies of the same species. The canebrake rattler of the southeastern United States has a reddish brown dorsal stripe, dark crossbands and a dark eye stripe like that of the timber rattler. The canebrake's favorite habitat is in southern swamplands.

The eastern Massasauga rattlesnake, although not found in Arkansas, is native to the northern three-fourths of Illinois and northeastern quarter of Missouri. Toward the northwestern quarter of Missouri, this snake, which averages 20 to 30 inches in length, gradually intergrades with the western Massasauga rattlesnake of Kansas, Oklahoma and Texas. This is a dark gray to gray snake with large roundish gray-brown to brown spots and blotches. The western subspecies is lighter in color. This snake lives in a variety of habitats ranging from dry woods to swamps, marshes and wet prairies.

Western pigmy rattlesnakes are not found in Illinois but are native to most of Arkansas and the Missouri counties bordering Arkansas. These are small snakes with small rattles and thin tails, averaging well under 2 feet in length. Dark irregular dorsal spots and a row or two of dark irregular spots on the sides are on a background of pale gray-brown. Many have a rusty stripe down the back. Pigmy rattlers usually live in cedar glades under rocks or in marshes and swamps near water. This is an extremely shy snake that you are not likely to see.

Chances are that you will never see any of these native poisonous snakes. Their habit of remaining motionless unless directly threatened makes them all but invisible. Most will retreat if discovered, only too happy to get away from danger—people are undoubtedly their worst enemies.

HOTSPOTS

Most people will want to be aware of habitats that are particularly likely to harbor populations of poisonous snakes. Combine a little knowledge of habitat with some of the keys to identification and you should be prepared to name snakes that you may see and also to treat them with respect. These populations are rarely large except in denning places where some of them gather in the fall as they prepare to go into winter dens.

The swampy sloughs and lakes of northeastern Arkansas in places like **Big Lake NWR** (see Chapter 1 for directions) and **Wapanocca NWR** (see Chapter 1 for directions) in northeastern Arkansas are places where you would be likely to see some of the region's poisonous snakes, including cottonmouths and canebrake rattlers. The bottomlands, bayous and sloughs of **Felsenthal NWR** also offer good prospects for seeing these snakes (see Chapter 2 for directions).

In southern Illinois, the extensive and varied land of **Crab Orchard NWR** (see Chapter 1 for directions) offers opportunities for seeing copperheads, cottonmouths and some of the rattlers. Eastern Massasauga rattlers might be seen in places with varied terrain such as **Starved Rock SP**, perhaps the most famous of all of Illinois' parks, located in north central Illinois (see Chapter 13 for directions).

A place with environments that vary from swamp to hardwood forest is **Mingo NWR** is southeastern Missouri (see Chapter 1 for directions). You are likely to find a variety of snakes at Mingo, including some of the poisonous ones. Another place for finding these unusual native animals would be **Cuivre River SP** in the Lincoln Hills of northeastern Missouri (see Chapter 13 for directions). Here you will find the kind of rugged landscape, sinkhole ponds and limestone glades more often found in the Ozarks—good places to see snakes including, perhaps, timber rattlers and copperheads.

39

Butterfly Counts

Summer marks the peak of the butterfly season in our region with many species appearing at the blooming flowers of prairies, woodland edges, roadsides and other places where butterflies' favorite flowers grow. Before the butterflies appear, people who are sharp-eyed and know the habits of butterfly larvae can find the caterpillar or chrysalis of some species, although the larva and chrysalis are often so well camouflaged that they are very seldom seen.

There are various species of butterflies in our three-state region—many of them are exquisite creatures painted with jewel-like tones. Surprisingly, little is known about the life cycles and habits of many butterflies, and new species are still being discovered and named.

Did you know that there have been butterfly counts in our country since the 1970s? They are sponsored by the North American Butterfly Association and the Xerces Society. NABA began publishing a quarterly newsletter in early 1993, called *American Butterflies*, which the association hopes will develop into a full-color magazine. Butterfly counts are held between June 12 and July 25—many groups plan to have their butterfly counts on the Fourth of July. You can join this young organization, NABA, for just $20 a year and learn more about butterflies and about participating in the annual butterfly counts (the address is in the Appendix). NABA charges a small $2.50 fee for each adult volunteer and provides count forms.

The reason for butterfly counts is that biologists can determine what kinds of butterflies are using different habitats and so get an idea of how abundant a species is. When counts are done for several years in the same locations, we begin to learn valuable information about butterfly distribution and population trends.

Butterfly counts are made within large circular areas (15 miles in diameter). Volunteers visit probable butterfly habitats within the circle to collect data on the species and number of butterflies they see. Volunteers use their own knowledge plus field guides to identify the butterflies. Unknown species are collected for later identification. The organization makes every effort to see that every circle's volunteers include at least one person who knows butterflies well. Reports are submitted to NABA by early September.

If you do collect and release butterflies, use a net and a delicate hand, not the hand alone. When you catch a butterfly in a net, quickly flip the net over so that it folds over the opening, capturing the butterfly within. Then you can study it, making any necessary measurements and notes, then gently release it.

If you wish to collect any that might be on a "watch" list, indicating that they are on the way to becoming either endangered or more populous, you must check with the visitors' center or headquarters of the park or refuge and get a permit if necessary. Those planning to volunteer for butterfly counts should plan to have pest repellent handy because chiggers, mosquitoes and other annoying insects are likely to be present.

During the 1993 butterfly count, the regal fritillary was found by the hundreds in some Missouri count circles. This butterfly is on the Missouri watch list, meaning that there is some cause to suspect that its numbers may dwindle. For that reason, this was exciting to the biologists at the Missouri Department of Conservation as well as staffers at The Nature Conservancy, both participating organizations in the butterfly counts.

Prime habitats for the regal fritillary in this count were the southwestern Missouri prairies that come into their greatest season of bloom during this time of year. Hundreds of these butterflies were seen in southwest Missouri—significant for this species because it is becoming rare in the eastern half of the United States. This butterfly is especially attracted to the flowers of common milkweed, butterfly weed and coneflowers. The orange-red front wings have black borders dotted with white spots and the hind wings are very dark with two rows of white spots. The regal fritillary begins life as a brownish yellow caterpillar with dark splotches and lines, yellowish bands and numerous branching spines that are pale and have black tips. The single brood of eggs is laid in late summer on violet plants. When newly-hatched larvae emerge during cold spring weather, they may hibernate until warmer weather arrives.

A similar, related butterfly is the great spangled fritillary, common throughout our region in forested lowlands. This handsome butterfly is also common in suburban gardens. The 3-inch butterfly is orange on top with black patterning edged by rows of dots and crescents. Underneath, the hind wings have a number of silver spots. The caterpillars, which feed on violets, are black with spines that are black with contrasting yellow-orange bases. Spangled fritillaries, like the regal fritillaries, overwinter in the caterpillar stage. The eggs are laid near violet plants upon which the young feed.

Delaware skippers are small butterflies of prairies and woodland edges where the young feed on grasses. Only an inch or a bit more in wing spread, they are usually dusky orange although they may be yellowish gold. In the orange phase, there usually is a dark band on the wings. The larvae are whitish with a black and white head and a black bar on the rear. The adult will search for nectar in trumpet vine flowers and other deep tubular flowers, one of the few butterflies to do this.

One of the many sulphur butterflies you may see in the Ozarks is the dogface butterfly, a 2-inch long butterfly that visits mud puddles as well as flowers. Easy to recognize, it is yellow with a dog-like profile on each front wing. In the Ozarks, the dogface produces two generations yearly. The female fall form of this butterfly is rosy and the dogface harder to see. In more northern parts of our region, this insect may be only a summer resident. Favorite food plants are prairie clover and false indigo.

You can expect to see a number of swallowtail butterflies at this time of year. Tiger, giant, spicebush, pipevine and zebra swallowtails all are medium to large butterflies that have tail-like lobes on their rear wings and hibernate in the pupal stage. Knowing how to recognize their favorite food plants will help you find the swallowtails. Tiger swallowtails are cosmopolitan eaters as larvae, being content with a number of different trees and shrubs including the hop tree, ash, cherry and tulip tree. Giant swallowtails tend toward the hop tree and prickly ash. Spicebush swallowtail larvae prefer sassafras and spicebush. Virginia snakeroot and pipevine are two favorites of the pipevine swallowtail. Zebra swallowtails are forest butterflies and are especially fond of pawpaws.

Look for flowering plants and you are likely to see butterflies, if you are patient. Butterfly weed and coneflowers, found in prairies and along roadsides, are two species well known for attracting a variety of butterflies.

HOTSPOTS

The many trails of **Pinnacle Mountain SP** in central Arkansas offer a variety of habitats from lush lowlands to wooded hillsides, making it a park where you are likely to see a variety of butterflies (see Chapter 28 for directions). This 1,700-acre park is known for the diversity of its plant and animal life. **Felsenthal NWR** in southern Arkansas (See Chapter 2 for directions) is another place with the kind of varied habitat that makes it good for studying butterflies. At this time of year, look especially for flowering prairie plants.

In Illinois, look for butterflies at **Pere Marquette SP**'s 54-acre natural area that is known as **McAdams Peak Hill Prairie** (for directions on reaching Pere Marquette State Park, see Chapter 13). Get a trail map from the visitors' center and you will see the trails leading to this special place that features prairie grasses and a bountiful supply of the prairie flowers. Of course, you are likely to see butterflies in other parts of this west central Illinois park as well, because it does have a variety of plant communities.

Goose Lake Prairie Nature Preserve in the Chicago area is another place to look for butterflies (see Chapter 34 for directions). Here you will find a variety of prairies and many wildflowers to attract butterflies. The majority of this 2,380-acre preserve is relatively unspoiled prairie. The remaining 767 acres offer good examples of plant succession in old fields.

Prairie SP in southwestern Missouri (see Chapter 34 for directions) has the variety of prairie wildflowers that make it a butterfly heaven. This is Missouri's largest remaining prairie. Some 3,000 native and restored acres give you some sense of the vastness of the original prairie that covered at least one third of the state.

Another good place for studying butterflies is the **Missouri Botanical Garden's Shaw Arboretum** in east central Missouri (see Chapter 2 for directions). The replicated prairie offers plenty of summer wildflowers that always attract many butterflies. The trail through the prairie leads to a lookout stand where you can see over the entire expanse of this experimental area.

40

Bird Nests from Ground to Treetop

Summer is a quieter time in the bird world than spring. Spring is the time for staking out territories and pairing up, while summer is the time for nesting and raising young. There's little reason for territorial singing in July, which makes birding more difficult since you can't mark a bird's presence by its song. For birders, it's an interesting time to look for adults feeding their young and exhibiting other parental behavior. Plan to bird early in the morning during hot weather—not only is it more comfortable for you, it is a more active time for the birds. They tend to hole up in a shady place during the heat of the day.

When you get too close to nests, the parents react in a number of ways, depending on the species. Some birds get visibly nervous, hopping from one branch to another, while others pull the old broken wing trick to try to lure you away from the nest area. Some birds get quite violent. Just recently, I inadvertently walked too close to the nest of a red-winged blackbird and was attacked—the bird flew at my head, rapping me with its beak as it clawed with its feet. I never did see the nest, but the bird accomplished what it intended—I moved away from the area.

A number of warblers can be found nesting in our region, including parulas, ceruleans, worm-eating and black and white warblers. Most warblers build their nests anywhere from 4 to 60 or more feet up in shrubs and trees, but some, including the black and white warbler, build their nests on the ground, in a hollow log or under a rock ledge. It makes you wonder how any of the young reach adulthood since they seem so exposed to predators.

The mimic thrushes, mockingbirds, brown thrashers and gray catbirds all make rough nest cups of twigs, leaves, stems and grasses in dense brush, thickets or shrubs. Their nests are fairly low, rarely above 10 to 15 feet high. They lay two to six pale greenish or bluish eggs. Like other birds, their parental instincts increase as hatching time approaches.

The tiny blue-gray gnatcatcher, only 4 to 5 inches long, summers and nests throughout our region. These small birds of lowlands and open woods catch gnats and other small insects on the wing, darting in pursuit with great agility. It builds its nest anywhere from 2 feet high to up in the treetops, weaving a compact cup of grass and other plant fibers. Learn their nasal call and you will be able to find them. The male stays close to the nest while the female is incubating, singing all the time. Even when he takes a turn on the eggs, he continues to sing—the song is soft, and hard to hear from any distance. These tiny birds have great courage, attacking any bird that threatens their nest—even blue jays and crows.

Carolina wrens and house wrens are favorite birds of summer in our region. The Carolina wren is a year-round resident, but the house wren spends its winters farther south. These little brown birds with their saucy behavior will make their nests in just about any kind of cavity—mail boxes, old hats, hollow trees or birdhouses. Both sexes work on the nest, preferring moist materials and lining it with moss or soft feathers. These birds are omnivorous, eating seeds and fruits as well as insects.

The chickadees, both the black-capped chickadee of the northern part of our region and the Carolina chickadee that lives from about the Missouri River southward, are permanent residents often seen at the edges of brushy woods where they nest in tree cavities wherever possible. The two species may hybridize freely in their border territories. They build their loosely-constructed nests of mosses, feathers and other plant fibers. Once they have raised their young they will band together in small flocks of a dozen or less birds. They remain with the flock until spring and, often, other birds— titmice, nuthatches, brown creepers and even warblers and vireos— will join this casual association. Experts believe that the flock gives individual birds a good defense system. Sometimes you can see the entire flock flee when a one member gives an alarm call.

The tufted titmice, often found in association with chickadees except during the nesting season, live in the same kind of habitat— brushy growth often at the edge of woods. These perky little year-round residents look for holes in trees to build their nests. Titmice eat insects during the warm season, switching to seeds during the winter.

Although it's an aggressive bully and incorrigible nest raider, the blue jay is one of the most beautiful birds of our woods. Its raucous calls loudly warn of other intruders; less well known are its remarkable soft songs and its mimicry of other bird songs. The blue jay's diet includes insects, fruit, seeds and nuts as well as baby birds and mice. The paired birds build their ramshackle nests of twigs, leaves and other plant fibers placed on a limb or in a tree crotch. Although blue jays are tough on other birds, they are generous with each other and make good parents. Blue jays are among the birds observed "anting," a peculiar habit that is not well understood. The bird will pick up ants and run them over its feathers or will sit among a group of ants and let them walk through its feathers. Some suspect that the formic acid in the ants will kill bird lice and mites.

In areas next to streams, rivers and lakes where there is an ample supply of small fish, tadpoles and frogs, you may be lucky enough to hear the rattle call of the belted kingfisher as it flies along the bank. This is a large flashy bird, about a foot long and chunky in appearance. The large strong bill, designed for catching fish and other small animals, is also a useful tool for digging the nesting burrow. The kingfisher has a large, obvious head crest, is blue-gray on top and white underneath with a blue band across its upper breast. The female also has a brown band across its chest. These are solitary birds except during the breeding season, when the mated pair shares the work of digging a nesting tunnel into the earth of the banks. The female lays five to eight white eggs on the bare soil of the nest chamber. Both sexes share in incubating the eggs for three to four weeks, then the female tends the young until they begin feathering out. During that early period the male feeds both the young and his mate, then the two share the feeding duties until the young are fledged at about five weeks old. They will learn to fish and otherwise fend for themselves in another couple of weeks, at which time they will leave to find territories of their own.

Some birds build no nests at all. The killdeer, one of the plovers, is an obvious example of this, laying its speckled eggs in grassy fields or on stony ground where they are so well camouflaged that you can barely see them even when you know where they are. The best way to tell where a killdeer is nesting is to walk around a field where they are active, waiting for the telltale broken wing trick to tell you that you are close to the nest.

Nearly all birds usually wait until their full complement of eggs is laid before beginning to incubate them. A few, including owls, begin incubating right away. Those that wait to incubate until the full clutch is laid have young that hatch all at once and so are of the same size. In the case of owls, the young hatch in the order in which they were laid, and so are different sizes. Owls feed the largest chick first, which means that when food is plentiful they can raise the full brood, but when food is scarce, the smallest chicks may starve.

Most small birds hatch in about two weeks and are featherless, blind and helpless for the first few days. Incubating and feeding the young are chores often shared by both parents. Even when the female shoulders most of the responsibility, the male bird remains close, often feeding her as she sits on the eggs. Some of the ground-nesting birds, including ducks, geese and most shorebirds, including the killdeer, are the exception to this—they are born ready to run and fully covered with down. They are able to find and peck away at food from the start, although the parent birds continue to look after the young and protect them from danger.

HOTSPOTS

The beautiful mountain settings of **Petit Jean SP** with its ravines, streams, and spectacular views offer good opportunities for summer birding (see Chapter 14 for directions). The visitors' center offers maps of the park as well as interpretive programs.

In southern Arkansas, **Felsenthal NWR** offers a great variety of habitats in its thousands of acres, everything from bottomland hardwood forests to a variety of waterside terrain. You might even chance to see wood storks, which are common during summer and fall. Felsenthal also boasts a year-round population of the rare red-cockaded woodpecker. (See Chapter 2 for directions.)

Morton Arboretum near Chicago (see Chapter 3 for directions) is a marvelous place for birding at any time of year. The 1,500-acre preserve offers a variety of woodland and wetland areas where you are likely to see all the birds described in this chapter and more.

An unusual nonprofit private park that is open to the public for a fee is **Wildlife Prairie Park** located ten miles west of downtown Peoria. Take Interstate 74 to exit 82. This park, with 2,000 acres of grazing land, lakes and forests, aims to present the plants and animals that are part of Illinois' prairie heritage. There are a number of trails that will take you to different habitats, including Hidden Lake Trail and Overlook Trail. There are interpretive programs and guided walks daily during the summer. This should be a good spot for summer birding. Within the city of Peoria, on Forest Park Drive, is the parent organization of the Wildlife Prairie Park, known as the **Forest**

Park Nature Center. This is a cooperative project of Peoria Park District and Forest Park Foundation. An urban preserve of 800 acres with seven miles of trails, it is situated in a hardwood forest with a healthy population of birds and animals. Naturalists can provide information on the best birding spots of the day. They also give regular programs and guided walks. To get there, take Illinois Route 29 3 miles north of downtown Peoria and exit on Gardner Lane which turns into Forest Park Drive just a quarter mile east of Highway 29. Watch for signs and A-frame visitors' center.

The varied terrain of **Crab Orchard NWR** in southern Illinois (see Chapter 1 for directions) offers everything from wooded wilderness to agricultural fields to wetlands, making this a good choice for summer birding. Stop at the visitors' center to get a map and get information on what specific places look promising.

Busch Wildlife Area west of St. Louis, Missouri, is one of the region's favorite places to go birding (see Chapter 10 for directions). Here you will find both evergreen and deciduous woods plus many lakes. The variety of habitat in this preserve makes birding a joy.

Near Kansas City, try **Powell Gardens'** extensive 835-acre property for summer birding. You might want to begin by checking in the 14-acre area around the visitors' center and the perennial gardens. You can get to Powell Garden by taking either Highway Z or Highway 131 south from I-70 east of Kansas City. Powell Gardens is on the north side of Highway 50 about halfway beween Lee's Summit and Warrensburg.

Mingo NWR (see Chapter 1 for directions) in southeast Missouri and **Swan Lake NWR** (see Chapter 8 for directions) in northwest Missouri are two other places that should offer good birding at this time of year. Check out the varied habitats of both.

41

July Shorttakes

Compass Plant

On the prairies, compass plants begin to bloom. This plant of the daisy or composite family turns its lower leaves to a north-south orientation, hence the name compass plant. Growing up to 8 feet tall, this elegant plant has huge, deeply cut leaves nearly 1 1/2 feet in length.

Blazing Star

On the prairies and along roadsides, blazing star, also known as gayfeather or liatris, begins to bloom. There are two species that bloom in our region, one with tufts of pinkish flowers along a long flower stalk, the other with a tall flower stalk that begins blooming at the top and works its way downward, the opposite of most flower stalks.

See also:

Chapter 42, Breakout: Berries and Fruits. Blackberries and many other tasty berries begin to ripen this month.

Chapter 50, Bird Migrations in Wetlands. Watch for shorebirds around shallow ponds and mudflats, as they are already beginning to work their way south for their fall migration.

42

Breakout:
Berries and Fruits

The fruits and berries of summer are ripening on shrubs, brambles and trees throughout our region. In the wild, many are eaten by birds and animals, including songbirds, turkeys, quail, deer, squirrels and others. Wild fruit is a treat for them as well as for us. Often, the animals will beat you to the ripening fruit. One day the berries or other fruit will be there, and the next day they are gone. It's as if the animals and birds have a telegraph system that tells them exactly when the fruit is perfectly ripe.

Always use caution when planning to eat wild fruit. In some plants, only the fruit is edible—the other parts of the plants may be highly poisonous. For example, the fruit of mayapple is edible but the rest of the plant is very poisonous. Wild cherries are wonderfully edible but the wilted foliage contains a serious poison. If you are unsure of identification of a plant, stay on the cautious side—*don't eat unknowns!*

Gooseberries and serviceberry fruit are usually already gone by July; watch for them to ripen in June. Gooseberries, small shrubs with thorns, have simple palmate leaves and are close relatives of currants. Look for them in rocky or open, dry woods just about everywhere except the lowlands of the Missouri Bootheel and eastern Arkansas. They make wonderful jams and pies if you can pick them when they are at the stage between green and reddish purple. Gooseberry leaves are good in salads, cut up and added raw.

Serviceberry fruits are like tiny apples, a fact that signals their membership in the rose family along with apples, pears, plums and cherries. These small understory trees have simple ovate leaves and smooth gray bark when young. Look for them on steep wooded slopes and in open woods. Their juicy small fruits are among the favorite treats of wild birds so you will rarely be able to find enough for yourself. This year I found a tree that had fruit almost ripe—it was laden with small red fruit. I ate a few and thought I'd wait until the following day—too late! The birds got them all, except for the few that the squirrels ate.

The hawthorn, another member of the rose family and the state tree of Missouri, has small hard fruits that ripen later in the summer. There are dozens of different species of hawthorns native to our region—be content to identify the genus. Hawthorn leaves are alternate and either oval or lobed, and many but not all species have thorns. You may want to identify some hawthorns now so that you can return later, in August or September, to pick the fruit. You can make a good jelly or fruit butter from hawthorn fruit.

Wild black cherries ripen at this season. Their toothed lancelike leaves grow alternately. They make a delectable jelly or cherry syrup. Look for black cherries in woods that lie along stream banks. The fruits are white or green at first, then turn red, and finally darken to purplish black when ripe. They grow in bunches a bit like grapes and each is about the size of a garden pea. They are quite sour when raw.

Wild strawberries are found in many places throughout our region. Usually, they have already fruited by the time July rolls around. Some people pick the leaves to use as a tea—they are good sources of vitamin C. In most places there are rarely enough wild strawberries to pick and take home, so you may as well enjoy them in the field, warm from the sun. Look for wild strawberries at the edges of woods, on open slopes and alongside streams.

You might wonder at the suggestion of American basswood as a source for edible fruits, but both flowers and fruits are edible. Look for this tree on slopes and alongside streams and rivers. The large simple leaves look like lopsided hearts. The fragrant flowers that appear from May to July may be used either fresh or dried as a tea. It is said that Indians ate the spring flower buds raw to quench thirst, and cooked them as a vegetable. The fruits can also be ground up and used as a chocolate substitute.

Deerberry, also called huckleberry, got its name from the fact that it is a favorite of the native white-tailed deer. This small branched shrub with alternate leathery leaves has bell-shaped flowers that hang down, a sign of its membership in the heath family. Deerberry thrives on the acid soils of sandstone and chert areas where you can find it on rocky slopes and glades. The small fruit is not very juicy and often quite sour. Many prefer making the fruit into jelly to eating the berries raw.

Both the flowers and fruit of elderberry are good to eat, but beware of the poisonous stems and foliage. Recognize this scrubby shrub by its compound leaves, each having two to five pairs of opposite leaflets and a single leaflet at the tip. The delicate white flowers grow in umbels at the ends of branches. The entire flowering umbel can be dipped into a fritter batter and fried. The green berries can be pickled. When the berries ripen from green to purple later in the summer, they will make great pies or jelly.

Although pawpaws and persimmons don't ripen until late summer or early fall, you would be wise to find the trees now and return to pick later. Pawpaws, the northernmost representatives of the tropical custard apple family, grow in moist bottomland woods and alongside rivers and streams in most of our region. Recognize them by their habit of growing in colonies and the immense size of the oval leaves—6 to 12 inches long and up to 5 inches wide.

Persimmons have a distinctive nubby bark and alternate oval leaves on short stems. Look for persimmons in open woods, at the edges of fields and in abandoned fields. Small insignificant flowers appear in late spring and the fruit ripens at around the time of the first hard frosts. This tree is a member of the ebony family and has wood that is prized for golf clubs. The pulpy fruit will make your mouth pucker if unripe but is sweet and tasty when ripe and soft.

The brambles, all plants in the rose family, are in a class by themselves. Raspberries, blackberries and dewberries all grow in our region and are very popular for use in jams and jellies, pies and tarts and syrup. The leaves of all are tasty when steeped into a tea. Raspberries are black caplike fruits growing on bluish white canes— the white of the cane rubs off revealing a shiny maroon surface. Look for them in thickets, fields and at the edges of woods. Their canes are less thorny and more delicate and graceful than those of blackberries. Raspberries are wonderful in any fruit dish or jam.

Blackberries grow on thorny, sturdy canes in abandoned fields, fence rows, roadsides and prairies. The seedy berries are delicious in pies, jams, cobblers and on cereal. Picking blackberries is an excruciating task compounded by hot sun, chiggers and ticks, but many people believe the results are worth every chigger bite. Dewberries are in the same genus as blackberries but have canes that sprawl along the ground rooting where the tips touch the soil. Blackberry canes are more inclined to grow tall and arching.

In rich bottomlands, fence rows and along the edges of woods, you may find wild grapes with their large heartlike leaves, viny growth and tendrils. The young tendrils are tasty when pickled and tender young leaves are good in salads when cut into small pieces. In some years the grapes are particularly plump and large. The jams and jellies made from this fruit have a tangy wild taste, making it worthwhile to take the time needed to pick and destem each small grape.

The fruits of summer are an added bonus to birding, botanizing or otherwise enjoying the plants and animals of our region. If we have had a rainy spring, these summer fruits should be plump and juicy. When springs are dry, the fruit often is wizened and hardly worth picking.

AUGUST

August Observations

43

A Different View of Stream Life

I know a way that you can enjoy studying nature on the blistering hot humid days of summer, days when the temptation to stay indoors in air conditioning is strong. A snorkel and mask will give you a whole new outlook on animals and plants that live under the water in our streams, rivers, ponds and lakes. At the same time, you will stay cool as long as you are floating or submerged in the water.

The spring-fed streams of the Ozark Mountains are the best for summer snorkeling—clear and cool. Some of the other streams and lakes in our region are clear as well. The clarity of the water is the single greatest requirement for summer snorkeling. If it has rained recently, you may find streams are turbulent and murky, no time to go looking for the fish, crustaceans, amphibians and insects you can see when the water is crystal clear.

Before heading for the water, take the time to buy a mask and snorkel that fits. Nothing is more aggravating than having a mask too tight, too loose or leaky. A snorkel with a mouthpiece that is too small or too large also is an aggravation. Once you find a mask and snorkel that fit properly, learn to adjust them and how to use the small gadget that attaches the two together.

Learn the techniques of snorkeling in a local pool, then apply them to clear streams and lakes of our region. In streams with a mild, steady current this is the easiest, most comfortable way to see underwater plants and wildlife.

In the pool, learn how to cruise along on the surface or just under the surface of the quiet water—beginning in a swift stream can be dangerous. Learn to go under the water and then clear the snorkel vigorously so that you can breathe through it once again. In some bodies of water, you may use your mask and snorkel just to peer at a particular area while you are standing in the water—for instance, you might want to watch the territorial and breeding behavior of sunfish, perch or bass at their cleared gravel nests, a common sight in shallow lake water at some times of the warm season.

Should you use swim fins to help you maneuver and move more swiftly? In calm waters, fins are marvelous—just a small flick of

The Black River of southeastern Missouri is one of many clear, spring-fed streams in the Ozarks which are ideal for canoeing, tubing and floating.

the feet carries you much farther than bare feet and hands alone. In swift water, fins, can be difficult, even dangerous to manage. The water pushes the fins, making it hard to stand up and more difficult to walk on a slippery rocky stream bottom.

The flotation devices required by the Coast Guard for boating can be very helpful if you just want to float along, studying the underwater wildlife as you go. They are a necessity for small children and anyone who is not a strong swimmer. An inner tube can be a valuable adjunct to snorkeling along rivers and streams, because you can be more easily seen by canoeists and others if you float along with one hand on the inner tube. Do not go snorkeling alone—go in a group of two to three people. On streams and lakes it's best to have a canoe or other small boat along with you: in addition to being better transportation than an inner tube when you're ready to go to your intended takeout spot, it's handy for storing food, drink and equipment.

Now that we've discussed the equipment, preparations and cautions for studying water plants and animals with the aid of a mask and snorkel, let's take a look at some of the joys of this method of observation. First of all, this kind of natural observation can lead to the tall tales normally reserved for fishermen because the water itself acts as a magnifying glass, making everything you see look about 20 percent bigger than it really is. If you should see a good-sized bass gaping at you from under a shadowy bank, you may be startled by its apparent size—it looks big enough to be frightening.

Look for crayfish on the bottom, especially in rocky places where they can easily hide under the nearest stone when disturbed. Watch for the strange looking larvae of mayflies, caddisflies and other insects as they cling to plants and stones on the bottom. Caddisfly larvae often look like underwater bagworms because they gather small bits of stone and plants to make a movable case that protects them.

You are likely to see small minnowlike fish in small groups or schools in lakes and streams. There are a number of different species of the minnow family including a handsome one called the bleeding shiner. The bleeding shiner has a dark stripe along its side, red on its gill covers, and bright red on its fins and tail—altogether a beautiful little fish. Duskystripe shiners also are brightly-colored minnows, each with a lengthwise stripe along its side and some red markings.

The sunfish species are all easily recognizable by their deep bodies that are slim from side to side, their prominent gill cover flaps—often brightly colored—and their double dorsal fin with the front half spiked, the rear half smooth. The green sunfish is the most common of this group throughout most of our region. This sunfish has a larger mouth than the others—it extends behind the eye. If you're lucky you may see it feeding on insects, small fish and crayfish. The longear, bluegill and redear sunfishes all are recognizable by their names, which describe their gill cover flaps. Look for the sunfish in places where there are abundant aquatic plants nearby.

The largemouth and smallmouth basses also are members of the sunfish family, although their bodies are longer and not so deep. The largemouth is distinguished by its mouth, which extends well behind the eye. In the smallmouth, the mouth extends only to the eye. Largemouth bass prefer the waters of lakes and slow-moving streams while smallmouth bass are the ones you will find in the clear, cool moving streams such as you find in the Ozarks. Look for bass at the edge of shady places, under overhanging banks and by big rocks.

You will soon discover that the mask and snorkel give you a unique view of the underwater world. You can learn much about the habits of the animals and plants that you see by exploring the fresh-water aquatic world in this way.

HOT(COOL!)SPOTS

The **Buffalo National River** in the Arkansas Ozarks is a beautiful, clear spring-fed Ozark stream that is a joy for naturalists with mask and snorkel. Watch out for places that are too swift for comfort. In between riffles and rapids are slower, wider deeper holes that will be easier to explore in the water. This unpolluted, free-flowing river, 137 miles of beautiful water next to springs, caves and colorful bluffs, was added to our National Park System in 1972. You can get to the major center for visitor activities, Buffalo Point, in the northwestern part of the state by going 17 miles south of Yellville on Arkansas Route 14. Headquarters for this national park is at Buffalo National River Headquarters, Federal Building, Walnut and Erie Streets, Harrison. Be sure to get maps of the area and information about the wildlife (Superintendent, Buffalo National River, P.O. Box 1173, Harrison, AR 72602-1173. Phone 501-741-5443).

Other places in Arkansas that offer lots of promise for under-water exploring with mask and snorkel would be many of the state parks featuring lakes with swimming areas such as the swimming beach at **Lake Ouachita SP** (see Chapter 3 for directions) and the swimming area at **White Oak Lake SP** (see Chapter 13 for directions).

In Missouri there are many clear, spring-fed rivers and streams in the Ozarks that are superb for aquatic investigation with mask and snorkel. A top-notch place to start would be the **Ozark National Scenic Riverways** in southern Missouri. This park includes both the Current and Jacks Forks Rivers, two of the prettiest rivers you'll ever see, 140 miles with caves, springs and tall bluffs. The Riverways is an easy drive from either St. Louis (175 miles) or Kansas City (250 miles). These rivers became part of the National Park System in 1964. Headquarters for the Riverways is in Van Buren in southern Missouri (Superintendent, Ozark National Scenic Riverways, P.O. Box 490, Van Buren, MO 63965. Phone 314-323-4236). Be sure to write for a pamphlet on the park if you plan to go—it's a big area and it will help you decide where to start.

Some of the other places in Missouri you might want to try with mask and snorkel are state parks with swimming beaches on lakes or rivers such as **Lake Wappapello SP** (see Chapter 19 for directions), **Lake of the Ozarks SP** (see Chapter 14 for directions), and **Cuivre River SP** (see Chapter 13 for directions).

44

Fossils Along the Highway

Most of the bedrock of Illinois, Missouri and Arkansas is limestone formed eons ago when the land was a seabed. Preserved in those limestone layers are the fossilized remains of ancient plants and animals. When dead plants and animals were quickly buried by mud, sand or other sediments, there was a good chance that they would become fossilized. Sediments collect all the time at the bottom of the sea which is why so many fossils are found in limestone rocks formed by marine sediments. Highway cuts, quarries and stream beds expose fossils in the limestone layers so that you can easily find them.

Sedimentary rocks such as limestones, dolomites and sandstones contain the majority of fossils. The sandstones are more likely to include significant remnants of vertebrates and plants while the limestones and dolomites are more likely to include remnants of marine plant and animal life.

Plants and animals that are quickly buried rather than eaten or decayed are likely prospects for fossilization, and hard tissues are far more likely to be preserved than soft parts of the organisms. Fossils develop in a number of ways. They may be petrified, in which case other minerals replace the original organic compounds. As water dissolves the substance of the creature or plant, minerals replace those organic substances while keeping the shape of the original object. In another form of petrification, minerals fill the air spaces in bone and shells without changing the shape of the original object. In the carbonization process of fossilization, the substances in the leaves and soft parts of plants and animals are replaced by carbon.

This highway cut demonstrates layered limestone, which may offer a number of different kinds of fossils and ancient imprints.

Molds and casts are another form of fossilization. When plants and animals are buried in mud, clay, or other materials that harden over time, the bodies of the organisms eventually dissolve, leaving hollow molds of the objects. Sometimes the hollows remain and sometimes they slowly fill with other minerals. Another major way that fossils are formed is by prints, molds of footprints left by animals; impressions of skin, fur or feathers left by vertebrates; or impressions of leaves and stems of plants.

Seldom are whole animals and plants found in fossilized forms. When the conditions are right for fossilization, gradually, over long periods of time, the shells, bones and other hard parts of plants and animals are replaced by other minerals. Shells, corals, snails and sea urchins are animals commonly found in fossilized form. Sea worm burrows and trilobite tracks also are found in the rocks that formed ancient seabeds. When you find limestone with lots of shells or other animal remains, you often see casts of the objects themselves plus fossilized imprints of the surfaces. In places where there are coal strip mines, fossils of plant parts are found.

The fossil reservoir of the region includes many *crinoids*, fossilized remains of marine invertebrates, plantlike organisms including sea lilies and feather stars. The crinoid is the official state fossil of Missouri. They had feathery radiating arms on stalks attached to hard surfaces. It is common to find crinoid stems—they have many thin rings making them look like piled up coins. Crinoid stems as large as pencils or even larger are found in some richly fossilized limestones in highway cuts throughout much of our region. You also will find an abundance of brachiopods in some areas. These marine invertebrates are bi-valves with dorsal and ventral shells. A brachiopod is easily recognized by the pair of armlike tentacles on either side of the mouth.

As of 1988, the official state fossil of Illinois was slated to be the Tully Monster, a fossil blob of an invertebrate discovered by an amateur archaeologist named Tully. He found this new species of invertebrate fossil while splitting rocks as he was searching for fossil plants and animals in northern Illinois outcroppings. Other new species of both plants and animals also were found in many of the fossil concretions. Concretions are elongated ironstone rocks that contain intriguing fossils. These concretions are abundant in spoil piles of coal mines. To break a concretion, set it on edge and tap the edge—it should break along its weakest point, which is where the fossil is located.

Local rock shops in your home area are good sources for both information, guide books and equipment. Although many people just sift through loose materials in their search for fossils, a good rock hammer will help you in serious collecting—be sure to wear safety goggles whenever you are using it. A hand lens will help in seeing details. If you moisten pieces of stone, you usually can see details better.

The study of fossils tells us about where ancient seas existed, what the climate was in a particular area, where plants and animals existed in ancient times and other valuable information about prehistoric life on our planet.

When studying fossils, make notes as to where you see or collect each specimen. Before collecting in parks and preserves, be sure to check with the visitors' centers or headquarters to see what the rules are for that particular property. If collecting is against the rules, you can photograph your finds.

HOTSPOTS

Look for outcroppings of limestone about a mile south of **Leslie** on the west side of U.S. Highway 65. The limestone bluff is about 20 feet high and goes along the highway for about a mile. About 4 feet off the ground you will find snail shells scattered through the stone. There are fossilized algal reefs in the northern part of the bluff, and crinoids can be picked out of the top layer.

Follow Arkansas Route 25 south of Batesville, past Locust Grove and about 1.6 miles past the intersection of Arkansas Routes 14 and 25. On the west side of the road is a ditch nearly 4 feet deep. Go past the ditch area to a pull-off area on the left where it is safe to park. The ditch contains a 50-foot length of exposed crinoid stems that can be picked out with only your fingers.

Watch for numerous outcroppings with plentiful fossils west of **Arkadelphia** near the intersection of Arkansas Routes 26 and 51. Look for gray marl, a mix of clays and limestones, in the roadside ditches 100 yards south of the intersection on Highway 51. You will find echinoids (sea urchins) and numerous other fossilized remains of marine organisms.

Newton County has limestone bluffs ripe for finding fossils. Go north on Arkansas Highway 21 through Ozone and Fallsville, then turn left to continue on Highway 21. Nine miles north of this intersection, just after you cross the bridge over Smith Creek, a tributary of the beautiful Buffalo River, you will find a series of large and small limestone bluffs. Look in the talus slopes at the foot of the bluffs for weathered invertebrate fossils. You may want to crack open a few of the rocks to find unweathered specimens.

Take U.S. Highway 64 about 3.5 miles east of **Altus**, Arkansas, in Franklin County to a roadside fill-dirt quarry on the north side of the road. Here you will find fossil plant impressions in the shaly rock. Look in the gray shale and use a knife blade to split the soft layers.

Starved Rock SP in north central Illinois (see Chapter 13 for directions) is a good place to study rock formations and find fossilized plants and animals. Check with the park visitors' center before doing any collecting. Many parks and preserves allow only looking, not collecting.

Near Starved Rock State Park and just south of Utica, Illinois, on Illinois Highway 178 at its intersection with Highway 34 is a quarry noted for fossil plants and animals of the Carboniferous Period of the Paleozoic Era some sixty million years ago. Similar places at Oglesby on Highway 71 at the Vermillion River have fossil plants and invertebrates in road cuts, stream beds, old quarries and spoil banks of abandoned coal mines.

Mastodon SP marks the location of one of the best vertebrate fossil finds of our entire region. In 1839 Albert C. Koch was the first of several explorers who discovered rare fossils here. He unearthed a mastodon at the base of a limestone cliff that, unfortunately, is on display at the Natural History Museum in London rather than in Missouri. More recently, excavations in the 1970s and 1980s yielded Clovis points, flint flakes, and bones from a variety of ancient mammals, evidence that experts believe proves an association of man and the mastodon on this continent. Visit this park for the entire story of the park and its archeological stories (for directions, see Chapter 16).

Cuivre River SP (see Chapter 13 for directions) in east central Missouri has stream beds known for their fossils as does **Rockwood Reservation**, a Department of Conservation preserve in west St. Louis County. To get to Rockwood, take Highway 109 north from I-44 at the Eureka exit a few miles west of I-270 in St. Louis County— the usually dry stream beds here are widely known for excellent trilobites, both rolled and open forms.

Stream beds, road cuts and gravel pits in the Kansas City area in western Missouri will yield a variety of marine fossils, both vertebrate and invertebrate. The same is true for the area around Springfield in southwestern Missouri. Road cuts are great places to look for fossils and also interesting, often beautiful minerals. Do not stop on major highways, but rather look for those with easily accessible outer roads where there will be places you can safely park the car. One of these is south of St. Louis on I-55, then 3 miles south of the I-55 exit to Barnhart along the service road next to the highway. Outcroppings here are known for their brachiopods, gastropods and other invertebrate fossils. For good fossil hunting, check out other road cuts along highways that have outer service roads paralleling them.

45

Prairie Grasses

Grasses become dominant features of prairies in our region in August. Until now the forbs (flowering plants) of the prairies dominated with their beautiful blooms and interesting foliage. Now the taller prairie grasses are reaching maturity, gaining height at the same time that their seedheads are forming.

There is a relationship between blooming time and height in the prairie grasses. Shorter grasses tend to bloom earlier in the year during the spring months while taller grasses bloom in the late summer and fall. Tallgrass prairies, the so-called True Prairie, originally existed throughout the northern three quarters of Illinois, the northern and western two thirds of Missouri, and the extreme northwestern tip of Arkansas. Beyond the tall grass prairies to the west were the Mixed Prairies of forbs plus short and medium-sized grasses.

Today there is increasing effort to preserve, restore and replicate different types of prairies in our region. People are learning more about managing prairielands with fire and fire substitutes such as mowing at the proper time. Recently planted prairies are being started and cared for by educational institutions, highway departments, corporations, departments of conservation, conservation organizations and individuals.

The dominant grasses of the True Prairies are indiangrass and big bluestem. Turkey-foot bluestem is another common name for big bluestem because of its three-branched seed head that resembles a big bird foot. This grass, the most prevalent of all the grasses, also has been called the "Monarch of the Prairie Grasses." The lower leaves are generally covered with fine hairs. Young shoots are fairly flat and the lower leaves curl when dry. Big bluestem is a warm-season perennial grass that begins growing in April or earlier and reaches a height of 8 feet or more by the time the seedheads develop and begin to ripen in August through October. Big bluestem plants turn reddish copper after fall frosts, providing color to the winter landscape. The roots, plentiful in the top 2 feet of soil, may reach a depth of 12 feet—this accounts for its ability to survive drought, heat and fire.

Indiangrass also is a warm-season perennial. This grass reproduces by both seeds and short underground stems. The silky golden seedheads on 5- to 7-foot stems are beautiful in the fall and winter, adding drama to the prairie. Next to big bluestem, this is the most important plant of tallgrass prairies. Indiangrass grows fast on any well draining soil, often maturing in only two years. It grows more erect than big bluestem and, like big bluestem, may grow in bunches and form patches of sod.

Little bluestem, another warm-season perennial, is a popular ornamental grass with leaves that range through a variety of greens and blues. The plants turn bright red in the fall and are topped by silvery white fluffy seedheads. Little bluestem's extensive root system may grow as much as 5 feet deep. Two- to five-foot seed stalks appear on the 2- to 3-foot plants from late August to October. In the early days of this country, little bluestem was the most prevalent grass of the prairies. It will thrive on mesic and dry soils.

Switchgrass, a sod-forming, native warm-season perennial, has vigorous roots and reproduces from both seed and underground stems. The easiest way to identify this grass is by the small area of thick short hairs where the leaf blade attaches to the sheath. The large airy seedheads grow on 3- to 6-foot stalks and are a lovely golden color in the fall. This grass will form a sod on fertile ground and, although it's tolerant of drought, grows best in moist soils.

Prairie dropseed, a perennial warm-season grass, is my favorite of all the native grasses. Its leaves grow in a large round tuft a foot or more in diameter and about a foot tall. The open, airy seedheads grow 2 to 3 feet tall in a sort of a halo over the leaves. This elegant plant is very popular with gardeners who cultivate native plants, making a great addition to just about any garden—it grows well in most dry soils.

Sideoats grama is a medium-sized, warm-season perennial grass that grows about 2 to 3 feet tall and has tiny purple and orange flower spikes, one of the handsomest of all the grasses. When the

Little bluestem is a major prairie grass, particularly in uplands areas, and forms bunches up to three feet tall.

seeds develop, they are all suspended on one side of the stem, which is what gives the plant its name. This grass thrives on dry soils.

These grasses stand out among the prairie grasses as very robust and adaptive plants; they are long-lived and will grow in a wide variety of soils and moisture conditions. They once covered most of the immense midwestern grasslands and, along with over a hundred different wildflowers, these grasses helped build the fertile soil that today produces record amounts of corn, wheat, beans and other important crops.

HOTSPOTS

In Arkansas, two joint projects of The Nature Conservancy, Arkansas Field Office, and the Arkansas Natural Heritage Commission are **Railroad Prairie State Natural Area** in the east central part of the state and **Warren Prairie** in the southeastern part of the state. (See Chapter 26 for directions to both.) Contact the field office for maps and plant lists. (The Nature Conservancy address and phone number are in the Appendix.)

Illinois has every right to be very proud of **Markham Prairie** in the Chicago area which has about 300 acres of native grasslands and wetland. This preserve is a National Landmark that is a property of The Nature Conservancy, Illinois Field Office, and is managed by

Northeastern Illinois University. Markham Prairie is the largest re-maining tallgrass prairie of top quality in Illinois (for directions, see Chapter 26). For the sake of this valuable habitat, be sure to stay on the trails when visiting.

Another prairie area west of Chicago is **Nachusa Grasslands** (see directions in Chapter 26). This preserve also is owned by The Nature Conservancy, Illinois Field Office. Western Illinois University manages this prairie that is just west of Rochelle and north of Franklin Grove, between Ashton and Dixon on the Lowden Road. There are several hundred acres of rolling prairie hillsides. Contact the Illinois Field Office of The Nature Conservancy before visiting either of these prairies to get brochures and trail guides. They sometimes have guided tours. (The address and phone number of the office are in the Appendix.)

Squaw Creek NWR (see Chapter 1 for directions) in north-western Missouri has upland prairie on the loess hills with good collections of native grasses. This refuge has both auto tour routes and hiking trails. **Pershing SP** in central Missouri has a rare example of bottomland wet prairie, a habitat that used to be common in river valleys. (For directions, see Chapter 26.)

The **Missouri Botanical Garden's Shaw Arboretum** at Gray Summit, west of St. Louis, has an impressive replicated prairie area that will have spring wildflowers. Stop at the gatehouse to get a brochure telling you how to get to the prairie. (For directions, see Chapter 2.)

Over in western Missouri in St. Clair County is **Taberville Prairie Conservation Area**, a property owned by the Missouri Department of Conservation that includes over 1,000 acres of prairie with more acreage being restored to prairie. In addition to upland Ozark border prairie with over four hundred plant species, this preserve has a permanent flock of prairie chickens in residence. This preserve is a Missouri Natural Area and a National Natural Landmark. To get there, go .5 mile east of Appleton City on Highway 52, then 2 miles south on Highway A, and 7 miles south on Highway H.

46

Sparrows—
Those Little Brown Birds

The sparrows, those little brown birds of woods and fields, are confusing to beginning birders—and to all of us—when they are viewed under less than ideal conditions. Sparrows are members of the same family that includes grosbeaks, finches, crossbills and buntings.

The birds of this family have wedge-shaped seed-cracking bills that are used with great dexterity to crack hard seed coats and extricate the tender embryos. The grosbeaks have very large thick bills, crossbills have seed-eating bills that actually cross at the tips, and the sparrows, finches and buntings have bills that are rather like those of Old World canaries. Small fruits, seeds and insects make up the diet of sparrows.

Favorites of Illinois, Missouri and Arkansas birders are the song sparrow, white-throated sparrow, white-crowned sparrow, chipping sparrow and field sparrow. Since the white-throated and white-crowned sparrows are winter residents, I'll take a closer look at them in a later chapter when they are inclined to be in our region. And what about the immigrant Eurasian tree sparrow that lives in limited areas of the St. Louis bi-state region? Although commonly called a sparrow, this bird with its distinctive black cheek spot is a weaver finch closely related to the English "sparrow," both part of a group of Old World birds that belong to a totally different family.

The sparrow family is the largest family of birds with between five hundred and six hundred species that are found in all parts of the world except Australia. As seed eaters, they are less affected by cold weather than are the insect eaters, whose favorite diet items either die or go into hidden hibernation during winter. Some sparrows are with us all year long, while others are migrants or are with us as temporary residents during one or more seasons. Some of our best avian songsters are in the sparrow family.

The chipping sparrow or chippy, also known as the hair bird because of its nest-building habits, is common throughout our region during the summer breeding season; it winters from our southern states down into Mexico and Central America. It is found year-round in southern Arkansas. This chestnut-capped sparrow with the plain pale breast is one of the tamest of all the wild birds, frequently nesting close to human habitation. It returns to its summer home in early April and its simple monotonous chant can be heard beginning early in the morning.

The chipping sparrow eats both insects and seeds, and is especially fond of fall weed seeds such as ragweed, purslane and plantain. The chippy is an enemy of several pernicious pests, including gypsy moth, army worm, canker worm, beet worm, cabbage worm and pea louse.

This bird builds its nest in shrubs or thick vines. The nest is a neat, hair-lined construction that holds three to five bright bluish green eggs that are spotted with dark brownish or black markings that are especially prominent near the larger end. Incubation, which is shared by both sexes, takes ten to twelve days. In only a week and a half, the young chippies feather out and show streaked breasts unlike the parents' pale breasts. As the young birds mature, the streaking fades.

These birds, well known near human residences, also frequent dry hilltops of the Ozarks and the bald cypress swamps of the southern lowland areas of our region. Chipping sparrows of the northern areas gather in weedy fields in the fall until winter winds drive them farther south.

The field sparrow is a permanent resident throughout our region, although some of these birds spend their summers farther north and winter farther south. Its field marks are the pink bill and legs, rufous upper parts with unstreaked breast and whitish underparts. The field sparrow is rather shy, frequenting old pastures dotted with bushy clumps and cedars. When alarmed it will fly off to land on a bare twig at or near the top of a bush or small tree. The song is clear and pensive, sounding like *cher-wee, cher-wee, cher-wee.*

Field sparrows build their cuplike nests of coarse grasses, small weed stalks and rootlets, placing them on the ground or in low bushes. The nest may be lined with hair or fine grasses. Three to five bluish white eggs speckled with brown are the usual clutch. The field sparrow and its young are enthusiastic eaters of insect pests and so are considered valuable birds by knowledgeable farmers and gardeners.

The field sparrow male is first heard at breeding stands during the first half of March. Both singing and nesting go on all summer and then, in late September, field sparrows gather in small flocks that may include other kinds of sparrows. Those that migrate leave by mid-November although some small troops regularly winter in the forests and woods of our region.

The song sparrow's other common names attest to its popularity—silver tongue, everybody's darling, groundbird, red grass-bird and swamp finch. While song sparrows are year-round residents throughout much of our three-state region, transient song sparrows also come through our area in the spring on their way to Canadian breeding grounds and in the fall on their way to winter grounds along the Gulf states to southern Arkansas.

This common bird is often found near or on the ground near undergrowth and, most often, near a brook or pond. If startled, the song sparrow flushes in jerky flight, pumping its tail as it heads for the nearest bush. The impatient *chink* or *tsink* of the call note is as diagnostic as the bird's spotted and streaked breast with one large dark spot in the center.

Weedy and grassy corners where there is an abundance of seeds are favorite places for these birds. Very retiring—except in song—they will slip into brush heaps and thick bushes almost before you can see them. About two thirds of their diet is seeds while the rest includes insects.

The great ornithologist of the turn of the century, Frank M. Chapman, called the song sparrow "the modest, lowly avian minstrel of the briar-patch—the most persistent singer of them all. The magic of his voice bridges the cold months of early spring." Some say its song says, "Maids! Maids! Maids! Hang up your teakettle-ettle-ettle," or, "Madge, Madge, Madge—put on the tea kettle-le-le." The male song sparrow is the leading performer but the female sometimes joins the chorus in the spring before nesting begins. Young song sparrows begin practicing the typical songs as soon as they fledge. They begin with random warbling, but soon add series of notes that resemble those of the adult. By spring, the maturing birds of last season will have perfected the notes and the stresses and be singing like pros.

In April the song sparrows build their nests of grass, setting them on the ground beneath grassy tufts of brambles or in bushes or low limbs of trees. The eggs are pale greenish white with thick markings of lavender, purple or brown. Too often, the cowbird finds the song sparrow nest and lays its larger egg. The cowbird baby then crowds the sparrow hatchlings out of the nest and the parents are left struggling to raise this large bird that has been foisted off on them.

Within only ten days the young leave the nest and are on their own soon after that. Song sparrows raise up to three broods a year. Those that raise multiple broods usually sing later into the summer than those with only a single brood. The August song is a husky warble, unlike the bright cheery spring carol of this bird. When their nest and young are threatened, song sparrows are brave little creatures. They stand fearlessly in a position of defense, with outstretched wings and depressed tails, guarding their offspring.

At the end of severe winters when snow and ice are still a part of the landscape and trees are bleak and bare, the song sparrow's bright song from the top of a small tree or bush brings cheer and the promise of spring into our lives.

HOTSPOTS

The three sparrows described above are found throughout the national wildlife refuges located all along the Mississippi and Illinois rivers. Here they find the kind of habitat in which they can thrive.

Wapanocca NWR in northeastern Arkansas includes at its heart the 600-acre **Wapanocca Lake** that is an old oxbow of the Mississippi River (For directions, see Chapter 1). Bottomland forests and the croplands of the refuge's farm unit combine with cypress and willow swamps to make this area an ideal haven for many birds, including sparrows.

The varied habitat of **Felsenthal NWR** (see Chapter 2 for directions) in southeastern Arkansas is another good area for sparrows as well as many other birds. Get the trail maps and hints as to good birding spots from the headquarters buildings or visitors' kiosk.

Visit **Petit Jean SP** in west central Arkansas between the Ozark and Ouachita mountains (see Chapter 14 for directions). Here you will find 3,471 acres of unusual natural beauty and likely habitat for a number of sparrows. A system of trails will take you easily to this park's natural secrets; along the way you may see wildlife of the area.

Chautauqua NWR (see Chapter 1 for directions) in west central Illinois, along with the Brussels, Gardner and Annada districts of the **Mark Twain NWR Complex** (see Chapter 3 for directions), are noted places to study sparrows. Get the maps and a few suggestions from staff at one of the offices before heading out into this giant refuge complex.

In northern Illinois, **Goose Lake Prairie State Natural Area** is another likely place to look for sparrows (see Chapter 34 for directions). This is a big, fairly new Illinois State Park that includes all types of prairies, marshes and potholes bordered by willows. In addition to birds, you will see prairie flowers, ground hogs, coyote, fox and deer.

Mingo NWR in southeast Missouri and **Squaw Creek NWR** in north central Missouri are great places in this state for seeking the sparrows as well as a multitude of other birds (see Chapter 1 for directions).

Another place in Missouri to check on wildlife, including some of the sparrows, is **Sam A. Baker SP** in southeast Missouri. This park in the St. Francois Mountains features an unspoiled wilderness surrounding Mudlick Mountain. Both Big Creek and the St. Francois rivers border the park. Check in with the nature center to see where the birding might be best when you are there. To get there, go 3 miles north of Patterson on Highway 143 in Wayne County.

47

August Shorttakes

Sumac Fruits

Watch for the fruits of smooth sumac to turn from green to rosy red to maroon as they ripen. They grow at the terminal of sumac growth, forming clusters of small berries.

Male White-tailed Deer

The antlers of the male white-tailed deer are maturing. They become itchy and the bucks remove the velvet from the tines by rubbing their antlers against small trees. Look for signs of these rubbing places at deer height on understory trees.

Fall Molting

Watch for cardinals, robins and other birds to look drab and shabby as they molt prior to fall. Sometimes I have seen birds with no feathers on their heads at this time of year—experts say that is the result of bird mites and lice influencing molting.

See also:

Chapter 20, Ruby-throated Hummingbirds. Watch for increased numbers of these birds this month as they begin to migrate.
Chapter 22, Spring Wood Warblers. The so-called "confusing"

fall warblers begin coming through our region this month—they all look alike!

Chapter 36, Breakout: Starry Nights of Summer. Look in the vicinity of the constallation of Perseus after midnight this month for the Perseids Meteor Shower.

Chapter 56, Waterfowl Migration. Mallards, gadwalls, teals, pintails and shovelers will be passing through or returning to our wetlands for the winter months.

Chapter 64, Accidentals, Rarities and Oddities in the Birding World. Look for unusual species of birds that wander or are blown off course into our region at this time of year.

48

Breakout:
Summer Flowers

The flowers of summer in our region are, for the most part, flowers of the prairies. They thrive on heat and sun which we usually have plenty of in this heartland part of the country. Where prairies have disappeared you will find these flowers along roadsides, in abandoned fields and, increasingly, in gardens since native plants have become so popular. In original, restored and replicated prairies there are multitudes of bright flowers at this time of year.

You will see many plants of the composite or daisy family, easy to recognize with their central disk flowers ringed by the outer ray flowers. Coneflowers, sunflowers, asters, black-eyed Susans—all are in the family of composites, probably the most-represented plant family in our region.

There are several coneflowers to enjoy in late summer. The gray-headed coneflower has yellow ray flowers that droop around the gray central disk florets. The pale purple coneflower has magenta, rosy or sometimes white ray flowers surrounding a knoblike center of disk flowers. Its ray flowers are sparse and thin. The purple coneflower has a purple-brown central disk surrounded by sturdy magenta ray flowers. Coneflowers are husky plants that have been taken into gardens with great enthusiasm—they will stand up to wind and storms better than most. Their flowers last a long time, bringing bright splashes of color wherever they grow.

Black-eyed Susans or rudbeckias also are sturdy flowers of prairies and other sunny places. The leaves of these plants vary from simple to lobed, from smooth-edged to serrate or toothed—the leaves are hairy and rough to the touch. The black-eyed Susan has ray flowers of a rich golden color surrounding a central circle of deep brown, nearly black disk florets. Actually, there are two black-eyed Susans, the common one and the smaller very hairy Missouri black-eyed Susan.

There also is a brown-eyed Susan that has smaller flowers than the others and also a central circle of disk florets that are more brown than black. Others in this group include the sweet coneflower and wild goldenglow or tall coneflower. Sweet coneflower has a semi-domed dark brown disk surrounded by yellow ray florets—this plant is tall, to 6 feet, branched, and grows in low moist sites. Tall coneflower, with a green disk center and under a dozen ray florets, also grows in low moist areas but it is usually not branched.

A number of asters grow in sunny sites such as found in prairies, fields and roadsides. New England asters may grow to 8 feet and are well branched, especially toward the ends of their stems. Narrow lance-shaped leaves clasp the green stems. The 1-inch-wide flowers have blue to purple or sometimes rose ray florets surrounding yellow disk flowers. White heath asters have many narrow leaves and flowers that consist of white ray flowers surrounding a yellow disk—they grow to a maximum height of 5 feet. The many-branched aromatic or oblong-leafed aster is shorter, rarely reaching 3 feet, and has blue to purple to rosy purple ray flowers around yellow disks.

Compassplant is a composite that grows to 8 feet. Its leaves are deeply lobed and huge, well over a foot long. During very hot weather, the leaves orient themselves in a north-south manner thus increasing the amount of sunlight they receive. The flowers have yellow disk and ray florets that develop at the ends of the branches.

The colorful tall ironweeds also are in the composite family. They grow in fields, glades, roadsides and riversides. Their leaves are hairy, alternate and lance-shaped with finely toothed or smooth edges. The rosy purple flowers have no ray flowers, just disk flowers with many florets to each multiple flowerhead. Both ironweed and great ironweed often grow in large spectacular clumps. Great ironweed blooms after ironweed. Tall ironweed and western ironweed are other species adding to the confusion of the several ironweeds.

The mint family is well represented in sun-loving plants of prairies, roadsides and fields. Mountain mint with its many small, opposite slender leaves has white flowers in thick half-domed inflorescenses. The plant smells delightfully like mint or sage. Monada is another mint family plant that blooms handsomely at this time of year. The opposite lance-shaped leaves are very slightly toothed. The lavender, lilac or rose flowers have minty lipped florets that develop in a circle. Prairie hyssop, another member of the mint family, grows to nearly 3 feet and has flowers in headlike clusters. Each small pale flower is spotted with purple.

Culver's root is an odd name for a handsome prairie plant that is in the same family as figworts, snapdragons and gooseberries. The plants grow to 6 feet with individual white to sometimes pink flowers on terminal spikes, several spikes rising from a single stem. The serrated leaves grow in whorls around the stems.

Representatives of the milkweed family bloom throughout the summer. These plants contain poisons that the monarch butterfly is immune to—they eat the milkweeds and so become poisonous themselves. Birds avoid them and the similar viceroy that is tasty, but resembles the monarch butterfly. The most beautiful of the milk-weeds is butterfly weed that does, indeed, attract many butterflies to its spectacular scarlet to orange umbel flowers. It has narrow, lancelike leaves that are very dark green and much smaller than the other milkweeds described here.

Two other milkweeds commonly in bloom in prairies, road-sides, edges of woods and other sunny sites are the purple milkweed and common milkweed. Purple milkweed has magenta to rose-magenta flowers in large terminal umbels above large, broad oval leaves. Common milkweed has large fragrant umbels of pink to rosy lavender flowers and large broad leaves. All of the milkweeds have long seedpods that when ripe release many seeds, each with its own "sail" of silky floss that will travel on the slightest breeze, spreading the plants far and wide.

Leadplant is a member of the pea or legume family that is brightly in bloom in late summer. Growing to 3 feet, it has gray, compound featherlike leaves and small purple and orange flowers that grow in tight spikes arranged loosely at the ends of stems. The name probably comes from its gray foliage. This plant is one of the very few woody shrubs found in prairies.

SEPTEMBER

September Observations

49

Mushrooms of Fall

In the fall the world of fungus brings a large assortment of the fruiting bodies we know as mushrooms. The fruiting bodies often are in colors, patterns and shapes that blend in perfectly with their surroundings. Some are very small and easy to overlook. Others appear underneath bark, logs and in other sheltered spots. Fungus often appears in dark damp places, adding to the mystery of this group of organisms that appear so dramatically and disappear as quickly.

Fungi are all around us. The microscopic spores float through the air all over the world. Where they land in hospitable environments, they begin to grow. Hospitable environments are those that have plant or animal matter upon which fungi can feed since they have no chlorophyll and are not able to manufacture their own food. The best time to find mushrooms and other fleshy fungi is the day after a rain when these fruiting bodies have grown in record style thanks to the moisture.

Some experts class the fungi in a separate grouping that is neither animal nor plant. In our region, some estimate that nearly eight hundred species of fungi with fleshy fruiting bodies occur.

The main body of each of these strange organisms is called *mycelium* and consists of a large network of threadlike growth mostly under the surface of the soil or organic matter upon which the fungus is growing. When the mycelium matures, the fruiting bodies appear and release fertile spores.

When you collect fungi, wrap the individuals separately or in similar groupings in a twist of waxed paper or put them in sandwich bags so that you can check identification later. Baskets are handy for carrying specimens. Spore prints made later are a surer way to help identify fungi.

If you want to learn about the wild edible mushrooms, be sure to learn from an expert. Even then, you should know that some people are strongly affected by certain fungal fruits that do not bother others a whit. It is wise to learn one kind of wild mushroom at a time and to proceed cautiously. There is an old saying, "There are no old bold mushroom eaters." Mycological society contacts are listed in the Appendix.

For those who have learned to prize and use the edible mushrooms, chanterelles are stars of summer and fall. The fleshy fruiting bodies appear in colors from pale smoky yellow to red. Many look like trumpets with gill-like folds that run at least part way down the stem. One of the most common groups of fungus, chanterelles bear spores on those gill-like folds underneath the cap.

Interestingly, chanterelles are more closely related to the coral fungi than they are to the true mushrooms. Coral fungi grow upright and often branching in colonies on moist soil, old dead wood or other plant debris. They look much like sea corals and grow in colonies up to a foot wide if conditions are ideal. More often they are smallish fungi of pale colors ranging from white to yellow or pinkish yellow.

Polypores are bracket fungi fruiting bodies that grow mostly on dead branches and stumps, and when parasitic, on living tree trunks. Many are very woody and decay slowly, therefore they are about the most commonly seen fungi of the woods at most times of year. They have pores on their under surfaces that contain spore-producing tissue. Unlike most fungi, some polypores are perennial, living for several years.

An unusual polypore is hen of the woods, a choice edible that is large and ruffly, grayish brown on top and white underneath. White stalks grow from a common base. You may find this fungus growing in huge clusters, some weighing several pounds, at the base of oaks and other hardwoods. A similar-looking fungus is chicken of the woods, which is orange on top and yellow or white underneath. It is considered a choice edible although some people may have allergic reactions to it.

Puffballs and related fungi are part of the fungal group called stomach fungi (gasteromycetes), identified by fruiting bodies that remain closed containers until the spores are mature and free within the sac. Most people are familiar with this phenomenon because of the way puffballs release their dark spores if you step on them when

This bracket or shelf fungus is growing on a dead branch that has fallen to the ground. This type of fungus may continue to grow for many years.

they are ripe. The bellows action of the outer sac makes the spores spew out. The fascinating fruiting bodies called bird's nest fungi, stinkhorns and earth stars also are in this puffball group.

Bird's nest fungi look like miniature birds' nests, complete with tiny "eggs" which are the spore-holding sacs. Common in summer and fall, these fruiting bodies have concave cups that hold the spore sacs until rain splashes them out and away from the cups. Bird's nest fungi range from pale buff to dark reddish brown with white to purple-brown spore sacs.

You will probably smell stinkhorn or carrion fungi before you see them. The unpleasant smell attracts flies and other insects that eat the foul-smelling slime that appears on the top or sides of the stalk. What a clever technique! The dark slime holds the spores and sticks to the insects. Thus the insects carry the spores both externally and internally, spreading stinkhorns to new sites.

Earth stars look like puffballs set within a star-shaped outer layer that has split and folded back from the inner fruiting body. Like the puffball, earth stars have spores that ripen within and then puff out of the central part of the fungus. Giant white puffballs, many the sizes of a soccer ball or even larger, grow at this time of year. During years with lots of rain, all fungi will be more plentiful, larger and fleshier than in dry years. Quite round, these are white fruiting bodies with no sign of an open pore such as you'd find in earth stars at the top of the dome.

True mushrooms, agarics and boletes are two kinds of fungi in the same botanical group, the club fungi (Basidiomycetes). True mushrooms have central stems and gills underneath their caps. The common cultivated mushroom of grocery stores is a true mushroom, as are a number of other delectable edibles, and also some that are deadly. Yet others will cause strong systemic reactions in some people but not in others.

Boletes as a group are common throughout North America with more than two hundred species known. Also known as fleshy pore fungi because of the pores rather than gills on the underside of the caps, these fruiting bodies are terrestrial and generally appear during the summer and fall, often in association with deciduous hardwoods such as oaks. The caps themselves, shallowly domed and generally on top of sturdy central stems, range from cream through yellow and orange to shades of brown. Being soft and often supporting a population of insect larvae, boletes decay and disappear quite quickly. The ripe spores fall from the pores and are scattered by the breezes to other sites. Some boletes are edible while others definitely are not.

Destroying angel and death cap are names of two of the more infamous mushrooms in the *amanita* family that includes many extremely poisonous species. The toxic amanitas cause the majority of fatal mushroom poisonings—experts recommend that you wash your hands after handling them. Amanitas often are recognizable by the veil or partial veil that originally enclosed the gills and often is left as a remnant or skirt around the stem just below the cap. Amanitas come in a range of cap colors from cream to yellow to scarlet.

There are a number of good mushroom guides available, including some written specifically for our region. If you are inclined to eat wild mushrooms, be absolutely *sure* of what you are eating.

HOTSPOTS

Throughout Illinois, Missouri and Arkansas there are plenty of places to hunt for fungi. Moist deciduous woods are prime habitat for fungal fruiting bodies. Specimens of different fungi grow almost everywhere especially when there's been plenty of rain. Because the microscopic spores are carried around the world through all climatic zones on currents of air, you will find fungi wherever the conditions are right for them. Whenever you visit a park or preserve, be sure to check with the visitors' center or staff to see if collecting fungi is allowed. If it is not, you still can "collect" with your camera.

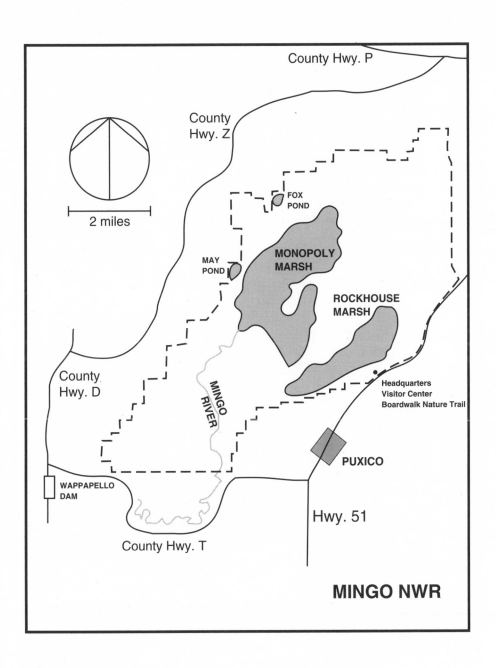

County Hwy. P

County
Hwy. Z

2 miles

FOX
POND

MONOPOLY
MARSH

MAY
POND

ROCKHOUSE
MARSH

County
Hwy. D

MINGO
RIVER

Headquarters
Visitor Center
Boardwalk Nature Trail

WAPPAPELLO
DAM

PUXICO

Hwy. 51

County Hwy. T

MINGO NWR

In southeastern Arkansas, the deciduous forests of **White River NWR** (see Chapter 15 for directions) should have a variety of summer and fall fungi for studying. The beautiful woods, springs, streams and ravines of **Petit Jean SP** (see Chapter 14 for directions) between the Ozark and Ouachita mountains in west central Arkansas offer a variety of habitat for mushrooming.

Bottomland forests along the Illinois River are likely places to look for mushrooms and other fungi in **Chautauqua NWR** (see Chapter 1 for directions) in west central Illinois. The Shawnee Hill country of **Trail of Tears State Forest** in southern Illinois is another place to look for mushrooms during the summer and fall (see Chapter 19 for directions).

Deciduous bottomland forests of **Swan Lake NWR** (see Chapter 8 for directions) in north central Missouri are good places to look for summer and fall fungi. **Mingo NWR** in southeastern Missouri is a great place for mushrooming (see Chapter 1 for directions). In the southeastern part of the state, **Lake Wappapello SP** offers plenty of good Ozark terrain for hunting down mushrooms and other fungi. (See Chapter 19 for directions.)

50

Bird Migrations in Wetlands

Shorebirds, those creatures you see in numbers on mud flats, poke in the sand and mud of shallow water and run along sandy or muddy shores. They tend to travel in flocks and often are tough to identify. Sandpipers of a number of species comprise the major birds included in the catch-all word, shorebirds. Plovers, oystercatchers, stilts and avocets also are shorebirds, but in our region most of the shorebirds you will see are sandpipers. Many of them are long-range migrants that we see only in the spring and fall as they stop to rest on their way to winter or summer homes in Central and South America or the far North.

In coastal regions, you will see shorebirds searching for the invertebrates that make up their diet in intertidal areas. Inland areas attract shorebirds to the gently sloping mud and sand flats of flood-plains, backwaters, sewage lagoons and other similar spots. In some places, you will meet the best birders at the sewage lagoons of the area.

Note that although fall is a high point in the migration pattern, many of these shorebirds begin migrating early, a few in early summer. The long-range migratory shorebirds are at home over a wide territory and thus may often be seen uncommonly far from their usual haunts—this of course, creates confusion among amateur and experienced birders alike. Most shorebirds are clad in similar tweedy patterns of brown and gray, and look much alike when you first see them puddling along hunting for invertebrates in the mud and sand. It's only when you take the time to observe them carefully and consult your fieldguide that you begin to see the subtle differences that will help you tell one from another.

A major key in identifying shorebirds is the shape of the bird, including not just the overall shapes but also the relative lengths of bodies and legs, of necks and bodies, of bills and heads. Knowing the shapes will also help you avoid misidentifications of birds that may have faded plumage, legs of a confusing color or other misleading features. Remember that fall plumage may be in sharp contrast to the breeding plumage of spring, another reason for using shapes as the primary identification characteristic.

Although it's exciting to find an unusual shorebird such as the slim, long-legged American avocet with its odd upturned bill, it's easier to get to know the more common shorebirds well. Let's take a closer look at some of the more common sandpipers. This group includes greater yellowlegs, lesser yellowlegs, solitary sandpiper, spotted sand- piper, semipalmated sandpiper, least sandpiper, sanderling, pectoral sandpiper, shortbilled dowitcher and longbilled dowitcher.

Sandpipers travel long distances to their breeding grounds far to the north, often well within the Arctic Circle. They are extremely gregarious except during the breeding season when each pair of sandpipers nests in its own territory and guards it fiercely. Most sandpipers have three distinct plumages: juvenile, nonbreeding and breeding. Sandpipers feed on mollusks, insect larvae, crustaceans, earthworms, seaworms, sandhoppers and, in some cases, on grass and grain seeds.

Greater yellowlegs and lesser yellowlegs do indeed have legs that are yellow to orange. The 14-inch greater yellowlegs is a larger stouter bird with larger leg joints than the 10-inch lesser yellowlegs, all of which you might guess from their names. The long bill of the greater yellowlegs is slightly upturned whereas that of the lesser yellowlegs is straight. In flight, both birds have dark wings with whitish rumps and tails. The greater yellowlegs also may be told by its three-note call that is said to sound like a strong exclamation: *Dear! Dear! Dear!* The lesser yellowlegs usually has a one- or two-note call and it is lower and less forceful. These birds are great travelers, win- tering in Argentina to Tierra del Fuego.

The 8-inch solitary sandpiper has white eye rings, olive green legs, dark wings and pale undersides with lower throat, breast and sides streaked with dark brown. It is seen both singly and in small groups as it passes through our region in the fall on its way to South America, although each pair nests in lone seclusion in the evergreen forests of the far North. Note the way it keeps its wings unfolded for a short time after it lands, and also the way it bobs its tail.

The small 7- to 8-inch spotted sandpiper in breeding plumage is gray-brown on top and has a white breast and belly spotted with black. In flight, the wings have a short white wing stripe and a short white trailing edge. Its bill is shorter compared with that of the solitary sandpiper. Both the spotted and the solitary sandpipers have calls that sound like *Weet! Weet!* they give while standing and in flight. The call of the solitary sandpiper is more shrill than that of the spotted sandpiper.

The sanderlings of fall and winter are our palest sandpipers, pale gray on top and white underneath. These small 7- to 8-inch birds winter all along the North American seacoast and nest in Arctic regions. These are birds you see in flocks rushing along the edges of ocean waves, endlessly running back and forth as they hunt for crustaceans and other food. In our region, we occassionally see them on mud flats, often with dowitchers, when they are passing through.

The small 6-inch semipalmated sandpiper has black legs and a short, stout black bill that looks almost tubular since it is somewhat expanded at the tip. In fall and winter, it is grayish on top and whitish underneath. It has a narrow pale eye ring and pale eyebrow. The sparrow-sized least sandpiper is very similar but smaller than the semipalmated sandpiper, only about 5 inches in length. The least sandpiper has a short thin bill that turns down slightly. This bird has a pale stripe lengthwise on each side of its brown back. The underparts of the least sandpiper are whitish with brown and buff streaks on the breast.

Pectoral sandpipers are larger 8- to 9-inch birds with breasts prominently streaked with dark brown against a buff background, in contrast to the belly that is solid white. The neck is relatively longer than that of the smaller sandpipers. The upper side of the pectoral sandpiper is a tweedy brown—its feathers are dark brown with paler edges. The pectoral sandpiper also has a pale eyebrow that broadens behind the eye, and beak and legs that are of a dull greenish yellow color.

Shortbilled and longbilled dowitchers are similar and used to be considered as one species. Recognize dowitchers by their chunky shapes, long bills and the white wedge that appears from the barred tail to the middle of the back in flight. Their tails are barred black and white or black and cinnamon. Their distinctive feeding pattern on mud flats is a fast jabbing motion almost as if they are imitating a sewing machine.

Studying the voices of shorebirds will reinforce your ability to identify these often confusing birds. When you hear birders refer to "peeps," you should know that they are lumping the several species of similar small sandpipers into a group of "little brown birds." In other words, they are content to know that these are small brown sandpipers and not worry about the specific species—you may as well do the same!

HOTSPOTS

The National Wildlife Refuges in Arkansas each has recorded at least one, and usually several of the sandpipers during the fall migration season. Look for fall sandpipers at **Felsenthal NWR** (for directions, see Chapter 2) in southeastern Arkansas, **Holla Bend NWR** (see Chapter 7 for directions) in the east central part of the state, **Wapannoca NWR** (see Chapter 1 for directions) in northeastern Arkansas and **White River NWR** (see Chapter 15 for directions) in the east central region of the state.

In Illinois, look for fall sandpipers in the **Brussels District** and **Gardener Division** of the **Mark Twain NWR Complex** (see Chapter 3 for directions). Perhaps the greatest place to study shorebirds in Illinois is **Illinois Beach SP** where more than 260 species of birds have been recorded over the past fifteen years (see Chapter 7 for directions). This park, which stretches along 6.5 miles of sandy beach on Lake Michigan in northern Illinois, encompasses the only remaining beach ridge shoreline left in the state. In addition to the great opportunities for birding, there are some 650 species of native plants in the rich natural areas of the park. When you visit Illinois Beach State Park, go first to the interpretive center located southeast of the main entrance to get maps and information on where birds are being seen that day.

One of the best places in Missouri to look for fall sandpipers is **Riverland EDA** near the new **Melvin Price Locks and Dam** on the Missouri shore in the east central part of the state (see Chapter 1 for directions). Here, the St. Louis Audubon Society, U.S. Army Corps of Engineers, and the Webster Groves Nature Study Society (WGNSS) have cooperated in developing a shorebird habitat area where gently sloping mudflats will be maintained for sandpipers, plovers and other shorebirds. Water will be lowered in some of the sloughs during the migration seasons in order to provide ample mudflats for shorebirds. Ornithologists have discovered that the birds will pass through the region without stopping if they can't find their favorite habitat.

Other good sites for finding shorebirds in Missouri include the National Wildlife Refuges. Look for shorebirds along the shallow mudflats and shores in the **Annada District** of the **Mark Twain NWR Complex** (see Chapter 3 for directions) in east central Missouri, **Mingo NWR** (see Chapter 1 for directions) in the southeastern part of the state, **Squaw Creek NWR** (see Chapter 1 for directions) in northwestern Missouri and **Swan Lake NWR** (see Chapter 8 for directions) in north central Missouri.

51

Lizards: Iguanas and Skinks

Our region is noted for an interesting group of native lizards that includes species more likely to be found in deserts. Lizards are grouped into the same biological order as snakes because they share certain characteristics. Both have lower jaws that are attached to the upper jaw in a special way that allows them to open their jaws very wide in order to swallow large animals they have caught. Both have scaly skins that are periodically shed and both are cold-blooded. In some ways, the so-called cold-blooded animals are more adaptable to their environments than the warm-blooded birds and mammals since they can conserve their energy better and need less food when weather turns cool.

The largest group of lizards in the western hemisphere is the family best represented by the iguanas, large lizards of Mexico and Central America. In our region we have three members of that family. Most common of them is the fence lizard, prevalent throughout Arkansas, southern Illinois and the southern half of Missouri. Fence lizards are small, usually about 6 inches long, and are usually some shade of tan, gray or brown. Females have wavy dark lines running from side to side on their backs and off-white bellies that may have pale spots. Males are dark brown or gray on their backs with very little or no markings and bellies that are an intense blue. Fence lizards eat insects and spiders, hunting most actively in the morning before the heat of the day and again when it begins to cool down in late afternoon and early evening. They are most often seen when they are sunning themselves on a rock or tree trunk. These lizards live in open woods or the edges of forests where they like to include dead trees, rock piles and brush piles in their range. When startled, they run very rapidly under rocks or up a tree, always staying on the far side of the trunk to avoid detection. If you catch one it may drop off its tail, which will wiggle for a while—a ploy that is used to decoy and escape predators.

The second iguanid is the Texas horned lizard, often called the horned toad, which is more common in the desert Southwest. In our region, the horned lizard is found in southwestern Missouri and western Arkansas. Adults are usually 6 inches or less in length. These stocky lizards have several sharp projections sticking out from the back of their heads. Their base color is tan to grayish to brown with two darker brown spots behind their heads and other brown spots on either side of a pale line down the middle of their backs. Look for these lizards on mornings when they are sunning themselves or hunting for their favorite food, ants—they also eat other insects and spiders. These lizards are active whenever it is hot and the sun is out. They prefer dry habitats with plenty of rocks or sandy soil. This lizard cannot break off its tail when threatened, but it has an equally bizarre habit of squirting small drops of blood from the corners of its eyes when caught.

Finally, the most spectacular of all the iguanid lizards of our region is the eastern collared lizard found in scattered populations in northwestern Arkansas and much of the southern half of Missouri, except for the Bootheel country. This lizard is large, 8 to 14 inches long, with a long tail and a large head. The males are yellow, tan, blue-green, or green with small pale spots on the body and legs—they are brightest during the mating season in May and June. Female collared lizards are less brilliant in shades of light brown or tannish yellow with small pale spots. Both sexes have two distinct irregular dark "collars" on their necks. You are most likely to see these large handsome lizards as they are basking in the sun on rocks and rocky ledges. When startled, they can run swiftly to escape and dart under a rock or into a crevice. If surprised in the open, they may run on their hind legs. Collared lizards eat insects, spiders, snakes and smaller lizards. They in turn are part of the diet of hawks, large snakes and, in the western part of our region, roadrunners.

Another group of lizards well represented in our region are the skinks. Skinks are shiny, smooth lizards that are alert and active— hard to catch. Their tails break off very easily and they try to bite when caught. The five-lined skink, usually 5 to 7 inches in length, is a common lizard in most of our three-state region. You will see the hatchlings and young adults most often because of their bright coloration—they are black with five yellow lengthwise lines and a bright blue tail. The adult female is brown with a dark lateral stripe, five tan stripes, and a gray-blue or blue tail. The adult male is tan or greenish brown with little or no striping on its body. These skinks eat insects and spiders. They live in open woods, edges of woods, near rocks or downed trees and generally on south-facing hillsides. It is common to see this lizard in trees where it may hunt for its prey.

The broadhead skink is a large lizard that grows to a length of 6 to 12 inches or slightly more. The young have similar coloration to the five-lined skink and the adults look similar as well. The broadhead skink has comparatively larger scales between its ear and its eye while the five-lined skink has a pair of small scales just in front of its ear hole. The adult male broadhead is greenish brown and, during the breeding season, has a reddish orange head that appears swollen—this is where the name came from. The female has a similar background color with light and darker striping on its back and sides. These lizards also eat insects and spiders. They spend most of their time on or near the ground near trees, logs, edges of woods and forests. Some people call this lizard "the scorpion" and think that it is poisonous but in actuality it is harmless, although it could give you a hard nip if caught.

These are the lizards you are most likely to see in Illinois, Missouri and Arkansas. Look for them on warm sunny mornings on south-facing slopes on rocks, downed trees and stumps when they are most likely to be sunning themselves and hunting their prey.

HOTSPOTS

Devil's Den SP in northwestern Arkansas (see Chapter 16 for directions) has plenty of rocky ledges and bluffs that make it a likely place to see some of the native lizards. There is an interpretive center where staff members may be able to tell you what lizards they see regularly in certain places. **Petit Jean SP** (see Chapter 14 for directions) in the central part of the state between the Ozarks and the Ouachita mountains also has rocky bluffs and ledges that make parts of its land a good habitat for lizards.

Castle Rock SP in northwestern Illinois (see Chapter 32 for directions) has spectacular sandstone rock formations and buttes that make its trails good prospects for seeing resident lizards. **Giant City SP** in the Shawnee Hills of southern Illinois (see Chapter 16 for directions) has unusual rock formations that early settlers thought looked like the streets of a giant city—here you also will find good lizard habitat. The rocks and bluffs of **Starved Rock SP** in the northwestern part of the state (see Chapter 13 for directions) also offer opportunities to see basking lizards.

Missouri's **Elephant Rocks SP** (see Chapter 32 for directions) has enormous granite boulders and ledges where you are likely to see lizards. The rocky, canyonlike "shut-ins" of nearby **Johnson's Shut-Ins SP** also offer opportunities for studying native lizards as well as other wildlife. **Lake of the Ozarks SP** in the Lakes Region of Missouri (see Chapter 14 for directions) has a variety of habitat including some rocky places and edges of woods where you are apt to see lizards— check at the interpretive center for trail maps and suggestions as to good sites. Johnson's Shut-Ins is just 8 miles north of Lesterville on Highway N in Reynolds County.

52

Broadwinged Hawk Migration

The last half of September is the best part of fall for watching hawks migrate. The ideal time and day for seeing a band of migrating raptors is midmorning on a bright day right after a cold front has gone through the area. It is then that you are likely to see hundreds—sometimes even thousands—of broadwinged hawks as well as sharp-shinned hawks, Cooper's hawks and others moving southward.

Broadwinged hawks are crow-sized, chunky buteos that can be identified by their white or buff underwings and the tail with white and black bands of the same width. The birds are 14 to 18 inches long and have a wingspread of 32 to 39 inches—they weigh less than 1 1/2 pounds. Its call is a high shrill *pweeee* that diminishes toward the end. Buteos are stocky hawks with broad, round tipped wings and wide, rounded tails that spend a great deal of time soaring in big circles high above the earth. The sexes are similar but the female is larger. The diet of buteos features mice, rabbits and other rodents as well as grasshoppers, small birds, amphibians and reptiles.

It is the migrating broadwinged hawks that you will see in the greatest numbers as they travel above ridges, shorelines and valleys where they can catch good updrafts. They often are so high that all you can see are masses of dark dots in the sky. They spend the summers throughout much of the eastern half of the United States, then travel south, mainly through Texas, to the American tropics where they spend the winter. Some winter in southern Florida.

The red-shouldered hawk and red-tailed hawk are permanent residents throughout our region although we may see some of those who spend their summers in Canada migrating southward. That is also true of the northern harrier as well as Cooper's hawk. Those we see migrating along with the broadwinged hawks are usually in lesser numbers. The sharpshinned hawk that spends its winters throughout our region summers in mountainous regions and Canada—it may migrate in larger flocks.

The broadwinged hawk is a woodland bird that perches on low limbs near ponds, lakes or streams while waiting for its prey to amble by. Since amphibians and reptiles are a major part of their diet, some 20 to 40 percent, they head south from their summer homes early in the fall before their cold-blooded prey go into hibernation.

When the broadwinged hawks pass through our region, it is one of the most spectacular sights you will see. At first, you see dark spots in the sky, then as they approach you see that they are high flying birds. Periodically you will see them turn and circle by the hundreds and thousands in a snarl of soaring birds that is called a kettle or a boil. The massive flocks then fly southward, funneling down toward Central America and following the narrowing land into the tropical forests of South America. In March they will reverse their trail, returning by the same paths to their nesting places in northern forests.

Broadwinged hawks live in our region from April until September and often nest here. When they do, they build shaggy nests of sticks. The mated pair are good parents, with both birds taking turns to incubate two to four eggs for about four weeks. The young hawks are feathered and ready to fledge in another four weeks or so.

Wildlife managers consider raptors such as the broadwinged hawk good indicators of environmental quality because they are at the top of food chains and thus show the presence of a healthy variety of plants and animals. Raptors help keep populations of their prey healthy by eliminating those that are sick, weak or simply surplus animals that the land can't support.

Hawks, eagles and other raptors share important characteristics that help them find, catch and eat prey species. They have exceptionally keen eyesight as you can tell if you've ever watched a hawk soar or hover, then dive down and catch a small animal that you couldn't see even if you were closer. Experts report that raptors can see 2 1/2 to 3 times better than humans and have amazing depth perception. They also have strong curved beaks that are well designed for tearing the flesh of their prey and strong, clawed feet with large, curved, sharp talons that efficiently catch and kill their prey.

HOTSPOTS

Felsenthal NWR in southern Arkansas (see Chapter 2 for directions) is a place where the broadwinged hawk migration is observed each year. Parks with high hills are good places to observe hawk migrations because the birds take advantage of the updrafts found on the upwind sides of hills after cold fronts pass through. **Mt. Nebo SP** (see Chapter 16 for directions) in west central Arkansas with its 1,800-foot Mt. Nebo is a spectacularly scenic place for seeking hawks in migration. **Pinnacle Mountain SP** (see Chapter 28 for directions) in central Arkansas near Little Rock is another place for watching migrating hawks on bright clear mornings in September.

Goose Lake Prairie Natural Area in west central Illinois (see Chapter 34 for directions) is a place where you are likely to see migrating hawks as well as many migrating waterfowl and shorebirds. Plan to visit **Chautauqua NWR** in west central Illinois (see Chapter 1 for directions) to see migrating hawks—the 100-foot observation tower there is a good starting place. Another likely place to look for kettling hawks is the bluff road along which you can drive. Visit the headquarters first to get descriptive folders, a map, and a checklist of birds—over 240 species have been recorded here since the refuge was established in 1936.

Birders commonly see broadwinged hawks kettling in the sky above **Busch Wildlife Area** in east central Missouri near St. Louis (see Chapter 10 for directions) after they have roosted in the area and are gathering to head south. **Swan Lake NWR** in the north central part of the state (see Chapter 8 for directions) is another place where broadwinged hawks are commonly seen at this time of year.

53

September Shorttakes

Swallows

Watch for mixed swallow species that band together in large flocks of one thousand or more. Tree swallows, barn swallows and roughwinged swallows gather before heading south for the winter to southern United States, Mexico and Central America.

Squirrels

As acorns and hickory nuts ripen, squirrels gather and bury them for later use as winter food.

See also:

Chapter 39, Butterfly Counts. Watch for gold and black monarch butterflies as they begin their migration to Mexico.

Chapter 57, Fall Color. Sumac, Virginia creeper and sassafras begin to show fall color this month, especially when they are growing on ridge tops. Dogwood, bittersweet and blackgum are also starting to change color.

54

Breakout:
Mammals of Our Region

Illinois, Missouri and Arkansas have rich and diverse mammal populations, most of which have increased in recent years. It takes sharp eyes and some awareness of appropriate habitat to see many of our native animals. Many are nocturnal and few are so bold as to go on about their business when humans are nearby. More often, they observe us far more than we observe them. Sometimes you can catch them at it. If you look at just the right spot in tree foliage in the forest or in a woodsy thicket, you will see a squirrel, raccoon or deer quietly watching you. Their colors blend in with their surroundings so well that you rarely see them until they move.

There are more white-tailed deer here now than there were in the days of early settlers. These two-toed hoofed creatures are our largest common mammals. They have antlers that are shed each winter after the fall breeding season. The reason you don't find antlers very often is that squirrels and other rodents eat them, a good source of calcium. Deer have become so common that they often are a nuisance to farmers and gardeners, browsing on just about anything green. In spite of that, there is nothing more beautiful than the sight of deer that you see in forests or the edges of woods. They stand at attention with their big ears bracketing the sight and sound of you, then spin and leap, bounding gracefully into thick cover.

Having just noted that the white-tailed deer is our largest common mammal, I must mention that our largest mammal is the black bear. Although it is the smallest of our North American bears, it is formidable with its length of 5 to 6 feet, height of about 3 feet at the shoulder, and weight of 200 to 400 pounds. They are black except for a "Y" on the breast and a brown muzzle. The black phase is most common but these bears occasionally also come in cinnamon and blue phases. Black bears are uncommon enough to make the news when they appear near civilization. Just this year, one was tagged the "Potosi Bear" because of the Missouri town where it was often seen. The Potosi Bear spread his charm over a 100-mile territory, appearing in backyards where women were hanging laundry, ambling along roadsides and startling people wherever he appeared. Although black bears aren't as truculent as their bigger cousins, the grizzlies, they do not like to be disturbed and sows with cubs are particularly likely to be cranky. It's safer to stay as far away from bears as you can—view them with binoculars.

Raccoons have made themselves thoroughly at home in cities, suburbs and public parks where they cadge food from trash and directly from people. These are big animals, weighing up to 35 pounds in their prime. Raccoons are most active at night. Their black masks and ringed tails against a grizzled gray background give them a clownish look, but don't be deceived. They are clever, cute, destructive and temperamental so don't mess with them—they will bite and scratch viciously if cornered. Raccoons have proliferated greatly because they are finding life easy near people—many people feed them regularly with fruit, dog food and other raccoon favorites, making them ever more bold. I am against feeding them and advise you to observe but not encourage the raccoon population.

The opossums are the only marsupials (pouched mammals) found in North America. The Virginia opossum is native through-out our region as you often can see by the number of roadkills along highways. These animals are strangely prehistoric looking and are not very bright. They are the size of a house cat and are grayish white to dark gray with papery black ears, beady eyes and a ratlike tail. Opposums are quite nocturnal. They will eat both plants and animals, preferring fleshy fruits when they are available. They live anywhere they can find shelter from the elements. Opossum babies are born in an embryonic state, travel to the fur-lined pouch and attach themselves to a teat where they live until they are fully developed.

Rodents are the most common wild animals throughout our region. They share that distinctive rodent characteristic of well-developed central incisors that continue to grow throughout their lives. They must gnaw on things in order to keep those sharp incisors ground down to a manageable length.

Cottontail rabbits, which aren't rodents but lagomorphs, need no description. Lovers of tender vegetation, they are not welcome in gardens where they have settled in with civilization as comfortably as raccoons. In preserves and refuges where there is a better balance of rabbits and their predators, cottontails are a natural part of the biome, the natural community of fields, meadows, edges of woods and thickets.

Squirrels are true rodents that have made themselves too much at home in towns and cities. Eastern gray squirrels are animals of eastern hardwood forests that have 8- to 10-inch bodies and heads, trailed by 7- to 10-inch tails. The bigger eastern fox squirrel is found in woods where there are nut trees. Fox squirrels are generally grayish with rusty yellow overtones, an orange or yellow belly and tail hairs tipped with dull yellow-orange. These two squirrels are chattery, aggressive animals that are most active by day.

You may never see them, but you've undoubtedly heard their soft squeaks at night and perhaps heard them running on roofs and in attics. Southern flying squirrels are gentle nocturnal creatures with big dark eyes, soft plushlike gray fur and a creamy white belly. They do not fly but rather spread folds of skin that go between wrist and ankle and glide from one tree to another or from trees to ground. They sometimes will come to bird feeders at night.

Eastern chipmunks are common ground squirrels through Illinois, Missouri and Arkansas. This small 5- to 6-inch animal has stripes on its face as well as on its sides and back and a red-brown rump. The chipmunk lives on or in the ground, preferring woods with rocky soil or plenty of dead wood. You often will hear its sharp *cheep, cheep, cheep* call before you see it—people often mistake it for a bird call. Chipmunks usually hibernate during the winter.

Woodchucks are found throughout Illinois and most of Missouri, less commonly in the Missouri Bootheel and Arkansas. They are more common in the eastern United States. This stocky short-legged rodent is yellowish brown to dark brown and has a paler belly. It looks larger than its 5- to 10-pound weight. Its big burrows have an obvious entrance with a mound in front plus one or more secret entrances hidden under brush or in thickets. This big rodent eats all sorts of tender vegetation and so can be a scourge of gardens. In less civilized places the woodchuck is content with grasses and other greenery found in fields and at the edges of woods.

There are a number of other rodents in our region. Voles and mice are very common. You will rarely see them but you may see signs, such as small tunnels under dead grass on the floors of fields and meadows. White-footed mice, deer mice, harvest mice and meadow voles all are small native rodents in our region.

The weasel family is represented here by the striped skunk, spotted skunk, longtail weasel, mink and river otter. You will seldom see the secretive weasel, mink and river otter. Native throughout our three-state region, you may smell the striped skunk before you see it because of its remarkable defense mechanism that lingers long after the encounter. This is an unusually diffident animal because it has such a good defense—it may walk boldly through campsites or backyards looking for grubs, one of its favorite foods. The spotted skunk is native to most of Missouri and all of Arkansas. Unlike its black-and-white-striped cousin, the smaller spotted skunk is black with a white spot on the forehead, one under each ear, and four lines of spots along the neck, back and sides. River otters are being reintroduced to the Ozark Mountains and so may again flourish as they once did years ago. These large playful creatures are fish and crustacean eaters.

The native canids in our region are the red and gray foxes and the coyote. Red foxes are handsome creatures with color variations that range from red-brown to black to silver. They have black legs and feet plus a white tip at the end of the bushy tail. The red fox roams most commonly in sparsely settled country, although in recent years it has become resident in many parks and refuges that are near towns and cities. The diet of the red fox consists mainly of mice, voles, grasshoppers and other small animals. The smaller gray fox is more common in woods and brushy areas of the West and South. Its long bushy tail has a black stripe down the middle and no white tip. The sides of its neck, backs of its ears, legs and feet are a rusty yellow color. Its habits are similar to those of red foxes.

Coyotes have in recent years not only made a comeback, they have grown in numbers far beyond what they were in early days. Looking like medium-sized dogs, they are gray or rusty gray with sharply pointed noses and lighter bellies. Their tails are bushier than dogs' tails and are held down loosely between the hind legs when they are running. Most often, you will see them endlessly trotting along the edges of fields where they meet woods and forests. If they are startled, they disappear into the brush in an instant. Their singing sounds like a group of demented souls, a cacophony of yelps, laughs, giggles and howls. These days you can hear them near cities and towns as well as out on the prairies and edges of agricultural fields.

In the feline department we have bobcats and, periodically, we get reports that someone has sighted a mountain lion. Bobcats are native to southern Arkansas and are found occasionally farther north. These 15- to 30-pound cats have short ear tufts and short tails tipped with black. They are tawny and lightly spotted with paler bellies. In western areas, bobcats are found more often in rocky, rimrock country while in more eastern territories, they prefer swampy habitat.

Even when you don't see the animals themselves, you may well see signs of their presence in tracks, droppings and in a number of other small ways. Learn to observe carefully for signs of animals in a variety of habitat—you can learn a lot about animals that you never see.

OCTOBER

October Observations

55

Northern Cardinal—
A Favorite Resident

Few American birds enjoy the popularity of the northern cardinal, that handsome crested bird whose liquid song is an integral part of our region's spring. Cardinals are permanent residents in Illinois, Missouri and Arkansas as well as most of the eastern half of our country. They are welcome winter visitors to bird feeders where they particularly enjoy sunflower seeds. During the warm season cardinals are omnivorous, adding insects and grubs to their cold-season vegetarian diet. The scarlet male is a bright note in the winter scene and the more subtle shades of the female are equally welcome. She is a yellow-buff color with a pink bill and a brush of red on her crest, wings and tail.

For years, the cardinal was split into the eastern cardinal, the Florida cardinal and the Louisiana cardinal. Currently, all three are considered one species—much simpler, don't you think? Biologists all agree that the cardinal is in the bird family with seed-cracking bills that also includes finches, sparrows, buntings, crossbills and grosbeaks. The cardinal's bill is thick and strong like that of the grosbeaks. Finches, sparrows and buntings have bills that are less imposing and more like the bills of canaries.

The coloring of the male cardinal with its scarlet plumage, red bill and black mask is spectacular. The cardinal is common enough and such a brilliant and beautiful bird that it is a favorite caged bird in Mexico.

The turn-of-the-century ornithologist, Frank M. Chapman, wrote poetically of the cardinal in his *Birds of Eastern North*

America: "As head of a family, the Cardinal is admirable, not only in his attentions to his lovely dove-colored mate, but in singing to her by the hour, and in protecting her from intrusion or danger. To the young in the nest, he is an untiring provider of worms and grubs, and thus most useful in a garden. Nothing can be more comical than his behavior when he first conducts his young family out into the world while his mate is engaged in her second sitting. He is as fussy as any young mother, hopping about in great excitement, and appearing to think that the whole world is thirsting for the life of his pretty little ones."

Cardinals originally were southern birds, little known north of the Mason-Dixon Line and most common in middle southern and southern midwestern regions. Arthur C. Bent, another noted early ornithologist, reported the spread of cardinal territory in the 1930s when cardinals began to appear in Iowa and even north to Ontario. The species was expanding its range northward in the Great Plains as well as the Northeast.

Favorite haunts of cardinals are lilac bushes and other shrubbery in parks and gardens as well as near houses. Streamside thickets, dense hedges, orchards, open woodlands with undergrowths of dense bushes—all are favorite nesting grounds of the cardinal.

Although many birds are loyal mates during the breeding season, some take a number of mates each season and yet others are casual about their mating habits. Cardinals, on the other hand, not only are monogamous, they remain paired throughout the year. Each spring the male courts the female, taking small bits of food to her which she gently accepts as their bills touch.

The bowl-shaped nests vary in quality and are built in dense thickets at a height of 2 to 12 feet above the ground. Some are well built while others are flimsy. The female, the primary nest builder, uses a variety of materials, including small pliable twigs and weed stems, grasses, rootlets and small vines, interwoven with leaves and paper.

Most nests are completed in three to nine days. As many as four clutches may be laid each season, each with as many as four eggs that are a dull white color or sometimes pastel green with brown or lavender speckles. The female does all the incubating but the male feeds her as she sits on the nest. Both birds work hard to feed the nestlings after they hatch. Once the youngsters are fledged and the female is brooding her second family of the season, the pair resumes the counter singing of its duets.

Cardinals are especially gregarious during the winter when several of both sexes and ages may come in to the sunflower feeders at once. At other times of year cardinals may be quite shy or even act pugnaciously, sending other cardinals off by flying at them or acting in other threatening ways.

Cardinal songs, consisting of a large number of whistling, single or double notes and songs, can be heard at almost any time of year, even in the heart of winter, but the main song period is from March through August. Both sexes sing but the female's voice is a bit softer than the male's. In the spring, the bonded pair sings a duet— first one and then the other will whistle several phrases that the other completes.

John James Audubon, America's first great authority on birds, also wrote glowingly of the cardinal: "How pleasing it is, when, by a clouded sky, the woods are rendered so dark, that were it not for an occasional glimpse of clearer light falling between the trees, you might imagine night at hand, while you are yet far distant from your home—how pleasing to have your ear suddenly saluted by the well known notes of this favorite bird, assuring you of peace around, and of the full hour that still remains for you to pursue your walk in security."

HOTSPOTS

In Arkansas, cardinals are abundant at **Felsenthal NWR** in the southern part of the state (see Chapter 2 for directions) and **Holla Bend NWR** (see chapter 7 for directions) in the central part of the state. Cardinals are common to abundant throughout the state.

Cardinals also are abundant at **Chautauqua NWR** in west central Illinois (see Chapter 1 for directions), common at **Crab Orchard NWR** in southern Illinois (see Chapter 1 for directions) and the **Brussels and Gardner Divisions of the Mark Twain NWR Complex** in west central Illinois (See Chapter 3 for directions).

In Missouri, cardinals are abundant in **Mingo NWR** in the southeastern part of the state (see Chapter 1 for directions). Cardinals are common in the **Annada Division** of the **Mark Twain NWR Complex** in the east central part of the state as well as in both **Squaw Creek NWR** (see Chapter 1 for directions) in the northwestern part of the state and **Swan Lake NWR** in north central Missouri (see Chapter 8 for directions).

56

Waterfowl Migration

Each spring and fall, ponds and lakes in our region are full of migratory ducks and geese that traverse the great Mississippi Flyway. Agricultural lands near water also are full of birds that come in to pick at the leavings of recent harvests. In some places you can't see the water because it is so packed with birds. Their quacking, honking and other bird conversation can be so loud that you have to shout to be heard. The fall migration of waterfowl is clearly one of nature's miracles. Unfortunately, migration is so well known that most people take it for granted that they will see thousands upon thousands of these handsome creatures as they travel to summer and winter grounds.

Think of how these birds fly unerringly from their summer breeding grounds to the same wintering sites each year and then back to the same nesting sites in the spring. Their inner compasses must be very precise for them to be able to do this. Extensive studies have been done by experts to try to understand how the birds navigate. Some experts believe that the earth's magnetic field somehow helps birds find their way, but there is still a lot to learn.

Best known of all the geese is the Canada goose, which is a migrant through our region as well as a year-round resident. In some places these large birds have become a nuisance because people feed them, encouraging them to inhabit city and town parks where they spend more time cadging handouts than acting like wild geese—as you can tell, I don't think highly of encouraging wild animals to become residents in artificial locations.

The Canada goose species includes a number of different varieties that vary greatly in size but all have black heads and necks marked by pure white cheek patches that go all the way under the chin. The body of the Canada goose is grayish brown and it has a white patch under the tail. These geese fly in a "V" at approximately 45 miles per hour, constantly chatting to each other as they go—I have often heard them before seeing them as they fly high overhead on their way south. The several subspecies of these geese range from 22 to 48 inches long with wing spans up to 5 feet. Their spring courtships are elaborate rituals that have long captivated birders. These are loyal birds that mate for life and defend their mates and young vigorously. Angry geese will attack any suspected enemy, even animals and people much larger than they are. The Canada goose eats grass, grain, aquatic plants and, sometimes, aquatic animals.

Snow geese travel through our region twice a year on their way to and from the Arctic north where they breed—they are not permanent residents in our country. These geese fly at altitudes of about 1,000 feet and in "U" patterns rather than the "V" of Canada geese. This species of goose includes the blue goose as well as two sizes called the lesser snow goose and the greater snow goose. These birds are 25 to 31 inches long and are white with black wing tips. The bill is pink with black "lips." The blue phase has a dark gray body with white head and neck. The white phase is white with black flight feathers in the wings. These birds have a different voice than the Canada goose, making high yelps as their major call notes. Their diet includes grasses, grain and aquatic plants.

Best known and most common of the ducks is the mallard, both a migrant and a permanent resident in our region. The male is yellow billed with a bright green head and chestnut breast. The female is sort of a brown tweed all over with an orange-mottled bill. Both have blue wing patches bordered by two white stripes. These birds are dabbling ducks that feed on seeds, small fish, insects and snails by tipping up so that the rear half of the duck is out of water and the front half is under water. Their well-known *quack* has become synonymous with the word "duck" throughout much of the world. Dabbling ducks can rise directly from the water into flight without the running start needed by some waterfowl.

Another common dabbling duck is the northern pintail, which has a brown speculum with a white stripe along its edge. The male has a brown head and white neck that continues as a thin stripe up into the rear of the head. The body is mainly gray and the tail long, thin and black. The female is a tweedy gray-brown with a shorter tail.

The bills of both sexes are gray. This bird is a permanent resident in northwestern Missouri and a winter resident throughout much of our region. The main breeding territory of the northern pintail is in the northern states and Canada to Alaska. Shallow ponds and potholes are favorite places of this and other dabbling ducks.

The green-winged teal, our smallest dabbling duck, and the blue-winged teal, slightly larger, show the colored wing patches for which they are named when in flight. The green-winged teal male has a chestnut head with a wide green patch that goes from the eye along the rear of the head and down the neck. The blue-winged teal male has a dark gray head marked by a white crescent that arches in front of the eye. The females are typically tweedy looking and can be identified through their small size plus the wing patches. Teal travel swiftly in tight "V" formations that move and turn as one bird. They eat insects, snails, aquatic plants and seeds.

The northern shoveler is an easily identified dabbling duck, more common in the West than the East. It looks like a strange mallard because of similar coloration and its odd, large shovel-shaped bill. The male shoveler has a green head and, unlike the mallard, a black bill and yellow eye. The bill is the identifying characteristic with this duck. The shoveler strains its food from the mud on pond bottoms, preferring insects, mollusks, crustaceans, seeds and aquatic plants.

This introduction to common geese and ducks is just that—an introduction. There are many other species of geese and ducks to be seen in our region during migration time.

HOTSPOTS

Millwood SP in southwestern Arkansas is one of the all-time best birding places in the entire state (See Chapter 10 for directions). Walk along the 1.5-mile trail called Waterfowl Way and you are likely to find more bird species than at any other single place. In addition to waterfowl, including canvasback ducks and others, you will see an active beaver lodge in one of the coves on the trail—you may see beaver at dawn or dusk. Go to the visitors' center first to get a map and any current information on migrating waterfowl.

Thousands of ducks and geese are present in large numbers during the winter at **White River NWR**. The 3- to 10-mile-wide refuge extends some 65 miles along the White River a few miles above its juncture with the Mississippi River (See Chapter 15 for directions). The refuge office is in DeWitt, Arkansas. It would be wise to check with the office before visiting because of possible high water or other adverse conditions. The habitats include bottomland hardwood forest, lakes, streams and impounded lakes and ponds. This refuge also includes farm land and recreation areas.

Goose Lake Prairie State Natural Area in northeastern Illinois, 2,380 acres of dry, mesic and wet prairies plus marshes and potholes, is a great place to find waterfowl in the fall and spring (see Chapter 34 for directions).The best places to look are around the potholes. The 7,000-acre lake at **Crab Orchard NWR** in southern Illinois (see Chapter 1 for directions) is a haven for huge populations of Canada geese and other waterfowl. There are many good vantage points along many miles of gravel and blacktop roads. Two observation towers along Highway 148, south of the refuge headquarters, provide excellent views of water and marshes.

Horseshoe Lake WR in southern Illinois is known far and wide as the "Goose Capital of the World." This Horseshoe Lake is an ancient oxbow of the Mississippi River surrounded by typical river bottomland. Bald cypress trees grow on the lake's edges. This area has been operating as a refuge since 1927, and it has numerous roads that are ideal for observing birds from the car. Note that some of the roads are closed during migration season in order to protect the birds, so be sure to check at the headquarters building before looking for waterfowl. To get there, follow Illinois Highway 3 south almost to the tip of the state. About 2 miles south of Olive Branch, the refuge entrance will be on your right—you will turn off onto the lake road.

In north central Missouri, **Swan Lake NWR** (see Chapter 8 for directions) is tops for observing waterfowl that gather there by the tens of thousands on their way to southern wintering ranges. **Riverland EDA** (see Chapter 1 for directions), a 1,200-acre refuge of agricultural floodplain, is being restored to a mosaic of bottomland marsh, native prairie and forest. Established in 1988, it is already proving to be one of central eastern Missouri's finest birding sites. **Table Rock SP** in the southwestern part of the state near Branson (see Chapter 7 for directions) is another good spot for observing the migration of waterfowl. In addition, this lake is known for the clarity of its water and the quality of its fishing.

57

Fall Color

When autumn comes to Illinois, Missouri and Arkansas you can easily tell the native plants from those that originated in Europe. The plants brought here from Europe fade from green to tan or brown while those that are native hail the cool weather of fall with a blaze of fiery colors. Golds, yellows, oranges, scarlets, reds and even purples shout their citizenship from tree tops, shrubs, grasses and forbs.

The only other places where fall color is a common plant characteristic are Korea, Japan and China. In fact, the plants of our midwest and northeast are more like the plants of the Orient than they are like the flora of California. The genes of these plants allow bright colors to flame when the chlorophyll green disappears from foliage. Rain, temperature, sunlight, soil quality and soil pH also have a bearing on the quality of fall color.

To be sure, the oak-hickory climax forest of most of our region is not as colorful in the fall as the golden birches, flaming sugar maples and other spectaculars of the New England autumn. Yet there is a special charm, a smoky beauty to our fall colors that are like a fire in check, ready to burst at any moment.

Days that are growing shorter and temperatures that are getting cooler are the factors that trigger the changing colors of the foliage. Corklike cells build up in a layer at the base of leaf stems, shutting down the transportation of nutrients and water to the leaves for manufacture into carbohydrates. Thus the manufacture of chlorophyll shuts down and there is no more green in the leaves. The green color begins to fade and as it does, the underlying colors begin

Smooth sumac is one of the first plants to show a hint of fall color. Grow-ing as it does on roadsides and along the edges of old fields, the sumac paints a bright red splash on the late summer and early fall landscape.

to show. The reds and yellows of the chemicals carotin and xantho-phyll appear in many leaves. When days are sunny and nights are cool—below 45 degrees Fahrenheit—reds and browns show up in foliage that has tannins. Leaves turn red when the corky layers of cells form before those tannins and sugars have a chance to drain back into the tree where they would have been stored.

Warm cloudy fall weather will result in fall color that is dull, and early hard frost will kill the foliage, cutting short the fall display. Heavy rains will wash the bright but water-soluble colors right out of the leaves. Generally plants reach their peak of fall color in the same sequence from year to year, but the length of the display and the brilliance of the autumn colors is variable, depending on many factors.

Among the earliest of plants to show fall colors is the red or swamp maple, noted for its bright red leaves each fall. Note that the fall color in some individuals may vary from greenish yellow and yellow to brilliant red as well. Smooth sumac, aromatic sumac and Virginia creeper also begin to turn red early, especially on rocky ridges where they may begin turning color in August.

Downy serviceberry is another plant of high color in autumn. Its foliage becomes a rich tapestry of reds, oranges and yellows. The sourgum or black tupelo, a native in the southern portion of our region, glows with an inner fire when its foliage turns scarlet or orange each fall. Warm yellow is the fall color of the tulip tree, a native in the eastern portions of our region. Some redbuds, native understory trees throughout our region, also have good yellow fall color. Our native sugar maples are glorious in the fall, ranging from golden yellow through hot oranges to bright red.

The oaks, though not noted for their fall display, do add to the symphony of color to some degree. Scarlet oaks are the brightest of fall oaks, their rich red leaves holding their color for a week and a half or so. Red oak leaves turn a deep red and then fade slowly to brown. The white oaks go through a stage where the leaves are a purplish-red that lasts for several days before fading to brown.

The native white ash varies in its fall color. It is usually yellow but sometimes the leaves—especially the outer ones that are more exposed to sunlight—turn an unusual shade of purple. This happened last fall, surprising many people who wondered what the unusual tree was and wondered also why they hadn't seen the exotic purplish fall foliage before.

The common dogwood, found as an understory tree in woods and forests throughout our region, is reliable for the beauty of its fall foliage. Red to reddish purple are the colors that crown the dogwood, making it one of the most handsome of fall trees. Another outstanding native tree for fall color is the sassafras, common along roadsides and the edges of woods, which lights up in a miracle of yellows, oranges, purples and scarlets each October.

HOTSPOTS

Pinnacle Mountain SP near Little Rock, Arkansas, (see Chapter 28 for directions) offers wooded hillsides and lush lowlands plus the cone-shaped landmark known as Pinnacle Mountain that rises over 1,000 feet above the Arkansas Valley. The vistas from the summit offer a panoramic view of fall colors in the hardwood forests. Get one of the trail brochures for this day-use only park so that you can find your way around.

Queen Wilhelmina SP in western Arkansas is in one of the state's most scenic areas, perched on top of the Rich Mountains nearly 3,000 feet above sea level. The drive to the park will offer you rugged scenery with the best of Arkansas fall color. To get there, go 13 miles northwest of Mena, Arkansas, on Highway 88. During inclement weather, take U.S. Highway 270 to Highway 272, then go south for 2 miles (a less steep, winding road). This park has a visitors' center and interpretive programs from Memorial Day through the time of fall foliage.

For fall color in Illinois, be sure to visit **Morton Arboretum** near Chicago (see Chapter 3 for directions). Here you will find the hardiest, most attractive trees, shrubs and vines of the Midwest, including both native and introduced species and varieties. The arboretum's 1,500 acres included natural areas as well as plantings organized according to their botanical groups, geographical origin and landscape types.

Pere Marquette SP north of Alton, Illinois, (see Chapter 13 for directions) offers a variety of terrain and habitats from magnificent hardwood forest to the famous McAdams Peak Hill Prairie, a 54-acre natural area. This is a good site for wandering about to enjoy fall color. **Starved Rock SP** in northwestern Illinois (see Chapter 13 for directions) is another great spot for fall color. Here you will find understory plants such as native witch hazels and hydrangeas under stands of red oak, basswood and sugar maple.

The rich and diverse plant life of **Hawn SP** (see Chapter 4 for directions) near Ste. Genevieve, Missouri, south of St. Louis, recommends it for fall color. Understory trees such as redbud, dogwood and serviceberry are common here as are scarlet oak and many other native trees, shrubs and herbaceous perennials. Note also that this park has rare stands of shortleaf pine—the finest in the state.

In the southwestern part of Missouri, you will find **Table Rock SP** near Branson (see Chapter 7 for directions) and a few miles west of that, you will find **Roaring River SP** near Cassville (see Chapter 13 for directions). Table Rock SP, although near the bustling entertainment center of Branson, boasts some of the prettiest country of the White River Valley. Although Table Rock Lake constitutes the greatest attraction of this park, there are plenty of places to walk and find quiet places to contemplate the changing colors of fall. Roaring River is one of Missouri's great trout parks where the fish are grown and regularly released in the waters for anglers. This park has several thousand acres of hardwood forests, glades and bluffs and a well-developed trail system to help you find the plants and animals you may want to see.

58

Liverworts

You have to think and observe on a different scale when you study organisms such as liverworts, miniature occupants of the forest floor. These delicate plants are green, which indicates that they use the sun to drive their manufacturing plant in making chlorophyll and carbohydrates. Liverworts and mosses are the two plant groups that are classed as *bryophytes*.

The liverworts and mosses are not like higher plants that have true leaves, stems, flowers and seeds. Their tissues don't conduct dissolved nutrients and carbohydrates as the higher plants do—they reproduce by spores rather than by seeds. In Chapter 32, I described some of the important factors in the spore reproduction of mosses—the same applies to liverworts.

Liverworts grow in damp shady places, on tree bark, rocks and, sometimes, in water. Look for them near springs, in seepage areas, along old mill races or similar structures and, in the case of some species, in shallow waters of streams, ponds and lakes.

Some liverwort plants look like miniature lobed leaves of flowering plants—the main body of the liverwort is called a *thallus*. Small rootlike structures that grow from the bottom of the thallus are called *rhizoids*. The rhizoids hold the plants on the surfaces where they grow. Rhizoids also take in water and dissolved minerals that are important nutrients for these plants.

Liverworts grow in two major forms. The group called thalloid liverworts grow flat against a surface in shapes like scales or ribbons. The other group, called leafy liverworts, branch in "Y" shapes and have parts that look like stems, branches and round leaves.

Thalloid liverworts may have small cupped organs called *gemmae cups* growing on their surfaces. These hold small pieces of liverwort that can reproduce vegetatively. The male and female organs needed for sexual reproduction, which involves the production of spores, develop on different thalluses. The female structures, called *archegonia*, grow from beneath the thallus, often on stalks and with lobes when ripe. The male structures, called *antheridia*, have two types, one that is stalked and the other resembling a wart.

There seem to be no common names for liverworts, which clearly shows how few people are aware of these tiny but interesting primitive plants. *Marchantia polymorpha* is a typical thalloid liverwort. Look for it on wet logs, rocks and soil. Its thallus is broad with flat lobes and edges that curl up. The thallus has rather obvious air pores spotting its surface. Older parts of the thallus may seem slightly translucent and are of a dark green to blue-green color. The reproductive parts of this liverwort all are obvious.

Conocephalum conicum is a liverwort found on very moist rocks and soil. Its generic name means conehead and its species name similarly means conelike, due to the conical shape of the archegonium. The thallus of this liverwort has large irregularly-shaped lobes that overlap each other. The surface of the thallus has many air pores that give it a scaly, even a bubbly look much like lizard skin. This is one of the largest thalloid liverworts, and its dry thallus has a spicy fragrance when crushed.

Reboulia hemispherica is a liverwort of rocks and soils. The shallow cuppings of the many lobes of each thallus give it its species name. The edges of the lobes are somewhat notched and darker, almost purple in color. When this liverwort dries out, the cupped lobes flatten. The surface of the thallus is smooth since the air pores are very small. The female reproductive organ appears in the spring and looks like an umbrella with a very long handle.

One of the floating liverworts is *Riccia fluitans* which is found in still shallow waters of every continent, from sea level to altitudes of over a mile above sea level. This liverwort doesn't look like most thalloid liverworts. The thallus of this one is long, flat and thin, with each lobe ending in a deep notch. It grows long and branches so much that it forms thick mats that some experts say resemble birds' nests.

Leafy liverworts often grow on trees and rocks. The several species of the *Frullania* liverworts will survive drier conditions than other liverworts. They are small and branching with rounded leaves that lie in alternate rows on either side of each main stem. Mature liverworts of this genus make lacy patterns against the surfaces on which they grow. The reproductive parts of these plants as well as the following liverworts are tiny and inconspicuous.

Leafy liverworts of the *Porella* genus grow on trees and rocks, and have many branches and round leaves that grow alternately on the sides of each stem. These liverworts grow in crowded mats rather than the netted patterns of the *Frullania*, are larger, brighter green and grow in moister areas than do the *Frullanias*.

When you are in the right kind of habitat for the lower plants I've described, look for mosses, liverworts and lichens. They make up an interesting group of plants that will surprise you with their unusual beauty and strange forms. These are delicate plants that thrive in special habitats—collect them with your camera or sketch pad only.

HOTSPOTS

The 2,000 acres of **Devil's Den SP** in northwestern Arkansas (see Chapter 16 for directions) offer spectacular Ozark scenery and a clear mountain stream. Check at the visitors' center for maps of the park and its trails including a wet-water trail that goes down Lee Creek. There are a number of places in the park where you are likely to find liverworts.

Logoly SP in southwestern Arkansas is a fairly new state park on 345 acres of forested coastal plain. It has long been famous for its purported medicinal waters that rise from mineral springs. This is the first of Arkansas' environmental education parks. The visitors' center, featuring both the history and the natural environment of the area, has maps of the park and suggestions as to where you might find primitive plants such as liverworts. To get there, take U.S. Highway 79 near the McNeil Highway junction 6 miles north from Magnolia and turn onto Logoly Road.

Mattheiessen SP in northwestern Illinois (see Chapter 33 for directions) is known for its liverworts, mosses and ferns. The huge sandstone canyons are worn and ribbed from thousands of years of water erosion, with mosses, liverworts and ferns covering the canyon floors. Spectacular waterfalls and rock walls, hundreds of species of birds and many wildflowers also are features of this beautiful park.

Moraine Hills SP in Illinois near the Wisconsin border is another park known for its primitive plants, liverworts, mosses and ferns. Leatherleaf Bog is a 10-acre area of kettle moraines, remnants of the glacial invasion. Here you will find all sorts of bog plants including many primitives. To get there go west on Illinois Highway 120 from McHenry or east on 120 from Woodstock and then take River Road south to Moraine Hills SP.

The moss- and fern-covered cliffs and shelves of the trails in **Hawn SP** near Ste. Genevieve, in east central Missouri (see Chapter 4 for directions) are wonderful places to study primitive plants. Trails in the Pickle Creek watershed offer opportunities to see a great diversity of other wildlife as well.

Roaring River SP in southwestern Missouri (see Chapter 13 for directions) features the Roaring River Spring from which flows more than 20 million gallons of water per day, the headwaters of Roaring River. On the limestone rocks near this and other water features, you are likely to find sizable collections of liverworts, mosses and ferns. This park has a well-developed trail system that makes it easier to study the treasure trove of plants and animals that it offers.

59

October Shorttakes

Spiders

Watch for spiders soaring on gossamer threads in the fall breezes. What a wonderful way to travel and find new territories.

Persimmons

Along the edges of woods, persimmon trees grow and, at this time of year, their fruit begins to ripen—look for the small golden globes of persimmon fruit.

Hard Frost

The first hard frosts usually occur this month, likely during the first half of October in the northern parts of our region and during the last part of the month or in early November in the southern reaches of our region.

Juncos

Winter birds are arriving from their summer homes in the North. Watch for juncos to begin arriving from Canada where they nest and raise their families.

See also:

Chapter 56, Waterfowl Migration. American widgeons, pintails and gadwalls arrive in wetlands, ponds and lakes this month. Snow geese are at their peak in refuges and preserves.

60

Breakout: Asters and Other Fall Flowers

Prairies, plains and other sunny sites blaze with color in the fall season as great numbers of native plants come into bloom. The buttercup family with its many representatives—anemones, columbine, larkspur, hepatica, crowfoot and meadow rue—is the champion plant family of spring. The composite or aster family clearly reigns supreme in the fall. Look around any site that receives three to four hours or more of sun daily and you will see countless composite flowers. *Asteraceae* is one of the largest of plant families with one thousand genera and twenty thousand species throughout the world.

Members of this broad-ranging family have flowers of three types. The classic daisy-type of flower has both disk and ray flowers. Some plants with both disk and ray flowers are the sunflowers, black-eyed Susans and asters. Disk flowers are the tiny florets with no long petals that develop in the central circle of the main flower. Surrounding the disk are ray florets with long petals. The second group has ray flowers only and includes chicory, hawkweed and wild lettuce. The final group, which has disk flowers only, includes pussy-toes, cornflower and white snakeroot.

Let's take a closer look at a few of these *Asteraceae* family plants. Those composite plants with both disk and ray flowers are well known to all of us. Yarrows, European natives that probably came here as uninvited guests in hay and straw, are common throughout our country. Their fernlike foliage and white, pink and yellow flowers grow in flat terminal clusters. Refined yarrows bred into elegant cultivars are garden favorites. The wild ones grow everywhere along roads and in fields and other sunny places.

The true asters, with both disk and ray flowers, are many and are also well known in the garden as well as along roadsides, in fields, in glades, in moist prairies and in places with disturbed land. Asters grow from 2 or 3 feet to as much as 8 feet tall, depending upon the species. They come in colors that range from whites to pinks, blues and purples. Asters truly are the glory of all the fall flowers. The plants, with narrow lance-shaped leaves, are weedy looking and nondescript until the flowers open, often covering the plant with bright blooms.

Tickseed sunflower looks like a leggy black-eyed Susan with eight golden ray florets surrounding the dark brown disk florets. The featherlike compound leaves have three to five leaflets. This plant of damp soils in prairies, roadsides and ditches is the one with seeds called beggar ticks—each seed has two sharp *awns* that will stick to animal fur and people's clothing with equal enthusiasm.

The coneflowers are handsome composites with daisylike flowers. These hairy plants have lance-shaped leaves that may be coarsely toothed. Flowers of the pale purple coneflower have slim ray florets of pink, magenta or sometimes white that hang down, surrounding the knobby disk florets that are brown with yellow stamens rising above them. Purple coneflowers have wider ray flowers in magenta shades, surrounding dark disks of florets that may appear yellowish because of protruding stamens.

The sunflowers of several species of the *Helianthus* genus are native in our region and bloom throughout most of the fall season. Sunflowers have large oval leaves that are coarsely toothed and usually alternate. Common sunflowers have hairy stems and are tall—to 7 feet—with large flowers having brown disks and often a double row of ray florets. The sawtooth sunflower is another large plant, growing to as much as 16 feet, usually branched with many terminal, all-yellow flowers up to nearly 4 inches in diameter. There also are 4-foot hairy sunflowers with lemon yellow flowers and 7-foot prairie or showy sunflowers with 1- to 3-inch flowers featuring yellow ray florets around purple disk florets.

The genus *Rudbeckia* includes black-eyed Susans and a number of similar plants including the gray-head coneflower, brown-eyed Susan, sweet coneflower and tall coneflower, also known by the intriguing name of wild goldenglow.

The goldenrods of the *Solidago* genus are composites with both disk and ray flowers. The plants of this group have very heavy pollen that does not float on the breezes. Goldenrods have been tarred with a wide brush because they are showy flowers that bloom at the same time as the ragweeds, whose light pollen drifts on every air current, causing untold miseries to those who are allergic. Look closely with a hand lens to see the details of goldenrod flowers. Our region has over two dozen species of goldenrod so you may be content to identify those plants belonging to the genus.

Chicory, which has ray flowers only, is also known as blue sailors and grows along just about every sunny roadside in our region. An Old World native, chicory's beautiful blue flowers an inch or more in diameter are open on cool days and during the morning hours of hot days. Extracts of the bitter roots are used to flavor coffee, especially in Louisiana. Chicory will continue to develop flowers even when it is mowed short and the flowers must grow only inches above the ground. Chicory normally reaches a height of about 3 feet.

The hawkweed species also have only ray flowers. These very hairy plants grow from 1 foot to nearly 3 feet in height and have flowers an inch or less in diameter in shades of yellow and orange. Hawkweeds grow in dry, rocky places in open woods and fields.

The wild lettuce species, migrants from Europe, are tall plants, growing from 2 to 6 or more feet in height, and are believed to be ancestors of our salad lettuces. The flowers develop in loose panicles with a dozen or more 1/2-inch flower heads of ray florets in pale yellow. The leaves may be simply or deeply lobed and both stems and leaves are prickly.

Asteraceae family plants with disk flowers only include the thistles, with their spiny leaves and pinkish bristly flower heads. Several species of thistles, originally from Europe and Asia, have made themselves too much at home in our region, growing and spreading in sunny places along roadsides and railroad rights-of-way. Musk thistle and bull thistle are two of the most common. You can tell them apart by the sharp spines that grow all the way up to the flower heads on the bull thistle.

There are a number of native plants in the *Eupatorium* genus that bloom in the fall and have disk flowers only. White snakeroot, a 4-foot, well-branched plant of rich woods, clearings and roadsides, has small white tufted flowers that appear in loose clusters at the tops of the plants. Late boneset and tall thoroughwort are similar plants, with boneset, having gray flowers in fewer numbers and the sturdy tall thoroughwort having only five florets in each loose cluster. Wild ageratum or blue boneset is common in open woods of bottomlands and alongside streams and lakes. This plant looks like a taller, looser version of garden ageratum.

Liatris, also called blazing star or gay feather, is another composite with disk flowers only. These prairie plants with their rosy purple flower spikes come in two forms, one with many small separate flower heads along the terminal spike, the other with the flower heads closely wrapping the flower stalk.

Liatris is a long-lived prairie plant of the aster family, growing three to four feet tall and having roots that may reach fifteen feet into the soil. Its spiky flowers have a strong pink color.

NOVEMBER

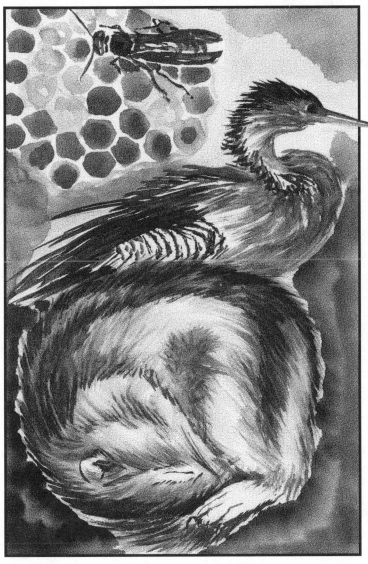

November Observations

61

The Patterns of Trees

The patterns of falling leaves are as varied as the trees from which they fall. When most of the leaves have fallen, you can once again study the growth patterns of the hardwood trees that formerly were dressed in green foliage. I'll describe some of the more easily recognized trees that grow in much of our region. Once you have learned to recognize them, you will feel more confident in adding others to your list. In Chapter 57, the reason for fall coloring was discussed and I explained that you can tell the native trees from those of European origin by their bright fall color. I also pointed out that many tree imports from places in Korea, Japan and China with climates similar to ours also have bright fall color.

Recognizing the pattern and overall shape of things, including trees as well as people and animals, is often called the gestalt method after Gestalt psychology, which holds that people tend to perceive whole things as organized patterns rather than separate parts that are added together. This theory says, therefore, that the whole is greater than the sum of its parts. In Chapter 4 we studied the winter patterns of tree buds and bark as clues to their identification. In this chapter we are looking at the overall growth patterns, branching patterns and general shapes. Keep this in mind when you look at trees in the fall. Look at the overall shape, study the way the branches grow, look for similarities in related trees, then look for the ways in which species differ. Notice also where the trees grow—this can be an important clue.

Some introduced trees have become so popular and are so widely planted that many people assume they are native trees. The classic example of that is the ginkgo tree discovered in eastern China and introduced to this country in 1784. Charles Darwin called it "a living fossil" because of its primitive fan-veined leaves and the fact that fossilized remains of this tree have been found dating back to the age of giant reptiles in the Mesozoic Era. The primitive ginkgoes are *gymnosperms*, plants that lack flowers and reproduce by means of naked seeds borne on special bracts rather than by seeds borne in ovaries like the flowering plants. Although this tree varies greatly in shape, it often is pyramidal when young and has wide-spreading large limbs as a mature tree. The leaves turn bright yellow in the fall and persist on the tree until one bright morning when there is a breeze, and all the leaves fall at once making a golden pool around the base of the trunk.

The common bald cypress of swamps throughout the southern part of our region is an easy tree to recognize. It usually grows in colonies in shallow water. Look for stout, straight trunks that are buttressed near the base. On older trees, look also for the "knees" that grow up near the trunk when the tree grows in water—no one seems to know the function of these knees. Mature bald cypress trees are tall and look like slim pyramids. You will see that, although they are conifers, they are deciduous trees that shed their needlelike leaves each fall.

A prevalent tree throughout our region and most common in the Ozarks is the red cedar, which is a juniper rather than a true cedar. This dense evergreen has needle leaves that are short and look like scales. Look for the overall shape of this tree to be pyramidal when young and ranging from columnar to a wide pyramid in shape when mature. This is the only tree of its type in the region, so identification is easy. Look for red cedars in association with sassafras and persimmon trees, along old fences and in old fields and frequently on dry limestone glades. Female trees may have bluish berries about the size of peas and are covered with a whitish bloom.

Common sassafras often grows in association with red cedar and others as mentioned above along the edges of fields, especially on rich moist soils. Once the leaves are shed, you can see green or reddish buds on fragrant greenish twigs. Note the zigzag lines of the branches caused by sympodial branching that also gives it the look of candelabra, a downward turn followed by an upward bend in the branches. This tree often grows in colonies that develop by means of root runners. When young the sassafras grows in a loose and irregular pyramidal form and when mature may be up to 60 feet tall with a 40-foot spread and an irregular form and somewhat flat head.

The American sycamore, a tree of bottomlands, has a characteristic bark which peels off in small plates when mature, leaving a mottled effect of tan, green and gray.

The American sycamore is hard to miss. Here is a towering giant of a tree that commonly grows in numbers on rich bottomlands where you also will find other trees that thrive on rich moist soil—river birch, silver maple, cottonwood and red maple. Once the large maplelike leaves drop off, you can better see the exfoliating surface of the trunk and larger branches that exposes a smooth white bark under scales of gray to greenish. The sycamore has an almost birchlike look because it is so white. The mature sycamore usually has a massive trunk and great height, often reaching 75 to 100 feet.

River birch, a native throughout much of our region, is another bottomland tree that you should recognize easily. The bark of this birch is thin on young trees and peels to reveal a white to pinkish to red-brown inner surface. Pyramidal as a young tree, it becomes more oval as it matures to a height of somewhat under 50 feet. Once the leaves are shed, you can easily see the extent of the exfoliating bark. On very old river birches, the bark of the main trunk may lose its scaling characteristic and appear furrowed and nearly black. Then you will have to look at upper branches to see the typically peeling paperlike bark.

Hackberry, an elm relative, also grows in rich bottomlands in most of our region. A common tree of moist soils, the hackberry grows 40 to 60 feet tall and usually has an equal spread. Two common characteristics will help you identify this tree. Look at the tree bark, which often has narrow, corky ridges that also appear as wartlike projections. When the leaves have fallen, look for "witches' brooms," dense, erratic bunches of small twigs caused by a cancerlike disease.

Flowering dogwood is a common small understory tree in many hardwood forests. This much loved spring-flowering tree usually doesn't grow much over 20 feet. Look for its horizontal limbs that have a layered effect and look somewhat like candelabra because of the way they turn up at the ends. Other clues are the buttonlike flower buds at the ends of twigs. The bark itself is singular, appearing broken into small squares and rectangles.

Musclewood, also known as blue beech and American horn-beam, is marvelously easy to recognize with its smooth gray sinewy bark that looks like gray stone with tendons and muscles rippling just under the surface. It is a small tree of the deciduous understory, seldom growing much over 20 feet and rarely attaining a diameter of more than 10 inches. Musclewood often grows in clumps with several trunks.

You can recognize many of the oaks by the way they hold their leaves through most of the winter. In some species, the leaves are so persistent that you may imagine that last year's foliage will fall off only when pushed off by spring's newly developing leaves. To identify the individual species, compare the leaves and buds with the aid of a good tree guide. Many of the oaks hybridize freely so you may find individuals that combine characteristics of two species and many with indistinct characteristics.

These are a few of the common native trees of our region that are comparatively easy to identify when the foliage has fallen. The combinations of characteristics including habitat, general shape, branching patterns, buds and bark are clues you can easily learn.

HOTSPOTS

Petit Jean SP in central Arkansas (see Chapter 14 for direc-tions) has an abundance of natural beauty in its woods, forests, ravines and streams, offering a variety of native trees for you to study. Go to the visitors' center first to get trail maps and guides to the park's plant and animal life. **Felsenthal NWR** in southern Arkansas (see Chapter 2 for directions) and **White River NWR** in southeastern Arkansas (see Chapter 15 for directions) are good places with ample wooded areas for learning to recognize the overall look of native trees.

Morton Arboretum near Chicago in northern Illinois (see Chapter 3 for directions) is a must for anyone interested in trees—its tree collections are the best in the entire region. Check out also the wilderness area of **Crab Orchard NWR** in the southern part of the state (see Chapter 1 for directions). **Chicago Botanical Gardens** (see Chapter 4 for directions) in northern Illinois is another place to study trees, especially if you would like to study those that are well labeled.

In eastern Missouri, both **Missouri Botanical Garden** in the City of St. Louis (see Chapter 4 for directions) and its own **Shaw Arboretum** a few miles west in Franklin County (see Chapter 2 for directions) are ideal for studying trees. There are trail maps as well as brochures showing you what you can expect to find. Near Kansas City, **Powell Garden** (see Chapter 4 for directions) is a good site for observing native trees. **Lake of the Ozarks SP** (see Chapter 14 for directions) is another top spot for seeing native trees in a lovely location.

62

Bird Nests

Now that the foliage has fallen from hardwood trees, a bonus of the season is that you can more easily see bird nests. The young of most of our songbirds are hatched from vulnerable eggs into a featherless, helpless stage. Both eggs and hatchlings are potentially tasty meals for many snakes, squirrels, foxes, cats, hawks, bluejays, crows and other birds and animals. That's why it is so important for the parents to build nests in places where there is good cover, and where the nest will be camouflaged by its natural materials blending in with the surrounding growth.

Camouflage is one way to keep the nest from being discovered and it is the one used most successfully by the greatest number of species. A second method, one more common to birds such as herons, cliff swallows and barn swallows, is to construct the nest in places that are inaccessible to major predators. Herons build their rookeries in tall trees. Cliff swallows put nests in tunnels in sandy banks while barn swallows build their nests of mud and straw on barn rafters and under bridges.

Once the nests are built and egg laying begins, the parent birds often go to great lengths to avoid being seen going directly to the nest. They may wait until no animals or birds are in sight before approaching the nest or they may take an obscure and circuitous path. Knowing the purposes of different kinds of nests will help you find them—even when the leaves are off, some of the smaller tree nests are hard to see.

The simplest of nests are barely nests. Pigeons, hawks and

eagles make nests that are little more than piles of sticks. Crows' nests are somewhat tidier and better constructed. They also are built of twigs and sticks, but have linings of rootlets that are carefully woven into the base. Woodpeckers nest in holes they have hammered out of old or dead trees—eggs are laid directly on the wood and wood chips at the bottom of the hole. Hummingbirds build tiny elaborate nests of plant down, lichens and other small pieces of plant material that are artfully woven and held together with bits of spider web.

Classic songbird nests are like those of robins or blackbirds. They are sturdily made of twigs, grass and other bits of plants all carefully woven together and reinforced with mud. In some cases the lining is smooth mud while in other cases, a fine textured lining is woven of delicate grasses and small roots. Wrens build domed nests, so when you see nests that look much like a small haystack and must be entered through an entrance hole, you may guess that it was built by a wren. The master architects of all our native birds are the orchard oriole and northern oriole, both of which nest in our region. Their nests are woven pouches carefully slung on outer branches of trees in open woodlands—the birds enter this nest from the top, below the handle that is woven over the branch. Orioles make their intricate nests of plant fibers and string, weaving each piece in and out of the nest.

You can tell the nests of chipping sparrows, called the hair bird by some, because it is a tidy cup in bushes or dense trees made of small stems, grass and tiny roots lined with hair that encircles the entire inside of the cup. Chippies prefer horse hair but will use hair from other animals and people if they can't find horse hair.

Grasshopper sparrows build their nests of grass, line them with tiny soft roots or hair, and often build an arch over the top to hide the eggs. These cups of woven grasses are built into the ground at the bases of tall grasses or other vegetation in old fields, pastures and other grasslands.

Barn swallow nests are easy to identify. Look for them on top of beams in barns or other outbuildings, under the eaves of buildings, under bridges and in other ledgelike locations. There usually will be several pairs nesting in the same locale, often very close to one another. The nests are plastered against a surface with mud and the nest itself is carefully made of mud pellets lined with grass and feathers.

Red-winged blackbirds nest in open marshes and grasslands. Look for their nests that are woven of grasses and carefully lashed to reeds or shrubby plants. In the case of this blackbird and, indeed, many birds, you can identify the builder of a nest as much by location as by any other factor.

If you find a domed nest made of leaves, small plant stems and grasses on the ground in hardwood forest or thickets and it has a side opening, chances are that you are looking at the creation of an ovenbird. This unusual warbler lives on the forest floor where you are likely to see it walking on the ground or on low growth rather than flitting through the tree tops the way other warblers do. The ovenbird nests throughout all of our region except perhaps southern Arkansas.

If you see a nest that is made of a mass of grass and twigs and includes a snake skin and possibly some waxed paper, cellophane or plastic as integral parts of the construction, you undoubtedly have uncovered the nest of a great crested flycatcher. This bird builds its nest, often in a tree hollow or even in a bird house, of just about anything, including twigs, leaves, roots and other bits of plant matter. The snake skin is thought to act as a deterrent to predators.

The American goldfinch builds a nest that is so thick and tightly woven that it will hold water. You might find goldfinch nests in bushes or trees. They are made of plant fibers and down such as that found on thistle seedheads, the seeds being one of their favorite foods.

If you have identified nesting birds during the breeding season at a location you can visit after the leaves fall, you will be able to find the nest and see what it looks like. Remember that location and habitat will help identify bird nests nearly as much as size, materials and construction.

HOTSPOTS

Look carefully along the edges of woods, in fields, in dense bushes and trees—all good locations for breeding birds to build their nests. Remember that in most parks you are allowed only to collect bird nests with your eyes and camera.

In southwestern Arkansas, **Millwood SP** (see Chapter 10 for directions) is widely known as a good birding spot, good for observing nests at any time of year. This also is a fishing hotspot if that will help lure other members of your family into taking a trip there. **Hot Springs National Park** in central Arkansas (see Chapter 22 for directions) with its many wooded trails is another good place to enjoy looking for bird nests after the leaves fall. Go to the visitors' center in the middle of Bathhouse Row to get trail guides.

Giant City SP in southern Illinois in the Shawnee Hills (see Chapter 16 for directions) also is known for its good birding as well as its spectacular rock formations. Get trails guides and information about the wildlife of the park at the visitors' center. **Morton Arboretum** near Chicago (see Chapter 3 for directions) is famous for its good birding and so should be fun for seeking out bird nests in the winter.

In Missouri, **Big Oak Tree SP** in the southeastern part of the state (see Chapter 22 for directions) is an excellent forested area for both summer birds and winter residents so it is a good site for finding bird nests during the cold season. The **Missouri Botanical Garden** in St. Louis (see Chapter 4 for directions) and its **Shaw Arboretum** southwest of the city (see Chapter 2 for directions) are good birding places as the area's many birders can attest. **Swope Park** in Kansas City (see Chapter 27 for directions) is another likely spot to look for birds' nests at this time of year.

63

Nests of Hornets, Wasps and Bees

The nests of some of our native stinging insects, especially those of the bald-faced hornets, are beautiful structures, geometrically perfect and made to instinctive plans that architects might well envy. Read on to find out why this time of year is ideal for taking a closer look at the nests of social stingers such as hornets.

I can't think of a more scary insect than the bald-faced hornet. The buzzing or even the mere sight of the giant paper nest of this creature makes even the bravest among us wary, more so even than the brown wasp. If you disturb the bald-faced hornets by hitting their nest or aggravating them while they are going about their business, they may take swift and painful revenge—and, unlike the honeybee, these powerful hornets can sting many times. A healthy respect is the best approach when observing bees, wasps and hornets. There are hundreds of species of wasps and bees in our region, and although most of the females can sting with their modified ovi-positors, only a few act aggressively and have stings that are painful.

Some of these stinging insects live a solitary life while others are called social insects. The social wasps, hornets and bees include honeybees and also yellowjackets, paper wasps, hornets and bumblebees. In the early spring the small nests of the native social species, excluding the introduced honeybee, each include just a single young fertile queen. By the time fall arrives, each colony may include from dozens in the case of bumblebees and paper wasps to thousands of adults in the case of yellowjackets.

Solitary bees and wasps (hornets are in the wasp family) may nest in the ground or in hollows in wood excavated by themselves or other organisms. Most of our stinging insects are solitary, that is, the entire small nest is cared for by a lone female. The solitary species don't make wax hexagons as nest cells but they do line the ground cells with a waxy substance and then seal the cell once an egg is laid and food stored for the young. Those that nest above ground in twigs or other wood hollows usually build lines of cells separated by walls of mud, pebbles and chewed-up plant materials. Mud daubers make their cell complexes of mud. The young of the solitary bees and wasps are the form that usually overwinter and emerge as adults in the spring. Very little is known about the nests and nesting habits of many of the solitary wasps and bees that nest in the ground.

In the case of the social species, only newly-fertilized queens survive hard freezes—all of the workers, the old egg-laying queen and any drones still around will die. The young queens endure the winter months sheltered in some protected site. At this time of year, after the leaves have fallen and there have been several hard freezes, all of the eggs, young and adults in the nest will be dead. That is why it is safe to collect and study the nests of these stinging insects during the late fall and winter. If you don't collect the nests, they will be broken into by birds, squirrels and other animals that eat the larvae and dead adults.

These highly respected flying, stinging animals are true insects and as such, have compound eyes, six legs, three body segments (head, thorax, and abdomen), and antennae. The wasps, bees and hornets belong to the order called *Hymenoptera* and occupy a valuable niche in the world. Honeybees, of course, serve by providing food for us at the same time that they pollinate flowers. Honeybees are not native to this country but have been introduced and cultured from European bees. Without pollinating insects, we would have far less fruit—fewer apples, peaches, pears, cherries and other bee-pollinated fruit. Other members of this group also may pollinate flowers. Some wasps are major predators of insect pests that otherwise would destroy more wild and cultivated plants.

Let's take a closer look at some nest-building social bees, wasps and hornets that are native to our region. Paper wasps are the best known of the social stinging insects. We've all had our ordeals with the several species of these nest-building, often brown stinging insects. They build their nests as single layers of cells hung upside down from a thin neck. Nests are made of paper made from small bits of woods scraped from old boards or branches and mixed with saliva.

The cells are open at the bottom until the young pupate—then the cells are closed. Nests are constructed anew each spring by one or more fertile females that have overwintered inside buildings or in crevices of tree bark. Nests are built in sheltered places under sills and eaves, often in places that are inconvenient for people—in mail boxes and on porch ceilings. Workers—infertile females—are produced first so that they can help with nest work of building cells and gathering food. It is the workers that so fiercely defend the nest when it is threatened. Fertile females and males are produced in late summer. These wasps feed their young with caterpillars and so are valuable allies in the garden.

Yellowjackets, those black and yellow bullets that are the size of bees and hover around food and drink on picnic tables in late summer and fall, are the worst menace among all the stinging social insects. By fall, a successful colony will have several thousand stinging workers, all ready to defend their territory if you should stumble upon it. The native species may nest in the ground or above the ground in wood piles or under steps. Each colony originates with a single female that has overwintered in a protected spot. The nests are like those of the paper wasp in that they hang down and open at the bottom but they are built in many layers of paper comb and then enclosed with a paper envelope made of wood fibers mixed with saliva. There are several species of yellowjacket living in our region. The introduced German yellowjacket prefers nesting in building walls, while the native species will nest wherever they find a suitable rodent hole or above-ground cavity. You won't often see these nests unless you have traced the workers to the sites before frost, then excavate them after frost.

The bald-faced hornet is clearly the most impressive of the social stinging insects. Its gray paper nest is a handsome globular creation that may get a foot or more in length with a diameter of 6 to 8 or more inches. Each large nest colony, carefully built onto branches of trees and shrubs, was founded by a single fertile queen that had overwintered in a sheltered spot. Layers of horizontal paper comb are enclosed by a thick outer layer of paper, similar to that of the yellowjacket, to which this insect is closely related. Unlike their smaller cousins, the bald-faced hornet is not aggressive away from its nest and does not make a nuisance of itself in searching for sweets. Pale yellow marks this predominantly black hornet that appears nearly twice as big as a honeybee. The colony will grow until there are hundreds of workers and, in late summer, young fertile females and males, as well as the old queen.

The bumblebee on this flower is one of several species that seek nectar and pollen from the flowers of the fields.

Bumblebees are social stinging insects that may nest in underground holes or above ground in brush piles, bird houses and other similar sites. A single fertile female that has overwintered in an underground place will start a new colony in the spring, building a large blob of a cell with wax and pollen. She lays eggs in the cell and stocks it with nectar and pollen, then incubates the eggs to rush their development. They develop into workers that maintain the nests, feed the young and collect nectar and pollen. They may store foods in empty cells. The several species of social bumblebees are important pollinators of many plants.

You will find bees, wasps and hornets everywhere in our region. Use some common sense when you find their nests before there have been hard frosts. Move slowly, wear shoes and light-colored clothing, avoid perfumes and schedule fewer picnics during the height of the yellowjacket season.

HOTSPOTS

You are likely to find the nests of wasps and hornets everywhere in our region. Most likely, you will be birding or botanizing and chance to come upon the large nest of bald-faced hornets or the pendulous paper comb of paper wasps. Parks and refuges with plenty of wildflowers will have more wasps and bees.

Felsenthal NWR in southern Arkansas (see Chapter 2 for directions) has varied habitat including much that is inhabited by a variety of social stinging insects. **Lake Poinsett SP** on Crowley's Ridge in the northeastern part of the state (see Chapter 13 for directions) is a good fishing spot as well as a likely place for finding wasp nests after hard frosts.

Castle Rock SP in northwestern Illinois (see Chapter 32 for directions) has a variety of habitat and a number of trails that go through spectacular sandstone formations, part of the Rock River valley, and is promising for finding paper wasp and hornet nests. **Crab Orchard NWR** in the southern part of the state (see Chapter 1 for directions) is another place you might want to visit in looking for wasp and hornet nests. That's a good place for observing waterfowl as well.

Mingo NWR in southeastern Missouri is a good place for just about anything to do with wildlife and native plants. So is **Squaw Creek NWR** over in the northwestern part of the state. Both offer opportunities to study a wide variety of plants and animals in varied habitats. (See Chapter 1 for directions to both.)

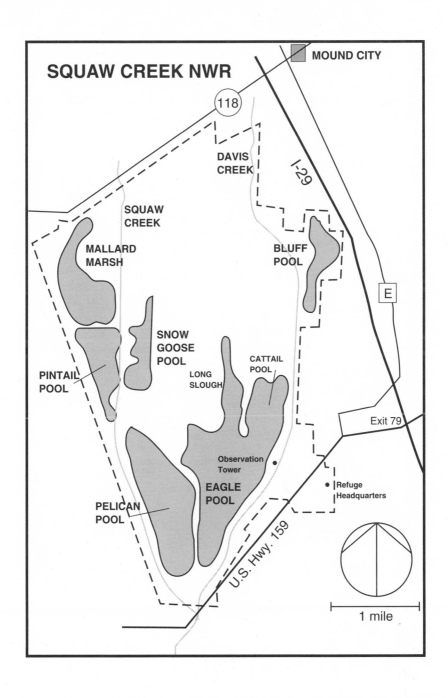

SQUAW CREEK NWR

MOUND CITY

118

DAVIS
CREEK

I-29

SQUAW
CREEK

MALLARD
MARSH

BLUFF
POOL

E

SNOW
GOOSE
POOL

CATTAIL
POOL

PINTAIL
POOL

LONG
SLOUGH

Exit 79

Observation
Tower

Refuge
Headquarters

EAGLE
POOL

PELICAN
POOL

U.S. Hwy. 159

1 mile

64

Accidentals, Rarities and Oddities

November is a good time of year to discuss a phenomenon that occurs most often with birds because flying gives them such freedom to travel. Every year, you will read of at least one rare bird being sighted where it has never before been seen. Sometimes such a rare bird, called an accidental or a "vagrant," will hang around for several days or even weeks, offering birders an opportunity to add to their life lists. Roger Tory Peterson was once asked why a particularly unusual bird—I think it was a flamingo—had appeared in the Boston area. He replied simply, "Birds fly."

The crossroads biology of Illinois, Missouri and Arkansas—a place where species of the East and West as well as the North and South meet—makes sightings of unusual birds nearly an everyday occurrence. During spring migrations, birds not only pass through our region, but many may unintentionally overshoot their regular breeding sites, landing hundreds of miles to the north. This will happen especially during unseasonably warm weather when winds are out of the south.

During the rush of the fall migration, which actually begins in August and goes on into November, you are even more likely to see accidentals and rarities. After all, when millions of birds are on the move, it's highly likely that a few will lose their way, get blown off their regular course or otherwise end up in what, for them, is the wrong place. Then birders will flag their hot lines and appear in droves to study the stranger. Some birders with both time and money for travel will go long distances to add accidentals and rarities to their lists.

During winter months, severe storms to the north and other conditions that might lead to a shortage of food may bring us birds that normally winter in more northern climes. The snowy owl is the classic example of this kind of rarity. The snowy owl prefers Arctic tundra for its winter home but, when storms or lack of prey drive it southward, one can sometimes be seen sitting on a small mound in the middle of an Illinois cornfield on a cold winter day.

In places where gulls congregate, experienced birders find unusual gulls for their areas with great regularity. Perhaps the gulls are more easily blown off course during stormy periods or perhaps they range over far wider territories than we have thought. Greater black-backed gulls, lesser black-backed gulls and Bonaparte's gulls are sometimes found in our region, far west and south of their usual winter territory, perhaps blown in by a northeaster. Glaucous gulls that usually range no farther south than the Great Lakes occasionally blow into parts of our three-state region. Occasionally little gulls that generally summer in the northern Great Lakes can be seen travelling through to their winter grounds along the coastline of our northeastern states. Once in a great while someone in our region will hotline a Franklin's gull that more commonly spends the breeding season in the northern plains and northern Rocky Mountains. This gull is occasionally seen on the Gulf Coast and in southern California, but is definitely a rarity in our region!

We often see common loons, especially in the northern parts of our region. It's not surprising that occasionally we see the red-throated loons in northern Illinois and the northern half of Missouri since they winter on the Great Lakes as well as the Gulf Coast and Atlantic and Pacific coastlines. But how do the yellow-billed loons of the Arctic and coastal Northwest manage to put in occasional appearances, especially in western Missouri and northwestern Arkansas?

As trumpeter swans are protected and reintroduced in refuges, you can expect to have more sightings of this rare waterfowl that normally is a year-round resident of Yellowstone Park and a migrating bird of Alaska and the Canadian Pacific coast. They occasionally appear in refuges in northwestern Illinois and northwestern and central Missouri.

Sandhill cranes are seen by the thousands in fall and spring in the Missouri River wetlands of Nebraska, where they rest on their way to and from summer grounds in northern United States, Alaska and Canada to winter grounds in southern United States and Mexico. These impressive 4-foot-tall cranes, gray with red caps, occasionally are seen as singles or in small groups elsewhere, but since their migration path is so narrow because of their traditional resting places, they are a rare sight. I once saw a pair in a small woodsy pond on a ridge in west St. Louis County—I was astounded by two gigantic birds taking off and looking like bombers with their necks and legs stretched out front and rear.

The Eurasian tree sparrow, an introduction from Europe in the last half of the nineteenth century, is a bird found only in parks, farmlands and suburbs in and around St. Louis and nearby Illinois. Unlike its close relative, the house sparrow, it has not made a nuisance of itself throughout the land. You can tell this bird from the house sparrow by the brown cap, black throat and black cheek patch of the Eurasian tree sparrow. Birders come from miles around to add this one to their life lists.

In warmer seasons, there are spots in western Arkansas and southwestern Missouri to occasionally find a number of birds more commonly residents of regions farther south and west. You will see the scissor-tailed flycatcher—watch for it sitting on utility lines. You will need no description to recognize this long-tailed bird for there is no other like it in our country. You also might well see the greater roadrunner, a ground-dwelling cuckoo of the desert Southwest. Again, this bird needs no description—if you see a large bird legging it down an open field or sunny path in an open area, that's the roadrunner.

Painted buntings are beautiful birds that summer in Arkansas and southwestern Missouri and may occasionally be seen farther north and east. They are uncommon and handsome enough to warrant attention wherever seen.

Mississippi kites are birds that spend the summer breeding season in the Mississippi Valley in the Bootheel of Missouri and throughout much of southeastern Arkansas. They often are found nesting farther north and west of their usual territory. Hardly a year goes by without someone reporting nesting Mississippi kites in the Missouri and Illinois suburbs of St. Louis.

The anhinga is a cormorantlike bird more usually found throughout the Gulf Coast and summering along the lower Mississippi Valley. It is one of the more common rarities found somewhat farther north in the big river valleys. Sometimes after raising it young the anhinga will wander well north and west of its breeding range.

The important thing about accidentals and rare birds is to know that you probably will see some of them, but look for more common identifications first. Only when the common identification doesn't fit should you look for the field marks of less common birds for your area. Since, as Peterson says, birds fly, you will be hard-pressed to prove a rare sighting unless you are with at least one experienced birder.

HOTSPOTS

In Arkansas, **Felsenthal NWR** in the southern part of the state (see Chapter 2 for directions) is a good place to see unusual birds including an occasional anhinga. Check out the trails of more open areas at **Table Rock SP** near Branson, Missouri, (see Chapter 7 for directions) for sightings of birds more commonly seen farther southwest.

Crab Orchard NWR in southern Illinois (see Chapter 1 for directions) is a good place to search for unusual birds and waterfowl that are more common in other regions. The **Illinois Beach SP** (see Chapter 7 for directions) is a good spot for unusual gulls. **Goose Lake Prairie State Natural Area** is a good site for hunting out unusual waterfowl and other birds that may be farther south than their usual winter range. (See Chapter 34 for directions.)

Busch Wildlife Area west of St. Louis (see Chapter 10 for directions) is a good place to look for unusual waterfowl and other rare birds. So is **Squaw Creek NWR** in northwestern Missouri (see Chapter 1 for directions). For unusual gulls, it's hard to beat **Riverland EDA** near the Melvin Price Locks and Dam, directly across the Mississippi River from Alton, Illinois (see Chapter 1 for directions).

65

November
Shorttakes

Voles and Mice in the Winter

Voles and mice continue to be active during the winter. They store grasses and the seeds of grasses and flowers near runs that they make under the snow and under the fallen growth of the past year's tall grass and other weedy growth.

White Pelicans

Migratory white pelicans leave northern refuges, especially during early fall, and pass through our region on the way to their winter headquarters along the Gulf of Mexico. These fish-eating birds spend the breeding season in the lake and pothole country of Canada and the northern plains states.

Bird Feeders

When bird feeders are set up at this season, year-round and winter residents alike soon come in to the seeds, fruits and suet. Many wildlife refuges and parks put feeders outside their visitors' centers so that we can sit comfortably indoors and watch the winter visitors that range from juncoes to grosbeaks to wild turkeys. For more on winter birds, see Chapter 68.

66

Breakout: Animals Seek Winter Shelter

Cold temperatures trigger winter behavior in animals. When Arctic Clippers—fast moving cold fronts—shoot south into our region, animals dive for shelter. Their responses to the coming winter are as varied as the animals themselves. While many stay active all winter, others hibernate throughout the cold season and yet others sleep sporadically. Apparently, hibernation occurs at several levels, depending on both the species and the temperature of the air.

Starting with the lower animals, there are many insects, crustaceans and other lower animals that hibernate all winter under shreds of tree bark, in the ground, in mud and under water. Some winter over as adults while others spend the winter as eggs or larval forms. Apparently there is something in the circulatory systems of these so-called cold-blooded animals that allows them to freeze, to go into a kind of suspended animation. The cells of their living tissues freeze but seem to have some kind of natural antifreeze that keeps them from rupturing with the cold.

When warm-blooded animals hibernate, their metabolism shifts into a much lower gear. Their body temperatures fall from slightly under 100 degrees Fahrenheit to between 40 and 60 degrees depending upon the ambient temperature. Their breathing and heart rates fall as well. Prior to going into hibernation, warm-blooded animals eat large amounts in order to store up enough fat in their body tissues to last through the winter.

Salamanders are animals that spend their larval lives in the water of still ponds and streams, their adult lives on land. There is little known about the entire life cycles of some of these animals, but we can assume that those going through the winter in larval forms would hibernate under dead leaves and in silty mud at the bottom of ponds. Those wintering over as adults would hibernate under moist leaves in damp deciduous woods, hidden under rocks and logs or dug into light moist soils. Some overwinter as eggs.

Green frogs and bullfrogs burrow into the mud in pond and stream bottoms during the winter. Their overwintering tadpoles, those that were late in hatching and those that take more than one season to mature and metamorphose, also nose into the leaves and loose mud at the bottom of ponds and inlets.

Other frogs and toads have varying winter habits. Some may winter over in wet mud at the edges of ponds while others move into caves where they have greatly reduced activity during the winter. Others may burrow under leaves, logs, rocks, old bark or any other place where they can be under enough cover to shelter them from the winter weather.

The winter habits of turtles depend on whether they are aquatic or land turtles. Aquatic turtles burrow into the mud, dead leaves and other plant materials at the bottom of ponds, streams and rivers. Their heart rate, breathing and general metabolism is very greatly reduced. Their activity, if disturbed, is sluggish at best—it takes spring sun to bring them back to regular activity. Land turtles, including the well-known box turtles, burrow as best they can into leaf litter and other organic duff on the forest floor.

Lizards and skinks will spend the winter in underground animal runs, hollow trees and limbs, rock crevices, under rocks and logs—any place they can find that will protect them from icy winds and buffer the temperature around them. They are true hibernators with a much-reduced metabolism through the cold season.

Snakes often spend the winter in underground dens where they are well protected from winter weather. The activity of these animals is totally dependent upon the air around them and the temperature of the materials upon which they rest. Therefore, throughout most of our region, snakes will be in deep hibernation for several months each winter. Caves and animal burrows are top choices for snakes seeking places to hibernate. Rock crevices in outcroppings and on rocky hillsides, hollow rotted tree stumps, abandoned quarries and abandoned cisterns also are likely places. When hibernating, snakes may be rather neighborly—you might find copperheads hibernating in the same small cave as black rat snakes, racers and rattlesnakes, for instance. Some snakes den together in intertwined masses. This may be due to the scarcity of appropriate denning places in some areas.

Our largest mammal, the black bear, spends the coldest periods of the winter months in a torpor in caves and hollows under fallen brush and trees. In more southern climes, the black bear's hibernation may be quite restless as it arises during warm periods, then returns to its den when the weather gets cold once again. Bears coming out of hibernation often are cranky and hungry.

Mammals that burrow into the ground are, as a rule, among those that hibernate. Chipmunks and woodchucks hibernate for an extended period each winter, as do striped and spotted skunks, both native to our region. Walk into almost any cave and you will see bats hanging upside down on the cave ceiling where they hibernate, many of them in large colonies. If you should see them, be careful not to disturb them—many are becoming more rare and are on the endangered lists. Some animals, including squirrels and gophers, are dormant sporadically, waking occasionally to eat some of the nuts and other seeds they stored, then going back to sleep.

Animals that do not hibernate have other ways of protecting themselves from the cold. You will see that they have grown winter coats and, in the worst of weather, will appear fat and fluffy as they hold the hairs of their fur out straight to increase the insulating power of their coats. Birds fluff up and also crouch down so that often all you can see of their legs is the toes.

Cottontail rabbits find thickets of dense bushes or brush piles where they can burrow far inside and be protected from wind, ice and snow. White-tailed deer move to southwestern slopes that are out of the wind and get the most sunshine when storms are past. These deer change from their tawny summer color to a much thicker grayish winter coat—deer hair is hollow, which also increases the insulating power of the pelt.

DECEMBER

December Observations

67

Owl Hoots

A large blocky shape swoops through the night without a sound, plunging from the skeletal trees to the snow-covered ground. A shrill squeak follows and the bird returns to the tree tops, a small rodent clutched in its talons. An owl has captured and killed a rodent too hungry to stay hidden in the winter landscape. Owls are successful predators that live on mice, voles, rabbits, rats and other animals that otherwise might overpopulate the land.

Perhaps it's the eeriness of their hooting or the way they fly through the night without a sound. Perhaps it's the way they sit straight in such an imposing way and look at you with their big round eyes, sometimes turning their heads completely around to see what's behind them. Whatever the reason, we have long associated owls with both mysterious and sensible traits and legends. The owl has long been a symbol of wisdom and also an omen of death—part of the tradition of witchcraft and Halloween for centuries.

Owls comprise only a small percentage of the world's birds. The total number of bird species in the world is estimated to be about ninety-seven hundred—only about 178 of those species are owls. In our three-state region, less than a dozen have been reported. Several are residents and, occasionally, a couple of other species make appearances in our region.

Owls have huge immobile eyes and large heads. Immobile eyes mean that the bird must move its head to see objects. The large eyes are good light gatherers, making the owls' night sight excellent. Having the eyes on the front of the head gives these predators good depth perception, the capacity to recognize distance and three-dimensional qualities. Their ears, directed forward like the eyes, also provide them with depth perception. The facial disks of owls are thought to help focus sound to the ears. Owls have fluffy feathers with serrated leading edges that baffle the air, making their flight nearly soundless, a great advantage in hunting their prey.

Owls typically hunt at night and rest during the day, perching quietly on limbs where they are rarely noticed unless they move. Owls commonly roost on the same limbs of the same trees every day. On the ground below those tree limbs, you will find owl pellets, regurgitated nuggets of bones and fur that will tell you what the owls' diet is. Another way to discover where owls are roosting is to watch for songbirds and crows to mob the owls. If you see or hear several making a din and diving at a certain spot, you may assume that they are mobbing an owl or some other foe. Once discovered, the owls have a poor chance of escaping torment.

Both talons and beak are strong, curved and sharp. The legs and feet are sturdy and powerful, tipped with long, sharp, black talons. Owls catch their prey with their feet, then return to the trees to tear the meat apart with their strong bills. They eat the entire animal, bones, fur and all. A few hours later, the 1- to 2-inch pellets of indigestible parts are regurgitated. Biologists learn a great deal by dissecting and identifying the animal fragments in owl pellets.

Most common of all the owls in our region is the great horned owl, a large yellow-eyed bird (22 inches or more in length) with a wing spread of up to 5 feet. As is the case with hawks and eagles, the female is larger. The large size and conspicuous ear tufts identify this forest bird. This year-round resident also may frequent open country and suburban lands. I love to hear the resonant hooting of the great horned owl—it consists of three to eight hoots, commonly in a pattern like *Hoo, hoo-hoo-hoo, hoo-hoo, hoo.* This bird is sometimes called the hoot owl, for good reason. Great horned owls begin courtship as early as November, adopt an unused hawk, crow or eagle nest, and lay one to six white eggs by January or February. The young leave their nest in about nine to ten weeks, before they can fly—parents continue to feed them on the ground. Their prey includes mammals up to the size of opossums and also reptiles, amphibians and birds.

The smallest eared owl east of the Rocky Mountains is the screech owl, which comes in two color phases, gray and red. Like the great horned owl, this small owl is a year-round resident with a generally barred appearance to its plumage. The screech owl is only about 8 to 9 inches in length with a wingspan of about 22 inches. This owl, often found in urban and suburban settings, lives in both woodlands and open land. Despite its small size, the screech owl can tackle animals as large as rats or quail successfully. Its usual diet consists of smaller mammals and birds, plus beetles, grasshoppers and sometimes crayfish. This owl's call, heard most often in spring and fall, is a mournful muted wail that descends the scale in pitch. The bird may be right over your head and yet the call has a quality that makes it sound much farther away. This bird nests in hollow trees or sometimes birdhouses and raises its young during the spring months.

The barred owl, nearly 20 inches long with a wingspan of almost 4 feet, is a chunky owl with dark eyes and streaky, barred foliage with no ear tufts. Another permanent resident in our region, the barred owl, is also often called hoot owl. This bird is the one whose distinctive call says "Who cooks for you—who cooks for you all." Its repertoire also includes an assortment of screeches, howls, squawks and yowls that can be hair-raising on dark nights in swampy forests. This bird is most often found in wooded swamps and forests but occasionally will visit more settled places. The barred owl eats mostly mice but also other mammals, amphibians, reptiles, small birds and large insects. Breeding and nesting take place in February and March when two to four eggs are laid in hollow trees or old hawk nests.

Barn owls are pale with yellow brown upper bodies and white to cinnamon underparts. They are about 17 inches long with a wing span of roughly 42 inches. They have dark eyes and a white round to heart-shaped facial disk. This owl does not hoot—its call is a raspy hissing screech with a sucking intake that some say sounds like it's sucking up soup. This is a rare endangered owl in our area and is being reintroduced by the Wild Bird Sanctuary of St. Louis and others. It prefers open grazing or croplands and often lives in buildings, but occasionally it will nest in hollow trees or nest boxes. Their breeding season is usually from February through July when three to five white eggs are laid.

Snowy owls, normally creatures of the northern tundra, are forced southward into our region in appreciable numbers about every four years when the lemming population crashes or when weather farther north is unusually severe. Then you may see this large (23 inches long with a wing spread up to 5 feet) white owl with its yellow eyes and rounded head sitting on open ground or on fence posts. You will commonly see this owl perching near or on the ground. It is also unusual in that it is most active during the day. Because it is so tame, the snowy owl is too often shot or run over by cars.

Other owls that are uncommon but have been sighted in our region include the small northern saw-whet owl, the long-eared owl and the short-eared owl. These are considered rare to uncommon winter residents.

HOTSPOTS

Felsenthal NWR (see Chapter 2 for directions), **Holla Bend NWR** (see Chapter 7 for directions), and **Wapanocca** (see Chapter 1 for directions) in Arkansas all have noted regular sightings of the more common owls.

In Illinois, **Morton Arboretum** (see Chapter 3 for directions) is a favorite of birders seeking owls. **Crab Orchard NWR** (see Chapter 1 for directions) and **Chautauqua NWR** (see Chapter 1 for directions) are noted for sightings of resident owls and occasional owls from other regions.

Missouri's **Mingo NWR** (see Chapter 1 for directions), **Squaw Creek NWR** (also see Chapter 1) and **Swan Lake NWR** (see Chapter 8 for directions) all have resident owls and occasionals from other regions. At this time of year, check cedar trees at Squaw Creek NWR for Northern saw-whet owls that are sometimes reported here. This also is a place where you might see both long-eared and short-eared owls in early winter along the dike road on the southeastern, southwestern, northwestern and western boundaries of the refuge.

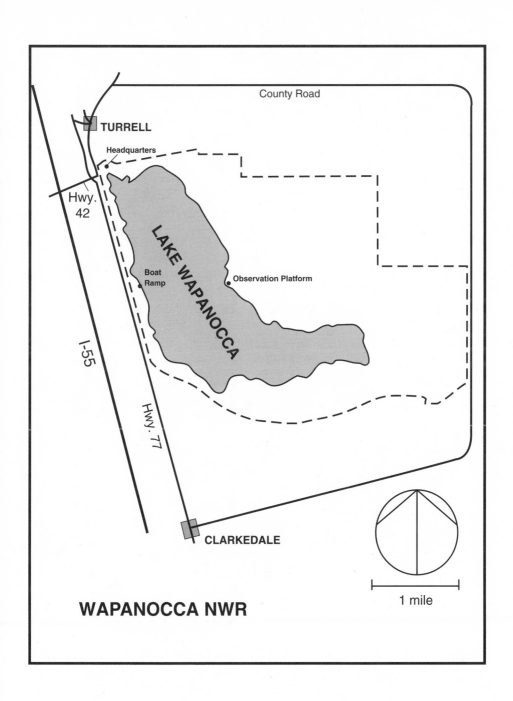

County Road

TURRELL

Headquarters

Hwy. 42

LAKE WAPANOCCA

Boat Ramp

Observation Platform

I-55

Hwy. 77

CLARKEDALE

1 mile

WAPANOCCA NWR

68

Winter Birds: Finches, Sparrows and Grosbeaks

With the advent of winter weather, a number of birds—our common winter residents—move southward from their summer breeding grounds. In addition, some of our permanent avian residents become more visible when deciduous trees drop their leaves. Many of the winter residents and year-round birds become frequent visitors to bird feeders, those set up near private homes and, increasingly, those established at nature centers, refuges and parks.

When learning to identify birds in the winter, remember that general body shapes are often different in the winter because of the way that birds fluff up their feathers to increase the insulating quality of plumage when temperatures are low and winds are strong. For instance, the plump northern mockingbird of winter doesn't look much like the slim bird of hot summer months. The same is true of American goldfinches, which are sleek and bright yellow trimmed with jet in the summer, olive drab and fluffily fat when weather is frigid. Likewise, cardinals are much plumper looking during cold weather.

The following are a few of the birds that are winter residents throughout most of our three-state region. Many are finches and sparrows that spend their summers in Alaska, Canada and northern states.

The finches best known to our region include the American goldfinch, pine siskin, purple finch, house finch and the evening grosbeak. These seed-eaters often have an undulating pattern of flight. Aside from our loyal goldfinch, a common permanent resident throughout our region, these winter birds are a bit erratic, appearing in some places one winter, another place the next.

The pine siskin looks like a thin, brown-streaked goldfinch and regularly hangs around with goldfinches. Notice the yellow at the base of the tail and on flight feathers—the yellow markings are noticeable in flight. Both goldfinches and siskins are easily tempted by niger (black thistle seed) at feeders. The siskin is quite erratic—some years I see none while other years they are as common as starlings.

The rosy red purple finch is a common winter visitor. The back is reddish and streaky, and the tail has a deep notch. This sparrow-sized bird is a common visitor at bird feeders. The female is a brown striped bird with a brown cheek patch.

The very similar house finch, originally native to the West Coast, is becoming increasingly common in our heartland states. It all began in the 1940s when pet store suppliers shipped a bunch of "Hollywood finches" to New York City. When the Audubon Society got wind of this, they descended upon the pet stores—to avoid the furor, at least one merchant released his house finches. Today, in some areas, the native west coast birds are only hundreds of miles from the east coast birds that have continued to pioneer westward. The male house finch has a raspberry-red head and appears somewhat thinner than the purple finch. The clear red bib is distinct from the streaked underbelly.

The evening grosbeak also is a finch, a large, plump noisy finch with a thick, strong yellowish bill. The male has a yellow eyebrow and forehead, yellow rump and belly. The head is brownish and the wings are black with a white patch. The female evening gros-beak is quite similar but duller, more grayish. These birds seem to be migrating farther south all the time—they are not uncommon at times in southern Arkansas and are sometimes seen in the rest of our region as well.

The commonly seen sparrows of winter include the white-crowned sparrow, white-throated sparrow, the dark-eyed junco, the song sparrow and the tree sparrow. Although the white-crowned sparrow nests farther north in Canada, Alaska and northwestern United States, I mention it because it's so much a part of the group of birds known as sparrows. This handsome bird spends its winters in our part of the world, throughout much of the southern half of our country including Arkansas, southern Missouri, and most of Illinois. A close relative of the white-throated sparrow, this bird has a gray breast, bright pink bill and prominently black-streaked crown with white stripes—the space between the eyes is black.

Its song is somewhat like the last half of the white-throated sparrow's familiar tune, repeated several times in a clear, clean whistle that sounds a bit sad. The song consists usually of five to seven notes that seem to say *more wet wetter wet chee zee.* In late summer and on warm autumn days, the white-crowned sparrow may sing sort of a whisper song that can be heard only when you are close.

This bird nests in cool brushy places of alpine and subarctic regions in our western mountains as well as the Pacific Northwest, Canada and Alaska. It is a common transient in our region passing through from April to early May and fall through early winter. In the spring you can often hear its curious song.

The white-throated sparrow, also known as the Peabody bird and Canada bird, nests in the spruce belt of Canada and as far south as Pennsylvania. It winters throughout southeastern United States including most of our region, all of Arkansas and all except the northwestern corner of Missouri and extreme northern edge of Illinois. The pure white patch on its throat is the most significant field mark.

This bird responds readily to whistled imitations of its song. The song consists of a series of clear, pensive whistles, diminishing toward the end. It sounds very much like *Poor Sam Peabody, Peabody, Peabody,* whistled in rhythm but varying in pitch, the last notes sometimes ascending, sometimes descending, or all on one pitch. This is one of the sweetest sounding of all our songbirds. If you whistle the song, white-throated sparrows will pop up from thickets, perching on outer twigs, to see the bird that called.

The white-throated sparrow is a ground feeder, devouring insect pests that include locusts, grasshoppers and beetles. Weed seeds and wild berries are also a major part of its diet, especially in winter months.

Song sparrows are little brown birds with streaked breasts and a dark spot in the middle of the breast. This is the best songster of all the sparrows with its many melodies and variations on different themes. Although this bird is a year-round resident throughout much of our region, it also migrates from Canada and northern states to more southern climes. Look for song sparrows along roadsides and in thickets.

Tree sparrows are little brown birds with pale gray breasts and a dark spot in the middle of the breast. They also have a chestnut crown and a stripe behind each eye. Although it's called a tree sparrow, this bird spends a lot of time on and near the ground. Their songs are mixes of twitters and warbles. This is one of the most common of winter birds in the central states, and you will see it browsing seedheads in frozen fields and prairies even in the coldest weather.

The fox sparrow winters in all three states of our region, a larger, darker bird than its cousins. This stocky bird is a rich rusty streaky creature with a bright rufous tail. These handsome birds frequent brushy forests, dense undergrowth and deciduous or conifer woods. Their spring songs begin in winter headquarters and are loud and rich, usually rising on the first notes and falling on the last. The songs usually are varied and short, combinations of trills and clear whistles. All sparrows scratch for seeds on the ground but the fox sparrow with its large strong feet really scratches deep into the forest humus where it finds seeds and tiny insects.

Another sparrowlike bird is the dark-eyed junco, often called the snow bird, which has a pinkish bill and white belly in sharp contrast to smooth dark grayish plumage everywhere else. In flight, you will see the white outer feathers of the tail flashing. Watch for juncos in shrubs, small trees and brush at the edges of fields.

All of the seed-eating finches and sparrows can be attracted to bird feeders through judicious offerings of a variety of seeds. See Chapter 6 for some tips on feeding the wild birds. Some are shyer than others. Some will thrive in suburban locations while others prefer wilder places. You can learn a lot about birds simply by watching their winter activities.

HOTSPOTS

Holla Bend NWR in east central Arkansas (see Chapter 7 for directions) has recorded many winter residents including sparrows and finches. Fox sparrows are among the sparrows regularly sighted here in the winter. The brochure on the area will show you how to get to the wildlife trail, auto tour, and observation tower. The hiking and auto trails of **Millwood SP** in the southwestern part of the state (see Chapter 10 for directions) will give you plenty of opportunity to see winter birds. Another good place to visit for winter birds is **Lake Fort Smith SP** in the northwestern part of the state. This park nestles in an Ozark valley near Ozark National Forest and offers spectacular scenery—the Ozark Highlands Trail begins here. Get a brochure at the visitors' center to help orient yourself to this dandy park. To get there, take Exit 13 off I-40 and go 12 miles north on U.S. Highway 71 to just north of Mountainburg, or from Fayetteville, take U.S. Highway 71 south for 35 miles.

Crab Orchard NWR in southern Illinois (see Chapter 1 for directions) is a great place to find the sparrows and finches of winter.

Goose Lake Prairie State Natural Area outside of Chicago (see Chapter 34 for directions) offers good winter birding. Look for sparrows and finches in the dense willows surrounding the potholes. Be sure to sign the register and check with the manager regarding possible restrictions.

Squaw Creek NWR in northwestern Missouri (see Chapter 1 for directions) and **Swan Lake NWR** in the north central part of the state (see Chapter 8 for directions) are two good refuges for birding in the winter. Squaw Creek has observation towers and a route for auto touring as well as varied habitat offering chances to see different types of birds—get an area brochure at the headquarters building. **Hawn SP** south of St. Louis in eastern Missouri (see Chapter 4 for directions) is another good spot for winter birding, one that is greatly undersung. Check the park brochure for trails—the Botkin's Pine Woods would be a good place to begin looking for winter birds.

69

Christmas Bird Counts

The National Audubon Society inaugurated its popular Christmas Bird Counts (CBC) at the turn of the century, before the days when most species of birds and animals were protected by law. Its aim was to promote the practice of observing and counting birds rather than shooting them for sport. When Frank Chapman set out to protest overhunting on that Christmas day in 1900, he could not have foreseen that tens of thousands of birders would annually join this census. The new awareness of the value and beauty of wildlife helped conservationists attain legislation protecting wild animals and plants.

By the early 1990s, the CBC had close to two thousand count areas and well over forty-three thousand observers. The annual Audubon Society event now includes all fifty states plus all of Canada, Central America, the Caribbean islands, Guam and other Pacific islands. Birders have chalked up a grand total of 628 bird species. They annually count well over one hundred million birds. When you sign up on a team for a CBC, you are assigned a "count circle" with a 15-mile diameter. The results are printed annually by the Audubon Society in *American Birds*, a publication with over one thousand pages of fine print.

Today we are realizing that these annual bird counts are somewhat valuable in assessing bird populations, a good measure of the health of the environment. As a result of these bird counts and scientific censuses, biologists around the world have focused more closely on songbirds, trying to understand and correct the declines in certain populations. Other bird censuses have grown out of the original CBC, some concentrating on certain species and others on certain territories or seasons.

CBC results, although not scientific censuses, are so all-encompassing that statisticians can build sub-studies of populations of certain species from the overall numbers. In 1992, for instance, two concentrated pockets of the Bohemian waxwing were identified in Quebec and British Columbia, but few appeared farther south.

A recent CBC in Arkansas called forth about 320 birders in eighteen teams who found over one hundred species. The groups in Arkadelphia, Pine Bluff and Texarkana got high marks, each tallying over one hundred species. Highlights and oddities included lingering migrants such as the lark sparrow, green-backed heron and night-hawk. Bald eagles turned up in nearly double the average numbers of the past and eastern phoebes were also up in numbers. Great egrets, on the other hand, were down in numbers by half. House finches, immigrants noted only in the past few years, appear to have become regular winter residents in Arkansas. A lone monk parakeet was seen near Fort Smith where there is a small resident population. Birders were pleased to see an increase in numbers of the rare red-cockaded woodpecker and also the belted kingfisher.

In Illinois, recent CBCs totaled forty-three groups and yielded 152 species. Top counts were ninety-eight species at Rend Lake and ninety-three species at Horseshoe Lake in southern Illinois. The most significant bird recorded in the Illinois count that year was an immature ivory gull, a bird that normally winters in the Arctic, found on the Chicago Lakefront. Other unusual sightings included the red-throated loon, fish crow and American pipit. Mild weather meant that waterfowl were numerous, including Ross' geese and greater white-fronted geese. Suspected trends noted were increases in the winter populations of double-crested cormorants, eastern phoebes, Carolina wrens, eastern bluebirds and northern mockingbirds. Here, as well as in Arkansas, the house finch is becoming the most successful non-native bird.

Birders on recent CBCs in Missouri also set records because of the mild weather that continued through early January. Some twenty-five teams of birders participated in this state. Unusual sightings were made of common loons and eared grebes. The house finch population continues to grow rapidly here also, but swamp sparrows are decreasing. Most unusual species included were the yellow-billed loon, white-winged scoter, sandhill crane, dunlin, margh wren, common yellowthroat, orange-crowned warbler, vesper sparrow and common redpoll. The team from St. Joseph reported an impressive 2,336 American crows and the team from Taney County listed an equally impressive 240 horned grebes. Not surprisingly, the team from Orchard Farm in St. Charles County was the only one reporting the immigrant European tree sparrow, most commonly found in the St. Louis region where it was introduced.

The American Birding Association (address and phone in the Appendix) sponsors a worldwide bird census competition titled Big Day. This competition is for those who like to see how many species of birds they can find in a single day. In 1992 approximately seventeen hundred people participated. These eager beavers start out before dawn and cover as many hotspots as they can during the day and even into the night. Competitions exist between states, counties and areas in various regions.

Other organizations that are striving to assess certain populations of birds include the Hawk Migration Association. For years, the migration of waterfowl has been studied by the U.S. Fish and Wildlife Service. The Second Annual North American Migration Count was held in May 1993, to census neotropical migrant songbirds.

On May 8, 1993, thousands of people gathered to celebrate and participate in the first International Migratory Bird Day, sponsored by the Smithsonian Migratory Bird Center and Birdlife International in Washington, D.C. This also is an effort to discover if neotropical migrants (migratory songbirds) have plummeting populations or not and, if so, to try and discover whether deforestation at both ends is the cause. In Washington that day, some eighty birders, including Roger Tory Peterson himself, sighted eighty bird species including thirty-five of the neotropical migrants. In southern Illinois in the Shawnee National Forest, three ornithologists spotted a record breaking thirty-two species of warbler on that single day. Perhaps things aren't as bad for these migratory birds as we had feared.

For most people, the CBCs are a dandy excuse to get outdoors during the winter. They provide a good method for finding out exactly what birds live here during the cold season—usually finding dozens of different species in their assigned areas.

HOTSPOTS

One good way to get in touch with the right people who can help you sign on with a bird census team for the CBC, Big Day competition or some other specialized census is to contact the birding hot lines or natural history organizations listed in the Appendix.

If you look up the National Audubon Society's annual Christmas Bird Count report, *American Birds,* you will find that many of the NWRs and other public parks we have been recommending in various chapters are sites for bird counts.

White River NWR (see Chapter 15 for directions) and the **Buffalo National River** (see Chapter 43 for directions) are regular sites for making censuses of native birds. **Chautauqua NWR** (see Chapter 1 for directions), **Crab Orchard NWR** (see Chapter 1 for directions), and **Pere Marquette SP** (see Chapter 13 for directions) all are used for CBCs and other wildlife counts. In Missouri, **Mingo NWR** (see Chapter 1 for directions) and **Swan Lake NWR** (see Chapter 8 for directions) both are sites for CBCs.

70

Christmas Ferns and Other Winter Plants

After a few hard freezes, most herbaceous plants die back to the ground. Herbaceous plants by definition are those that are not woody shrubs or trees but rather have green foliage and stems that do not survive winter weather, but grow back from their roots each spring.

Some of the lower plants are evergreen in our region. A few ferns are quite winter hardy, staying green through much of the winter season. Some of the mosses look gloriously green all winter long.

Christmas fern is the most obvious and largest of the evergreen ferns in our region. Snow may flatten its fronds to the ground but, once the snow melts, the Christmas fern will reappear in all its dark green glory. The past year's foliage does not usually crash until new fronds have started to grow in late winter. You can find Christmas ferns in colonies on either moist or dry, usually shady, wooded slopes. These ferns prefer acid soil that drains well. Favorite sites for these handsome ferns are near the bottom of valleys with rain creeks. You can recognize Christmas fern by its lance-shaped frond that is pinnate. The leaflets, properly called *pinnae*, are themselves lance shaped with earlike projections on each outer pinna base. The stems are covered with rust-colored scales. The fronds grow erect at first, then arching and, finally, prostrate.

Common polypody is another evergreen fern that grows in our region. The lance-shaped foot-long fronds are somewhat arched in their growth and have pinnae that are smooth edged and not completely separated at their bases but are broadly attached to the stem or stipe. This fern spreads by means of creeping roots, growing on mossy rocks, logs and downed trees. New fronds usually begin growing in early summer.

Some woodferns of the genus *Dryopteris* are evergreen and others are not. These ferns spread by means of underground roots that send up new clusters of fronds irregularly. One woodfern is known as marginal fern because of the way its fruiting bodies or *sori* appear on the underside edges of the pinnae or leaflets. Marginal ferns, native in much of our region, have leathery fronds that are bipinnate, that is, there are leaflets and subleaflets but no further divisions. These ferns are common in rocky woodlands and occur less commonly in prairie regions.

One of the most evergreen mosses is the juniper hairy cap moss that also is the largest of all our mosses, growing as much as 4 inches tall. This is the moss that looks like tiny evergreen trees all packed together and growing rigidly vertical. You may find this moss thriving in upland open woods with filtered shade. Where it finds the right spot, it may grow in large cushiony clumps that look so soft and inviting that you are tempted to lie down and take a nap. There are a number of other mosses that remain quite evergreen throughout the winter. Refer to Chapter 32 or a field guide to mosses for more information.

Although they are primitive plants and not green, the shelf or bracket fungi that grow on trees, stumps and fallen logs are very much a part of the winter scene because they are so obvious when the foliage is off deciduous plants. Fungi of the genus *Stereum* and their allies, which sometimes grow in bracket forms, could be called smooth fungi because of their smooth undersurfaces that usually face towards the ground. Some are known as skin fungi because they grow so tightly on logs, twigs and logs. Their flesh is pale and leathery. Some have top surfaces of various shades of brown or tan, from pinkish tan to bright rust and are often very attractive.

Most common fungi that you will see in the winter are the true bracket fungi, the polypores and their allies. Their common name is for the pores on the underside of the fruiting bodies of most species. These are long-lived woody plants, some continuing to grow larger for years. One of the common ones is known as artist's fungus because when you draw upon the undersurface, it turns brown where marked. There also are a number of polypores known commonly and collectively as turkey tails. They have multicolored concentric zones on the upper surfaces of the fruiting bodies that grow in large colonies on logs, stumps and tree trunks throughout our region.

Prairie grasses, while not evergreen in the true sense of the word, are very appealing in the winter scene, including little and big bluestems, Indian grass and prairie dropseed. These grasses hold their shape, standing erect through all but the worst of blizzards. They are crowned with handsome seedheads that gradually drop their seeds, not only reseeding their kind in the open prairielands but also feeding great numbers of winter birds as well as mice, voles and other mammalian seed eaters. For more about prairie grasses, see Chapter 45.

HOTSPOTS

Look for evergreen and other interesting plants of the winter scene in just about any public park or preserve. Remember that you are not allowed to pick plants in many public properties—it can be more fun and more lasting to "collect" with your camera.

In Arkansas, you can find interesting winter plants in **Lake Poinsett SP** in the northeastern part of the state (see Chapter 13 for directions). An interesting side trip to take when you go to Lake Poinsett SP is the **Hampson Museum SP** in the town of Wilson which houses an extensive collection of Nodena Phase Indian artifacts from the Mississippian Period.

Lake Ouachita SP in central Arkansas not far from Hot Springs (see Chapter 3 for directions) in the pine forests at the east end of the lake is another place that would be fun for appreciating the plants of winter. Bonuses at this park are the year-round cabins overlooking the lake.

The rare beauty of **Petit Jean SP** (see Chapter 14 for directions) in central Arkansas, north of Lake Ouachita offers a mountain setting and abundance of woods and spectacular views, obviously a great place for finding interesting winter plants. This park also has good facilities in its Mather Lodge plus a number of great trails. Begin your visit by getting a park brochure at the visitors' center.

Don't miss **Ferne Clyffe SP** in southern Illinois in the Shawnee Hills south of Marion, Illinois. To get there, take I-57 9 miles south of Marion, then I-24 to the Goreville exit. Go west to Goreville—the park is just south and a bit west of Goreville. This park features the **Round Bluff Nature Preserve** and has fascinating plants, including just about every fern found in the region.

Matthiessen SP in northwestern Illinois (see Chapter 33 for directions) is noted for its ferns and mosses as well as spectacular geological sights. Be sure to stop at the visitors' center first to get a brochure and other information about this beautiful park.

Chautauqua NWR in west central Illinois (see Chapter 1 for directions) promises good winter plants in its floodplain as well as the upland oak-hickory forest.

Mingo NWR in southeastern Missouri (see Chapter 1 for directions) is a great place for all sorts of plants and would be a good place to visit in December. Mushrooming is excellent there.

Roaring River SP in the southwestern part of the state (see Chapter 13 for directions) is another top spot for ferns and mosses. Look near the spring and along the waters below the spring. This park is at the western end of Table Rock Lake while **Table Rock SP** (see Chapter 7 for directions) is near the booming town of Branson at the eastern end of the lake. It is worth the trip to see the huge Roaring River Spring from which twenty million gallons of water gush forth every day to form the headwaters of the Roaring River. This is one of Missouri's famous trout parks where rainbow trout are raised and released.

71

December
Shorttakes

Woodpeckers

The woodpeckers that are common winter residents in our region will come to feeders, especially those that are supplied with suet and peanut butter. You also will see them in the trees and on tree trunks more commonly now that the leaves have fallen. For more about woodpeckers, see Chapter 2.

Squirrels

When winter weather is cold and wet with icy winds blowing around the clock, squirrels will gather in their leafy nests, usually built high in the crotches of oak and hickory trees to conserve energy. Raccoons, which prefer dens in hollow trees and logs, also seek shelter during winter's severe weather.

See also:

Chapter 1, Bald Eagles. Bad weather brings eagles to the open water at refuges and also the locks and dams of the Mississippi River. Watch in area newspapers for announcements of eagle counts that are scheduled each year.

Chapter 6, Breakout: Birds at Feeders. Many birds gather at bird feeders at this time of year, especially during and after storms when natural food is scarce or hidden.

72

Breakout:
The Skies of Winter

Crisp clear winter nights often offer the best astronomical sights of the year, and some of the winter constellations are glorious. For the best stargazing, find a place away from city lights during a time of the month when the moon is small or has set.

From now until March, the great hunter, Orion, dominates the southern sky with the most bright stars of any constellation. You can't miss Orion's belt—three bright stars in a straight line. From the belt hangs a sword, and you can trace Orion's legs from the end stars of the belt. Follow the form of Orion upward to the bright stars of his shoulders and you will see his raised arms holding a shield and a bow. Bluish white Rigel, Orion's right foot, is the brightest star in this constellation and Betelgeuse, a reddish star in the left shoulder, is the second brightest. Rigel is a giant star many times larger than our sun and over 500 light-years away—you are seeing its light from the fifteenth century.

The story of Orion in Greek mythology begins with a physician Asklepios, who had never lost a patient. When he tried to revive Orion, who had been bitten by a scorpion, Hades, the god of the underworld, prevailed upon Zeus to strike Asklepios with a bolt of lightning because Hades feared unemployment. As a result, Asklepios was transformed into a constellation in the northern skies to keep him away from Orion in the southern skies. When you see one, you cannot see the other.

If you follow Orion's belt line to the left, it points to Sirius, the Dog Star, only 8 1/2 light-years away, one of our closest celestial neighbors. Only twenty-six times as bright as our sun, it is as bright as Rigel because of its nearness to Earth. Sirius is the throat star of the constellation Canis Major (Big Dog). Look above, below and to the left of Sirius to see the body, legs and tail of Big Dog. This constellation is so close to the southern horizon that it takes a particularly dark clear night to see all of its stars.

Locate Orion and look above his upraised arm where you will find Gemini, the Twins. The heads of the Twins are bright Magnitude One stars. The one on the left is Pollux, a yellowish star that is brighter than the head of the other twin, Castor, a white star. To find Gemini from the Big Dipper, draw a diagonal through the bowl from the handle.

Another major constellation of the winter skies is Perseus, located to the left of his bride-to-be, Andromeda, and below and to the left of Cassiopeia, his future mother-in-law. Perseus is in the Milky Way and looks like a man with a pointed cap. His left arm beckons while his right arm looks as though he is about to grab Andromeda's foot.

The largest constellation of the zodiac is Taurus, the Bull. This constellation is between Orion, up and to his right, and Perseus, below and to his left. This constellation is best known for the Pleides, a group of six small stars that make up the tip of the right horn. Alderbaran, the brightest star of Taurus, is orange-red and located at the Bull's throat.

Locate the Great Square of Pegasus, a landmark of the night skies, by striking a line from the North Star (see Chapter 36 for the keys to finding the North Star) through the last star in Cassiopeia's "W" and beyond. The Great Square is one of the more obvious figures in the night skies. Pegasus is located to the southwest of Andromeda. The triangular wing of Pegasus includes the southwestern three stars of the Great Square and is fastened to the horse's rump. The head, body and legs of Pegasus are below and to the southwest of the Great Square.

The zodiac constellation of Aries, the Ram, is inconspicuous, located above and to the right of Taurus, below and to the right of Perseus. The two brightest stars of Aries are halfway between the Pleides and the Great Square of Pegasus.

When you are studying the night skies, take the time and make the effort to be comfortable. Sit or, better yet, lie down so that you don't become dizzy or get a crick in the neck or back. Chairs and blankets will come in handy for studying stars. Be sure to dress for the weather at this time of year. Binoculars will give you an even better view of more stars on clear nights.

Remember that constellations, as well as the sun and the moon, look much larger when they are near the horizon than when they are high in the sky. The skies appear to revolve around the Polar Star and so constellations may appear upside down at times.

Planets appear in the night skies with great regularity. Because they wander around among the constellations, they usually are not noted in sky charts. Of the sun's planets, including our own earth, five can be seen with the naked eye. You will hardly ever see Mercury because it is so close to the sun, but Saturn, Jupiter, Mars and Venus are often visible, sometimes at dawn, sometimes in the evening. Watch your newspapers for alerts of these sightings.

APPENDIX

The following includes addresses and phone numbers for national wildlife refuges, parks, preserves and organizations, many of which are mentioned in the text.

NATIONAL WILDLIFE REFUGES

Big Lake NWR
P.O. Box 67
Manila, AR 72442
(501) 564-2429

Chautauqua NWR
Route 2
Havana, IL 62644
(309) 535-2290

Crab Orchard NWR
P.O. Box J
Carterville, IL 62918
(618) 997-3344

Felsenthal NWR
P.O. Box 1157
Crossett, AR 71635
(501) 364-3167
(Also headquarters for Overflow NWR)

Holla Bend NWR (office in town)
115 S. Denver St.
P.O. Box 1043
Russellville, AR 72801
(501) 968-2800

Mingo NWR
Route 1, Box 103
Puxico, MO 63960
(314) 222-3589

Northeast Arkansas Refuge Complex
P.O. Box 279
Turrell, AR 72384
(501) 343-2595
(A U.S. Fish and Wildlife Service refuge administrative office and information source for Big Lake, Cache River and Wapanocca NWRs. The office is located at the Wapanocca refuge.)

Overflow NWR
(c/o Felsenthal NWR)

Squaw Creek NWR
P.O. Box 101
Mound City, MO 64470
(816) 442-3187

Swan Lake NWR
P.O. Box 68
Sumner, MO 64681
(816) 856-3323

Wapanocca NWR
P.O. Box 279
Turrell, AR 72384
(501) 343-2595

White River NWR (office in town)
704 Jefferson St.
P.O. Box 308
DeWitt, AR 72042
(501) 946-1468

NATIONAL PARKS, FORESTS AND RECREATION AREAS

Arkansas Post National Memorial
Route 1, Box 16
Gillett, AR 72055
(501) 548-2432

Buffalo National River
P.O. Box 1173
Harrison, AR 72602-1173
(501) 741-5443

Hot Springs National Park
P.O. Box 1860
Hot Springs, AR 71902
(501) 624-3383

Lewis and Clark
    National Historic Trail
(in Illinois, Missouri and other states
to the west)
National Park Service
700 Rayovac Drive, Suite 100
Madison, WI 53711
(608) 264-5610

Mormon Pioneer
    National Historic Trail
(in Illinois and also Iowa, Nebraska,
Wyoming and Utah)
Rocky Mountain Regional Office,
    NPS
12795 W. Alameda Parkway
P.O. Box 25287
Denver, CO 80225
(303) 969-2828

Oregon National Historic Trail
(in Missouri and also Kansas and
other states to the west)
Pacific Northwest Regional Office,
    NPS
83 South King St.
Seattle, WA 98104
(206) 553-5360

Ozark National Scenic Riverways
P.O. Box 490
Van Buren, MO 63965
(314) 323-4236

Pea Ridge National Military Park
Pea Ridge, AR 72751
(501) 451-8122

Wilson's Creek National Battlefield
Route 2, Box 75
Republic, MO 65738
(417) 732-2662

Riverland Environmental
    Demonstration Area
Riverlands Area Office
P.O. Box 337
West Alton, MO 63386-0337
(314) 899-0405

STATE AGENCIES

Arkansas Game & Fish Commission
    Information Department
2 Natural Resources Drive
Little Rock, AR 72205
(501) 223-6351

Illinois Office of Tourism
620 E. Adams St., 3rd Floor
Springfield, IL 62701
(217) 785-1032
(800) 223-0121

Arkansas Department of
    Parks & Tourism
#1 Capitol Mall
Little Rock, AR 72201
(800) 482-8999 (in state)
(800) 643-8383 (out of state)

Missouri Department of Conservation
P.O. Box 180
Jefferson City, MO 65102
(314) 751-4115

Arkansas Natural Heritage
    Commission
1500 Tower Building
323 Center Street
Little Rock, AR 72201
(501) 324-9619

Missouri Department of
    Natural Resources
P.O. Box 176
Jefferson City, MO 65102
(800) 334-6946

Illinois Department of Conservation
    Chicago Office
100 West Randolph, Suite 4-300
Chicago, IL 60601
(312) 814-2070

Missouri Division of Tourism
Truman State Office Building
P.O. Box 1055
Jefferson City, MO 65102
(314) 751-4133

Illinois Division of Wildlife Resources
Lincoln Tower Plaza
524 South Second Street
Springfield, IL 62706
(217) 782-6384

MISSOURI DEPARTMENT OF CONSERVATION
NATURE CENTERS AND WILDLIFE AREAS

August A. Busch Memorial
  Wildlife Area
2360 Highway "D"
St. Charles, MO 63304
(314) 441-4554

Runge Conservation Nature Center
Missouri Department of Conservation
2901 West Truman Boulevard
Jefferson City, MO 65109
(314) 526-5544

Burr Oak Woods Conservation
  Nature Center
Missouri Department of Conservation
1401 Park Road
Blue Springs, MO 64015
(816) 228-3766

Springfield Conservation
  Nature Center
Missouri Department of Conservation
4600 S. Chrisman
Springfield, MO 65804
(417) 882-4237

Powder Valley Conservation
  Nature Center
Missouri Department of Conservation
11715 Cragwold Road
Kirkwood, MO 63122-7000
(314) 821-8427

Taberville Prairie Conservation Area
Missouri Department of Conservation
Route 4
Clinton, MO 64735
(316) 885-3246

STATE AND MUNICIPAL PARKS AND MANAGEMENT AREAS

Dr. Edmund A. Babler Memorial
  State Park
Chesterfield, MO 63005
(314) 458-3813

Cave-In-Rock State Park
P.O. Box 338
Cave-In-Rock, IL 62919
(618) 289-4325

Sam A. Baker State Park
Patterson, MO 63956
(314) 856-4411

Cossatot River State Park–
  Natural Area
Route 1, Box 170-A
Wickes, AR 71973
(501) 385-2201

Big Oak Tree State Park
East Prairie, MO 63845
(314) 649-3149

Cuivre River State Park
Troy, MO 63379
(314) 528-7247

Bull Shoals State Park
P.O. 205
Bull Shoals, AR 72619
(501) 431-5521

Devil's Den State Park
11333 West Arkansas Highway 74
West Fork, AR 72774
(501) 761-3325

Castle Rock State Park
R.R. 2
Oregon, IL 61061
(815) 732-7329

Eagle Creek State Park
P.O. Box 16
Findlay, IL 62534
(217) 756-8260

Elephant Rocks State Park
Belleview, MO 63623
(314) 697-5395

Ferne Clyffe State Park
Box 708
Goreville, IL 62939
(618) 995-2411

Giant City State Park
R.R. 1
Makanda, IL 62958
(618) 457-4836

Goose Lake Prairie (Natural Area)
5010 N. Jugtown
Morris, IL 60450
(815) 942-2899

Graham Cave State Park
Montgomery City, MO 63361
(314) 564-3476

Grand Gulf State Park
Thayer, MO 65791
(314) 548-2201

Hawn State Park
Ste. Genevieve, MO 63670
(314) 883-3603

Horseshoe Lake (Alexander County)
Box 77
Miller City, IL 62962
(618) 776-5689

Illinois Beach State Park
Zion, IL 60099
(708) 662-4811

Jackson Park District
6401 South Stony Island
Chicago, IL 60637
(312) 643-6363

Lake Catherine State Park
1200 Catherine Park Road
Hot Springs, AR 71913
(501) 844-4176

Lake Chicot State Park
Route 1, Box 1555
Lake Village, AR 71653
(501) 265-5480

Lake Fort Smith State Park
P.O. Box 4
Mountainburg, AR 72946
(501) 369-2469

Lake of the Ozarks State Park
Kaiser, MO 65047
(314) 348-2694

Lake Ouachita State Park
5451 Mountain Pine Road
Mountain Pine, AR 71956
(501) 767-9366

Lake Poinsett State Park
Route 3, Box 317
Harrisburg, AR 72432
(501) 578-2064

Lake Wappapello State Park
Williamsville, MO 63967
(314) 297-3232

Lincoln Park
2200 North Cannon Drive
Chicago, IL 60614
(312) 294-4660

Logoly State Park
P.O. Box 245
McNeil, AR 71752
(501) 695-3561

Mammoth Spring State Park
P.O. Box 36
Mammoth Spring, AR 72554
(501) 625-7364

Mastodon State Park
Imperial, MO 63052
(314) 464-2976

Matthiessen State Park
Box 381
Utica, IL 61373
(815) 667-4868

Meramec State Park
Sullivan, MO 63080
(314) 468-6072

Millwood State Park
Route 1, Box 37AB
Ashdown, AR 71822
(501) 898-2800

Moraine Hills State Park
914 South River Road
McHenry, IL 60050
(815) 385-1624

Mount Nebo State Park
Route 3, Box 374
Dardenelle, AR 72834
(501) 229-3655

Pere Marquette State Park
Grafton, IL 62037
(618) 786-3323

Petit Jean State Park
Route 3, Box 340
Morrilton, AR 72110
(501) 727-5431

Pinnacle Mountain State Park
11901 Pinnacle Valley Road
Roland, AR 72135
(501) 868-5806

Prairie State Park
Liberal, MO 64762
(417) 843-6711

Queen Wilhelmina State Park
HC-07, Box 53A
Mena, AR 71953
(501) 394-2863

Roaring River State Park
Cassville, MO 65625
(417) 847-2539

Starved Rock State Park
Box 116
Utica, IL 61373
(815) 667-4726

Swope Park
6601 Swope Parkway
Kansas City, MO 64130

Table Rock Lake State Park
Branson, MO 65616
(417) 334-4704

Thousand Hills State Park
Kirksville, MO 63501
(816) 665-6995

Tower Grove Park
4255 Arsenal St.
St. Louis, MO 63116
(314) 771-2679

Trail of Tears State Forest
R.R. 1, Box 182
Jonesboro, IL 62952
(618) 833-6125

White Oak Lake State Park
Route 2, Box 28
Bluff City, AR 71722
(501) 685-2748

Washington Park Botanical Garden
Springfield Park District
P.O. Box 5052
Springfield, IL 62705
(217) 544-1811

Wildlife Prairie Park
Forest Park Nature Center
5809 Forest Park Drive
Peoria Heights, IL 61614
(309) 686-3360

PRIVATE PRESERVES AND ORGANIZATIONS

Chicago Botanic Garden
P.O. Box 400
Glencoe, IL 60022
(708) 835-5440

Morton Arboretum, The
Route 53
Lisle, IL 60532
(708) 968-0074

Memphis Botanic Garden
750 Cherry Road
Memphis, TN 38117-4699
(901) 685-1566

Powell Gardens
Route 1, Box 90
Kingsville, MO 64061
(816) 566-2600

Missouri Botanical Garden
P.O. Box 299
St. Louis, MO 63166
(314) 577-5100

Shaw Arboretum
Missouri Botanical Garden
P.O. Box 38
Gray Summit, MO 63039
(314) 742-3512

NATURE CONSERVANCY FIELD OFFICES AND PRESERVES

Arkansas Field Office
300 Spring Building, Suite 7171
Little Rock, AR 72201
(501) 372-2750

Markham Prairie
(Contact Illinois Field Office for
information)

Missouri Field Office
2800 S. Brentwood Blvd.
St. Louis, MO 63144
(314) 968-1105
(Contact for preserve details and
visitor regulations)

Cedar Glen Eagle Roost (contact
Illinois Field Office for information)
Resident Manager
P.O. Box 150
Warsaw, IL 62379

Illinois Field Office
79 W. Monroe Street, Suite 900
Chicago, IL 60603
(312) 346-8166

Nachusa Grasslands
(Contact Illinois Field Office for
information)

Pershing State Park
Laclede, MO 64651
(816) 963-2525

Railroad Prairie State Natural Area
(Contact Arkansas Field Office for
maps and plant lists)

Warren Area
(Contact Arkansas Field Office for
maps and plant lists)

OTHER PRIVATE NATURAL HISTORY ORGANIZATIONS

For information on Christmas Bird Counts, butterfly counts and other special activities, contact the appropriate organization for details as to times and places.

American Birding Association
P.O. Box 6599
Colorado Springs, CO 80934
(800) 850-2473

Arkansas Mycological Society
5115 South Main St.
Pine Bluff, AR 71601-7452

Illinois Mycological Society
c/o Serra 562 Iroquois Trail
Carol Stream, IL 60188

Missouri Audubon Society
c/o Randy Washburn
659 Oak Creek Court
Jefferson City, MO 65101

Missouri Mycological Society
2888 Ossenfort Road
Glencoe, MO 63038-1716

North American Butterfly
   Association, Inc.
c/o Ann Swengel, NABA Treasurer
909 Birch St.
Baraboo, WI 53913

North American Mycological
   Association
Kenneth W. Cochran,
   Executive Secretary
3558 Oakwood
Ann Arbor, MI 48104-5213
(313) 971-2552

Webster Groves Nature
   Study Society
P.O. Box 190065
St. Louis, MO 63119

BIRDING HOTLINES

These hotlines rely on reports from experienced birders in the area and are provided as a public service by a number of organizations. Taped bird hotlines provide information on rare bird sightings and may also provide general reports on migration and population trends. Most hotline tapes are updated on a weekly basis.

Arkansas (statewide)
(501) 753-5853

Audubon Society of Missouri
(314) 445-4925

Burroughs Audubon Society
Greater Kansas City
(913) 324-BIRD

Central Illinois
(217) 785-1083

Chicago, Illinois
(708) 671-1522

Kansas City, Missouri
(816) 795-8177

Missouri (statewide)
(314) 445-9115

Tyson Nature Line
(314) 935-8432

This small prairie grass forms a foot-tall clump that is topped by late-summer seed heads that rise up to nearly three feet. In some upland prairie-type communities, this grass can become the dominant species.

SELECTED BIBLIOGRAPHY

I have called upon the resources of many individuals, organizations and publications in writing this book. While I have not listed every flier, folder and brochure that has been helpful, I have listed the departments or organizations that produced those printed pieces. The following books have been especially helpful in seeing that I included correct information.

Buczacki, Stefan. *Fungi of Britain and Europe*. University of Texas Press, 1989.

Cliburn, Jerry & Ginny Klomps. *A Key to Missouri Trees in Winter*. Missouri Department of Conservation, 1990.

Denison, Edgar. *Missouri Wildflowers*. Missouri Department of Conservation, 1989.

Dodson, David and Sarah. *Rockhounding in Arkansas*. The Dodsons (14 Elmcrest Court, Little Rock, Arkansas 72211, $4.00), 1974.

Flader, Susan, editor. *Exploring Missouri's Legacy, State Parks and Historic Sites*. University of Missouri Press, 1992.

Hawker, Jon L. *Missouri Landscapes: A Tour Through Time*. Missouri Department of Natural Resources, 1992.

Jones, John Oliver. *Where the Birds Are*. William Morrow & Co., 1990.

Key, James S. *Field Guide to Missouri Ferns*. Missouri Department of Conservation, 1982.

Lobik, Paul H., editor. *Bird Finding in Illinois*. The Illinois Audubon Society, 1975.

Missouri Botanical Garden. *Birds of Missouri.* Botanical Garden and Tower Grove Park, St. Louis, MO, 1992.

National Audubon Society. *American Birds, the Ninety-Second Christmas Bird Count.* 1992

National Geographic Society. *Field Guide to the Birds of North America.* 1983.

Perrins, Dr. Christopher. *Birds, Their Life, Their Ways, Their World.* Reader's Digest Association, Inc., 1991.

Rey, H.A. *The Stars.* Houghton Mifflin Company, 1962.

Settergren, Carl and R.E. McDermott. *Trees of Missouri.* University of Missouri-Columbia, 1972.

Thomas, Lisa Potter and James R. Jackson, Ph.D. *Walk Softly Upon the Earth (A Pictorial Field Guide to Missouri Mosses, Liverworts and Lichens).* Missouri Department of Conservation, 1985.

Unklesbay, A.G. and Jerry D. Vineyard. *Missouri Geology.* University of Missouri Press, 1992.

Zeitner, June Culp. *Midwest Gem, Fossil and Mineral Trails Midwest States.* Gem Guides Book Company, 1988.

Zeitner, June Culp. *Midwest Gem, Fossil and Mineral Trails Prairie States.* Gem Guides Book Company, 1989.

INDEX

NOTE: Boldfaced entries denote directions.

ABOUT THE AUTHOR

Barbara Perry Lawton's interest in natural history began when she was a child spending the summer with family in the northern Adirondack Mountains. Later she majored in zoology and worked as a manager of publications at the Missouri Botanical Garden. She has written columns, articles and books on gardening and natural history for over two decades. She lives in Kirkwood, Missouri.